CHURCH, CONTINUITY
&
UNITY

CHURCH, CONTINUITY
&
UNITY

BY

H. BURN-MURDOCH
LL.D. Cantab.

FIAT VOLUNTAS TUA

CAMBRIDGE
AT THE UNIVERSITY PRESS
1945

CAMBRIDGE
UNIVERSITY PRESS

University Printing House, Cambridge CB2 8BS, United Kingdom

Cambridge University Press is part of the University of Cambridge.

It furthers the University's mission by disseminating knowledge in the pursuit of education, learning and research at the highest international levels of excellence.

www.cambridge.org
Information on this title: www.cambridge.org/9781107458727

© Cambridge University Press 1945

First published 1945
First paperback edition 2014

A catalogue record for this publication is available from the British Library

ISBN 978-1-107-45872-7 Paperback

CONTENTS

Part One

The Church in the light of Scripture: a living organism, the sacramental outward of an inner and spiritual reality

Part Two

Continuity in the organic life of the Church through the centuries

A. CONTINUITY UNAFFECTED BY DIVERSITY OF CIRCUMSTANCE AND METHOD

B. KNOWN CONTINUITY FROM THE SECOND CENTURY ONWARD

C. CONTINUITY FROM PENTECOST TO THE SECOND CENTURY

Part Three

Continuity an essential of the Church and its unity

PREFACE

In this century a sense of the need for Christian unity has steadily strengthened. A happy outcome of discussion and conference in recent years has been the discovery of closer doctrinal agreement than had been expected: but agreement does not extend to the doctrine of the Church, or connected questions of Order.

A platitude needs to be reiterated, because so many have not grasped it, that unity is not uniformity. As Dr G. W. Broomfield has lately written (*Revelation and Reunion*, p. 214), 'the order and practice of the united Church must be such as to preserve everything of real and permanent value in the organization and customs of the bodies which are now separated from one another...unity is to be sought not by readiness to minimize—much less to abandon—the things which distinguish us from our brethren, but rather by an eagerness to discover whatever is true and valuable in the things which distinguish them from us'. The *Appeal to All Christian People* from the Lambeth Conference of 1920 said:

> The vision which rises before us is that of a Church, genuinely Catholic, loyal to all Truth, and gathering into its fellowship all 'who profess and call themselves Christians', within whose visible unity all the treasures of faith and order, bequeathed as a heritage by the past to the present, shall be possessed in common, and made serviceable to the whole Body of Christ. Within this unity Christian Communions now separated from one another would retain much that has long been distinctive in their methods of worship and service. It is through a rich diversity of life and devotion that the unity of the whole fellowship will be fulfilled.

If then unity admits of great elasticity and variety in *organization*, what is the visible and practical one-ness, the unity needed to fulfil our Lord's prayer that we may all be one that the world may believe? It has come to be increasingly recognized on all sides that the answer to this depends upon the further question, what is the true nature of the Church in the world?

This is an attempt to find an answer to that question in the teaching of the New Testament. Organism is wholly distinct in principle from organization. The Church, or new Ekklesia, was left by our Lord with no organization whatever, but He left it a living society with an organism of His provision which is still its distinguishing endowment.

The New Testament also teaches clearly that the Church is sacramental, that is to say, it has both an outward, visible, identifiable
materiality, and an inward, spiritual reality; for this visible body of
most imperfect saints is at the same time the invisible and mystical
Body of Christ.

A paramount catholic doctrine of all sacraments is that God is not
tied to them (although we are); that is conspicuously true of the
sacramental Church. Grace abounding overflows all limits of sacrament and sacramental Church, but this does not make them unnecessary to us and, moreover, without them there cannot be that unity
which we know to be the divine purpose for the winning of the world's
belief.

An important step towards a recognition of the 'outward part' of
the sacramental Church was made at the Second World Conference
on Faith and Order, at Edinburgh in 1937. Agreement was arrived
at 'that every sacrament should be so ordered that all may recognize
in it an act performed on behalf of the universal Church', and that
'To this end there is need of an ordained ministry recognized by all
to act on behalf of the universal Church in the administration of the
sacraments'.

I have tried in this book to show, what seems to me plain, that the
one-ness of the Church must be a humanly perceptible one-ness, not
only in the time present, but also in its continuous and unbroken life
in the world: we must be perceptibly one with the Church of Pentecost
in order that we may also be one with our scattered brethren throughout the world to-day; unity must, as it were, be vertical in order that
it may be lateral.

Through half a lifetime I have longed for unity. The thought and
study of many years impel this attempt to express their outcome.
Lacking many qualifications for it, I can claim one, a real understanding
of, and high respect for, the wholly different outlook and opinions
of others, with some of whom I have close ties of friendship, kinship,
and affection.

As the table of contents shows, there are three divisions in this book:

1. The Church in the light of Scripture: a living organism, the
sacramental outward of an inner and spiritual reality.

2. Continuity in the organic life of the Church through the
centuries.

3. Continuity an essential of the Church and its unity.

The second of these divisions includes a survey of what is known of the hundred years following the time of St Paul's death. The history of that rather obscure period has been the subject of much speculation and controversy. It only need be remarked here that the main theme of the book does not depend upon acceptance of an exact historical theory of that period.

On some points additional matter may be found, if desired, in notes placed at the ends of chapters; these are indicated by an asterisk in the text.

I wish to express my thanks to the Very Rev. W. Perry, D.D., who read the typescript (in 1942), and has given me wise and kindly counsel.

H. B.-M.

August 1943

SOME ABBREVIATIONS USED FOR REFERENCE
IN THE NOTES

Ainslie=J. L. Ainslie, B.D., Ph.D., *The Doctrines of Ministerial Order in the Reformed Churches of the Sixteenth and Seventeenth Centuries.* Edinburgh, 1940.

Anglo-Russ. Sym. = *The Church of God: an Anglo-Russian Symposium,* by members of the Fellowship of St Alban and St Sergius, ed. E. L. Mascall, pref. by W. H. Frere, D.D., bishop of Truro. London, 1934.

Bright=W. Bright, D.D., *Notes on the Canons of the First Four General Councils.* Oxford, 1882.

Carnegie Simpson=Professor P. Carnegie Simpson, D.D. (Westminster College, Cambridge), *The Evangelical Church Catholic.* London, 1934.

Episcopacy A. & M.=*Episcopacy Ancient and Modern,* ed. Claude Jenkins, D.D., and Bishop K. D. Mackenzie. London, 1930.

Essays on Early Hist. = *Essays on the Early History of the Church and the Ministry,* by various writers, ed. H. B. Swete, D.D. London, 1918.

Flew=R. Newton Flew, D.D. (Principal of Wesley House, Cambridge), *Jesus and His Church: a Study of the Idea of the Ecclesia in the New Testament.* London, 1938.

Forsyth=P. T. Forsyth, D.D. (Principal of the Congregational Theological College, and Chairman of the Congregational Union of England and Wales), *Lectures on the Church and the Sacraments.* London, 1917.

Gore and Turner= *The Church and the Ministry,* by Bishop C. Gore, new ed. rev. by Professor C. H. Turner, with an Appendix. London, 1936.

Hamilton=H. F. Hamilton, D.D., *The People of God.* Oxford, 1912.

Harnack=Adolf Harnack, *The Constitution and Law of the Church in the First Two Centuries,* English trans. by F. L. Pogson. London, 1910.

Headlam=A. C. Headlam, D.D., bishop of Gloucester, *The Doctrine of the Church and Christian Reunion* (Bampton Lectures for 1920), 3rd ed. London, 1929.

Hort=F. J. A. Hort, *The Christian Ecclesia.* 1897.

Lightfoot, *Clement*=J. B. Lightfoot, D.D., bishop of Durham, *The Apostolic Fathers,* Part I. (2 vols.) London, 1890.

Lightfoot, *Ignatius*=*ibid.* Part II. (3 vols.) London, 1889.

Lightfoot, *Christian Ministry*=*Dissertation on the Christian Ministry*, in Commentary on *St Paul's Epistle to the Philippians* (1868), rev. ed. 1908, p. 179. Published separately, 1901.

Lightfoot, *Apostle*=*Note on the Name and Office of an Apostle* in Commentary on *Galatians*, 2nd ed. rev. 1866.

Lindsay=T. M. Lindsay, D.D., *The Church and the Ministry in the Early Centuries*, 4th ed. 1902.

Lockton=W. Lockton, *Divers Orders in the Church.* 1930.

Macgregor=Principal W. M. Macgregor, D.D., *Christian Freedom* (Baird Lecture for 1913), new ed. London, 1931.

Maclean=*The Doctrine of the Twelve Apostles*, trans. by Charles Bigg, D.D., with a new introduction and revised notes by Bishop A. J. Maclean. 1922.

Manning=Bernard L. Manning, *Essays in Orthodox Dissent.* London, 1939.

Moberley=R. C. Moberley, D.D., *Ministerial Priesthood*, 2nd ed. 1910.

Moffatt=Professor James Moffatt, D.D., *The Presbyterian Churches.* London, 1928.

Story=Principal R. H. Story, D.D., *The Apostolic Ministry in the Scottish Church.* 1897.

Streeter=B. H. Streeter, D.D., *The Primitive Church.* 1929.

Warr=C. L. Warr, D.D., *The Presbyterian Tradition.* London, 1933.

Wordsworth=Bishop J. Wordsworth, *The Ministry of Grace.* 1901.

CHURCH, CONTINUITY & UNITY

Part One

The Church in the light of Scripture: a living organism, the sacramental outward of an inner and spiritual reality

CHAPTER I. GOD & 'INSTITUTIONAL RELIGION'

I

EVEN among earnest Christians, very few are willing to give much thought to problems of Church and ministry, so many regard them as unessential, of 'merely ecclesiastical' importance. Let us be candid, we fight shy of the ecclesiastical. The word is often used in mild reproach; we apply it mostly to things clerical, and especially to faults or foibles that we dislike, such as the parsonic voice. Of course there is no other adjective for 'church', except perhaps 'churchy'; we should indignantly deny that we are churchy, and we certainly do not think of ourselves as 'ecclesiastical persons'. Nine out of ten lay folk will say, not that so-and-so has become a minister, or has received Holy Orders, but that he 'has gone into the Church', thus revealing unconsciously that, at the back of our minds, we do not think of ourselves as having come into the Church, although we were baptized into it.

II

Since the great fact and privilege of membership in the universal Church is thought of so lightly, it is natural that problems of Church and ministry are widely deprecated as the concern of 'institutional religion', despised as mechanical and unspiritual. There is a half-truth behind this, one-half of a great truth, the other half of which is often not understood. Religion is spiritual, not material—inward,

not outward. *It is the spirit that quickeneth; the flesh profiteth nothing.*
To many people who fully believe in the spiritual reality of the
Church, any kind of organism, so far as it involves human action,
seems to be alien to that spiritual reality. They think, for example,
of the laying on of hands as only a mechanical action in the material
sphere, and they cannot conceive of it as in any way indispensable
to accompany the bestowal of heavenly grace for the work of
ministry. A modern theologian has written that 'One bane of the
whole question of the Sacraments is the obtrusion of the material
elements'.[1]

From time to time in Christian history, some have mistaken this
half-truth for the whole truth. The Friends, with all their high-
minded spirituality, have abandoned all sacraments. It led to the
heresy of Docetism, at so early a date that there are allusions to it in
the New Testament;[2] to the Docetists, even the catholic doctrine
that the Word was made flesh seemed to be materialistic, and they
ended by denying the truth of the Incarnation as a fact in the visible
world.

The other half of this truth is found in the sacramental principle.
Sacrament★[3] is a meeting-place of divine Spirit with humble matter,
and the sacramental principle extends far beyond the solemn rites
of the Church. This indeed might seem to follow from the mere
fact of our dual nature, the fact that we, who live in material bodies
in the concrete world, are at the same time spiritual beings. *Know
ye not that your body is a temple of the Holy Ghost which is in you,
which ye have from God?*[4] We ourselves are sacramental beings: but
the great and all-comprehending sacrament was the holy Incarnation
of the Son of God, the Word made flesh. From that greatest of all
sacraments depends the truth and reality of all others. Our Lord
has once for all ennobled humble matter into a new union with
Spirit. This duality, this, to us, mysterious relation of spirit and
matter, pervades the whole life of the Church and its members.
When, for example, the presbyters pray over the sick, *anointing him
with oil in the name of the Lord,*[5] their use of a humble material
accessory is not formal or 'mechanical' any more than is the use of
water in Holy Baptism. It is the appointed accompaniment of a
spiritual grace, an 'outward and visible sign' of a sacramental

---

[1] Forsyth, p. 133.   [2] I John iv. 2; II John 7.
[3] Note A. *Sacrament* (p. 5).   [4] I Cor. vi. 19.
[5] James v. 14.

character. It is right and necessary to guard against materialism and formalism, to keep the emphasis on the inward and spiritual rather than on the outward form; but it is necessary also for the spiritually minded to guard against a well-known tendency to exaggerate the antipathy of spirit and matter. The whole Church throughout the world is sacramental. Whatever we may believe to be the marks distinguishing it as visible in the world, so far as it is so, it is an outward and visible sign of an inward and spiritual reality.

III

Even if we have understood the sacramental principle, and have come to perceive that the visible Church and ministry are closely linked with that principle and with the sacraments themselves, we may still have failed to grasp the whole of another truth, of which we have seen only half.

We often recognize beauty of life and character in men and women who, though they seem to remain apart from the life and fellowship of the visible Church, are nevertheless much richer than ourselves or most churchgoers in what we must acknowledge to be true Christian grace. *By their fruits ye shall know them.* Surely then, the Church and all things ecclesiastical must be 'unessentials'? If the visible Church is, as St Paul says it is,[1] the household of God in the world, how is it, we ask ourselves, that there are very many of God's elect outside that visible household? If the sacraments are means of grace of His particular appointment, how is it that grace is often and abundantly vouchsafed to Friends and other devout Christians who do not resort to them? If God has appointed a visible stewardship for His household, how is it that notable prophets and evangelists are raised up outside its ranks?

Such questions often face us, and the answer is clear and manifest, that God is not tied to His Church, or its sacraments and ministry, as channels of His grace. That is neither new and original, nor in the least degree unorthodox; it has been the teaching of the Church from the earliest times. Those who suffered martyrdom for the Faith were believed to have received Baptism in their own blood. Crusaders were taught that, when wounded and dying in the field, if they but plucked and ate three blades of grass with faith and prayer, it was

[1] Eph. ii. 19.

as if they had actually received the consecrated Host. The Church continues to teach the reality of spiritual communion, when actual sacramental reception is impossible; it is plainly taught in the Anglican book of Common Prayer.* In the old Latin book this spiritual act was expressed in the phrase 'only believe and thou hast eaten'. It was held at one time that confessors, i.e. those who had survived chains and torture, should rank as presbyters without actual ordination by the laying on of hands.*² Those too who hold most firmly that there is no safety, no security, for us outside the household of God, *nulla salus extra Ecclesiam*, are also the first to acknowledge with thankfulness that many who have lived aloof from that household will hereafter be found among the elect.*³

The great truth proclaimed in all these ways is, and always has been, the doctrine of the Church; it has for long been expressed in the theological maxim, *Deus non alligatur sacramentis*, God is not tied to His sacraments.*⁴ This can never be too distinctly stated, because there are many good people who imagine that insistence on the necessity of Church, sacraments, and ministry involves a terrible and indeed shocking doctrine that God's hands are tied to these means of grace, and that His omnipotence is somehow limited. They see that such a doctrine must be false, that it is almost blasphemous; they rightly recoil from it; but they are mistaken in supposing that it is held by churchmen of any school of thought.

Half a truth has again been mistaken for the whole. God is not bound to His appointed channels of grace. That is one half. *But we are.* That is the other half, which completes the truth. We are not to forsake the household of God, or its sacraments, although the grace of God can and does overflow the special channels to which His promises are attached. If we refuse to drink of a fountain provided for us, because He is able to bring water for us out of the rock in the wilderness, we greatly err. It is written, *Thou shalt not tempt the Lord thy God.*⁵ What are 'unessentials' for God are not therefore unessentials for us. Are we then to judge those who have not known, or have not recognized, the household, or the fountains of grace made ready for those within it? God forbid. But for those who have seen and understood, it would be a grave presumption to remain

¹ Note B.   *Spiritual Communion* (p. 5).
² Note C.   *Confessors as presbyters without ordination* (p. 6).
³ Note D.   '*Nulla salus extra Ecclesiam*' (p. 6).
⁴ Note E.   '*Deus non alligatur sacramentis*' (p. 7).
⁵ Matt. iv. 7; Deut. vi. 16; Exod. xvii. 2, 7.

aloof. To despise and reject appointed channels of grace, counting upon God's power to bestow it in other ways, is to 'tempt' Him.

IV

Divergent views of the nature of the Church and the due credentials of its ministry are a chief obstacle in the way of Christian unity, but those who look upon these problems as 'merely ecclesiastical', unessential, will not give time to studying them.[1] Are they to wait for Christendom to come round to their way of thinking? It will be suggested in a later chapter how the sacramental principle helps to explain the nature of the Church in the world; no study of the Church as the household of God can have any meaning without some appreciation of that principle. Also it is first necessary to see that we may be bound to follow appointed ways although God cannot be bound. That does not, of course, establish the truth of the old belief that a continuing stewardship has been divinely appointed for the household, but it is necessary before there can be any serious examination of that belief.

[1] 'In recent generations Reformed churchmen have been little interested in questions of catholicity and indeed, in many cases, have not believed in the Church in any recognizable Biblical or traditional sense.' (D. T. Jenkins, *The Nature of Catholicity*, pp. 14, 15.)

NOTES TO CHAPTER I

A. SACRAMENT

The Latin *sacramentum* and *mysterium* are used in the Vulgate, apparently indifferently (e.g. Col. i. 26, 27), for 'mystery', to translate μυστήριον from the original Greek of the New Testament; but 'sacrament' is not used in the English translations. The word has come into Christian use in the same way in which the wording of the Creed has been evolved, in order to express conceptions and truths that are implicit in the Bible. For the stages in the meaning of the word, see Archbishop R. C. Trench, *On the Study of Words*, pp. 137 f., and W. Bright, *Sermons of St Leo the Great*, p. 136.

B. SPIRITUAL COMMUNION

In the office for the Communion of the Sick, instruction is given that 'if a man, either by reason of extremity of sickness,...or by any other just impediment, do not receive the Sacrament of Christ's Body and Blood...if he do truly repent him of his sins, and stedfastly believe...he doth eat and drink the Body and Blood of our Saviour Christ profitably to his soul's health, although he do not receive the Sacrament with his mouth'. This teaching was given in the first vernacular Prayer Book of Edward VI in 1549, and has ever since been retained. Dr W. J. Sparrow Simpson deals with this subject in *The Ministry and the Eucharist* at pp. 72 and 99 f.

C.   CONFESSORS AS PRESBYTERS WITHOUT ORDINATION

Some writings on Church order and worship dating from about the third century assign 'the honour of the presbyterate' to confessors without actual ordination. See Gore and Turner, p. 134, and Bishop W. H. Frere in *Essays on Early Hist.* pp. 289 f. It was expressly stated that they could not be made bishops without laying on of hands, possibly because a bishop is himself the minister of ordination.

D.   'NULLA SALUS EXTRA ECCLESIAM'

'Nearly all the great Fathers of the Church used to say: "Nulla salus extra ecclesiam." That phrase does not necessarily mean that no one can be ultimately saved who is not on earth in visible communion with the Church, but it does mean that God's grace is ordinarily given to us, not as mere individuals but as members of a body....If we are to attach a true and useful meaning to the phrase, we must remember that the Church is a society infinitely wider than people commonly suppose. It is certainly not to be identified with the Church of England, or the Church of Rome, or the orthodox Churches of the East, or even with these taken together as being one visible body, though now, unhappily, divided.

'The Church must include, at least, all those who have been baptized with water in the Name of the Father, and of the Son, and of the Holy Ghost; and we certainly need not deny that the grace of God can and does overflow the special channels to which the promises are attached. We may distinguish, as Dr Pusey was accustomed to distinguish, between the soul and the body of the Church. I know of no wider and more beautiful conception of the Church than that contained in one of his University sermons (on the "Responsibility of the Intellect in matters of Faith", preached in 1872, pp. 37-44, *University Sermons*, vol. III):

The soul of the Church includes, we cannot doubt, a great multitude which no man can number of all nations, and kindreds, and peoples, and tongues, who did not on earth belong to its body; as contrariwise believers, who led to the end bad lives and died impenitent, belonged, it may be, visibly to its body, but not to its soul.

For the Lover and Father of mankind, Who willeth not that any should perish, has not one way only of bringing home His lost sheep. All who shall be saved, shall be saved for the sake of that Precious Blood, which has redeemed our earth and arrayed it with Divine glory and beauty. Varied and beautiful, each with its own special loveliness, will be the choirs of His elect. In those ever open portals there enter, day and night, that countless multitude of every people, nation, and language; they who, in the Church, were by His grace faithful to Him, and they who knew not the Church of God, whom the Church below knew not how to win, or, alas! neglected to win them, but whom Jesus looked upon and the Father drew to Himself, whom His inner light enlightened, and who out of the misery of our fallen state, drawn by His unknown grace, looked up yearningly to Him their "unknown God", yet still their God, for He made them for Himself.

There, out of every religion or irreligion, out of every clime, in whatever ignorance steeped, in whatever hatred, or contempt, or blasphemy of Christ nurtured, God has His own elect, who ignorantly worship Him, and whose ignorant fear or longing He Who inspired it will accept.

'It is remarkable that these eloquent and tolerant words were written, not by a so-called *broad* Churchman, but by the man who did more than any one else in the last century to bring back the English Church and the English people to full belief in the importance and reality of sacramental grace, which is assured only to those who are in full communion with the Church.' (M. Cyril Bickersteth, *Letters to a Godson*, Second Series, chapter XVII.)

E. 'DEUS NON ALLIGATUR SACRAMENTIS'

This is sometimes expressed more generally, *non alligatur mediis*. It is found in substance in the teaching of St Thomas Aquinas (1227–74) that, under certain circumstances, a man is sanctified by the interior act of God *cuius potentia sacramentis visibilibus non alligatur.* (*Summa* III, Quaestio lxviii, Art. ii.)

CHAPTER II. WORDS & NAMES

SOME words that must be used in any discussion of Church and ministry are commonly understood nowadays in meanings quite different from their meaning in the New Testament. This is true especially of the word 'Church' itself. It will be found too that some names or descriptions, such as apostles, and overseers or bishops, did not originally have the same significance that they have since acquired.*[1] It will be generally agreed that our surest guidance to a true interpretation must be looked for in the thought and language of apostolic and sub-apostolic times, particularly in that of the New Testament itself. There are other necessary words that are ambiguous and are used, often unwittingly, in different meanings by writers on these subjects, who therefore are sometimes found to be at cross purposes.

'CHURCH'

Not long ago a newspaper in a large provincial town contained notices of the religious services of over forty different denominations, nineteen of which used the word 'Church' in describing themselves. The word has come to be used very loosely. Even of Communism it has been said, by Berdyaev, that it 'wishes to be not only an organized Society, a State, but a Church as well'. It is useless to quarrel with such extended use of the word, or to try to confine it to the historic Church; Sir Thomas More, saint and scholar, wrote of 'the churche of the Paynims'.[2]

Even within the limits of orthodox Christianity, the idea of nationality has developed in a way unknown to the primitive Church. In the New Testament we do not read of the Church *of* Ephesus, the Church *of* Rome, and so on, but of the saints *at* Colossae, or *at* Philippi, the Church *in* Ephesus, or the Church that is in the house of Nymphas, or of Aquila and Priscilla. It is one and the same Church, visible and organic, that is found welling up everywhere throughout the old world. It is like the sea; we may go to the sea on various coasts of our own or other lands. We shall find it at Berwick or Blackpool, Biarritz or Bermuda, but it is all the same

Note A. *Changed meanings of words* (p. 13).
Sir Thomas More, *Heresyes*, II. Works, 178/2.

sea. We do not speak of the sea of Berwick, or of Bermuda. It is true that we may observe variations in its appearance. The sea at Berwick has a different colour and temperature from those of the sea at Bermuda, but it is all the same sea. If you sail from one place to another you will find exactly the same salt water; if you found some harbour where the water was very different, you would know that it had become contaminated and was not pure sea water. Similarly, in apostolic times, there was no distinct Church of Jerusalem, or of Rome, or of Philippi. They were all visibly and organically one body, whose membership only was localized.★[1]

The great subject of Christian reunion is closely concerned with a question that may be asked in regard to each Christian communion: Is it organically and recognizably *one* with 'the Church in Ephesus' or 'in the house of Nymphas'? On the one hand, all Christian communions that can claim to be truly and organically one with 'the church and the apostles and presbyters' at Jerusalem must also, it is plain, be truly and organically one with each other. In other words, the Apostolic Church of the first century is continuously one with the Apostolic Church of to-day; so this question vitally concerns every Christian communion. On the other hand, every Christian communion that cannot truly make that claim, however faithful and devout its members may be, must be lacking in something that is essential for organic unity with the Church of the apostles and essential, therefore, for Christian unity to-day.

It is clear that the mere adoption of the word 'Church' by a religious body settles nothing. Nor can it be admitted that a religious society or communion possesses organic unity with the Apostolic Church merely because it has been founded and carried on by sincere Christian believers. The members of a society, whether it is large or small, may all have been baptized into the universal Church, and yet their society, as a society, may not truly form part of the Church. Consider the following examples: the Society of Friends (Quakers); the Society of Jesus (Jesuits); the Society for the Propagation of the Gospel; the Salvation Army; the Church Army; the Congregational Union; the Wesleyan Connexion. That is a very varied list. The members of some of these societies have remained faithful to the life and worship of the historic Church, which others have deserted. The members of some of these societies have never even been baptized into the Church. All these societies have, in various ways,

Note B. *The Church localized* (p. 14).

manifestly been used as instruments of divine grace. None of them
is a 'Church' in the New Testament sense, or in any sense that
would have been recognizable to the early Christians.

The point which it is sought to bring out here is that we must
rid our minds of some present-day conceptions in order to grasp
clearly what the Church means in the New Testament. Thus, for
example, there is mentioned at Ephesus and Pergamum a sect of
Nicolaitans which, in the language of to-day, would be classed as
a 'denomination' and would probably be called 'the Nicolaitan
Church'; it might even find favour with the State and become
'established', when it would be called the Church of Ephesus. But
to the early Church, such a description would have been impossible
and unthinkable.

The true nature and meaning of the Church in the New Testament
must be considered more fully in the next chapter.

'CATHOLIC'

The expression 'the Catholic Church' first occurs in the letter of
St Ignatius to the Smyrnaeans, written about A.D. 110, where it
means the one Church 'throughout-all', as opposed to local groups
of its members, its local 'Churches'. Later, when heretical Christian
sects were formed, the word acquired the additional meaning of the
one and faithful Church, and that is its settled historical meaning.*[1]
The famous *Commonitorium* of Vincent of Lerins in the fifth century,
after speaking of the sufficiency of Scripture and the occurrence,
nevertheless, of various errors, says that in the Catholic Church
'we hold that which has been believed everywhere, always, by all'.
The word 'Catholic' will here be used in this acceptance, *ubique,
semper, ab omnibus*, which, incidentally, is thought to afford the
shortest and simplest disproof of claims subsequently asserted for
the bishop of Rome. These were unheard of in the first few centuries,
and they have never been admitted everywhere or by all. Rome,
which maintains that the great Roman Church is the whole Church,
is now quite consistent in claiming a monopoly of the word
'Catholic', but that claim cannot be admitted by other Christians,
among whom, strangely enough, it is most often those most bitterly
opposed to the Roman claim who verbally concede it by speaking
and writing of 'Catholic' as if it meant 'Roman Catholic'.

[1] Note C. *The Catholic Church* (p. 14).

'APOSTLE'

The word 'apostle', which means one who is 'sent forth', is very commonly supposed to refer only to our Lord's inner circle of disciples, 'the Twelve', with the addition of St Paul. Its actual Bible meaning calls for careful examination in a later chapter; it will be found that it is used in the New Testament in a considerably wider sense, and that it includes many others such as Silvanus, Timothy, James the 'brother' of the Lord, who were among the chief pastors of the Church in the New Testament period.

'BISHOP'

This is, of course, a contraction of a common Greek word *episkopos* which means 'overseer'; it has come to have a suggestion of dignity. In studying Christian origins we should remember that at first it carried no sense of grandeur or great pre-eminence. In the first century, in Asia Minor and Greece, where the supervision and guidance of the apostles and their successors could be given only from time to time, the presbyters were necessarily the local overseers or managers of the congregation and were often described as over-seers. (They do not seem to have been so described in Palestine, where apostles were resident.) From the beginning of the second century onwards, presbyters are not referred to as overseers. In most important towns or districts there was now a resident chief pastor, superior in the ministry to both presbyters and deacons, and he was now known as 'the overseer' or bishop. For a thousand years or more, these overseers were regarded as successors in ministry of the apostles, not of the first-century overseers, the presbyters. It is certain that this transference of the name or description of overseer occurred; how the transference came about is a major problem of early Church history, which will be explored later.

'EPISCOPACY'

In the first century, the chief pastors of the Church were the apostles and their immediate successors. They were not called overseers or bishops. Except in Palestine they were itinerant. Presbyters were resident local ministers and outside Palestine they were often called overseers, a description that well fitted one aspect of their duties as the managers and pastors of congregations.

By the beginning of the second century, members of the chief pastorate were becoming settled in resident oversight of the Church in most large towns and districts. From that time onwards, presbyters generally were never described as overseers. The name of 'the overseer' became attached to the chief pastor of the local Church, who had succeeded to the earlier oversight of the itinerant chief pastors in what is usually called 'diocesan episcopacy'. Some writers use the expression 'monarchical episcopacy' to express the fact that Churches came under the oversight or 'rule' of a single overseer, replacing the oversight of itinerant apostles, but the word 'mon-episcopacy' is preferable; 'monarchical' conveys an impression out of keeping with the paternal and constitutional character of the Catholic bishop, which is that of the father of his family or flock.

The name 'episcopacy' is applied, not perhaps very aptly, to denote acceptance of the chief pastors, now called bishops, as an organic part of the Church. From earliest times they have been regarded as successors to the chief pastorate of the apostles of the first century. The chief pastors of the Church, from the apostles to the bishops of to-day, have almost always had a leading voice in the administration of the Church, as well, of course, as in its spiritual guidance. Nevertheless it is an error, although a common one, to think of episcopacy as a mere system of government. Thus in the custom of the Irish or Celtic Church, although the bishops possessed spiritual authority higher than the rest of the ministry and they alone could ordain, abbots, who were not always bishops in order, 'ruled' the Church in matters of administration. In the immemorial belief of the historic Church, bishops, as chief pastors and as the only ministers of ordination, are essential to its continuity by the handing on of its stewardship in ordination. On a true analysis, that is the essential function of bishops in the historic Church; the name 'episcopacy' has to serve, although it is not merely 'oversight' that it stands for.

'VALIDITY'

'Valid' and 'validity' are unlucky words. 'Valid' has long been used by theologians in the sense of 'firm' or 'assured', as equivalent to the Greek word *bebaia*,*[1] in which its contrasted opposite, 'invalid', does *not* mean void or ineffective. Thus we require of a physician that his skill and learning shall be attested in certain approved or recognized ways, although there are doubtless some

[1] Note D. '*Valid*' (p. 14).

skilled and competent men who cannot produce 'valid' qualifications. A man who has not received due credentials may possess high actual qualifications.

But the word 'valid' shades into a further meaning. Thus if a will is not properly witnessed, the testator's intention goes for nothing and his will is 'invalid', not now merely unsure, but ineffective and void. That is the legal sense of 'invalid', and is also its most ordinary use. When a railway ticket has ceased to be 'valid' it is useless.

Unfortunately, theologians persist in using 'valid' to mean 'sure', while their readers insist upon taking its opposite 'invalid' as meaning 'ineffective',[*1] and so, it may be, involving an insufferable aspersion upon their particular ministries and sacraments. The theologians have repeatedly explained that 'invalidity' is not equivalent to 'inefficacy', and that it does not involve the aspersions it is supposed to convey;[*2] nevertheless it is an unhappy word and has often unintentionally caused pain and aroused needless indignation. One cannot help wondering if it is not sometimes wilfully misunderstood.[3] If 'authentic' were substituted for 'valid', it might perhaps serve the purposes of discussion without involving wrongful implications. Archbishop Davidson thought it right, and adequate, to distinguish 'regular' and 'irregular'. 'I purposely avoid the words "valid" and "invalid", as I have always found myself unable, without a feeling of intolerable presumption, to give to that phrase the meaning which in popular parlance it would seem to carry. The word "invalid" has, except when applied to physical health, drifted far from the original force of the Latin adjective.'[4]

'SUCCESSION'

This word is used variously in different senses, which has caused some obscurity, particularly in discussion of 'apostolic succession'. In chapter XIX an attempt is made to distinguish these meanings.

[1] Note E. *Implications of 'invalidity'* (p. 14).
[2] Note F. *'Invalidity' in theological use* (p. 15).
[3] Manning, p. 75, 'If God acts at all he cannot act invalidly'.
[4] *Kikuyu* (1915), p. 30.

NOTES TO CHAPTER II

A. CHANGED MEANINGS OF WORDS

'Ill and unfit use of words wonderfully obstructs the understanding.' (Francis Bacon, *Novum Organum*, xliii.) 'One of the difficulties of thinking clearly about anything is that it is almost impossible not to form our ideas in words which have some previous association for us; with the result that our thought is already shaped along certain lines before we have begun to follow it out.' (A. A. Milne, *Peace with Honour*, p. 12.)

B. THE CHURCH LOCALIZED

'The local Church was but the outcrop there of the total and continuous Church, one everywhere. The total Church was not made up by adding the local Churches together, but the local Church was made a Church by representing there and then the total Church. It was just where the total Church looked out at one point.' (Forsyth, p. 60.)

C. THE CATHOLIC CHURCH

'In its earliest usages therefore, as a fluctuating epithet of ἐκκλησία, "catholic" means "universal", as opposed to "individual", "particular". The Church throughout the world is called "catholic", just as the Resurrection of all mankind is called "catholic". In its later sense, as a fixed attribute, it implies orthodoxy as opposed to heresy, conformity as opposed to dissent. Thus to the primary ideas of *extension* are super-added also the ideas of *doctrine* and *unity*. But this later sense grows out of the earlier. The truth was the same everywhere, "quod semper, quod ubique, quod ab omnibus". The heresies were partial, scattered, localized, isolated.' (Lightfoot, *Ignatius*, ii. pp. 310, 311.)

D. 'VALID'

βεβαία is so rendered in Lightfoot's translation of St Ignatius, *Ep. ad Smyrn.* 8, 'Let that be held a valid eucharist which is under the bishop or one to whom he shall have committed it', ἐκείνη βεβαία εὐχαριστία ἡγείσθω. (Lightfoot, *Ignatius*, ii. pp. 309, 569.) It is translated as 'sure' in the New Testament, *to the end that the promise may be sure*, Rom. iv. 16, εἰς τὸ εἶναι βεβαίαν τὴν ἐπαγγελίαν, *firma* in the Vulgate, *ut...firma sit promissio*.

E. IMPLICATIONS OF 'INVALIDITY'

'Invalidity' is constantly understood as meaning void, not merely unassured. Thus the presidential address to the Methodist Conference at Liverpool in July 1939 condemned as the greatest hindrance to Christian reunion 'the belief that, through episcopal ordination, a grace is conveyed without which the administration of the Lord's Supper is lacking in validity', by which the speaker evidently meant 'efficacy'. Referring to this, a contemporary religious weekly paper remarked that efficacy 'is the sense incorrectly, but almost invariably, attached to it by Free Churchmen', and went on to remark: 'About episcopal ordination the English Church is certain. About other methods of appointment to the ministry it is not. It affirms the positive. It declines to affirm the negative. The opposite of certain is uncertain. It is not false. What graces may be granted through irregular ways must be left to the Giver of all good gifts to decide.' (*Church Times*, 28 July 1939.)

F. 'INVALIDITY' IN THEOLOGICAL USE

'To say "God's grace is not tied to His own appointed ordinances" is one thing. To say "other than Church ordinances may, perhaps, be His ordinances, only we are not sure of it" is quite another.' (B. J. Kidd, *Validity: Name and Thing*, p. 9.)

'In other words, ordinances administered without due commission, e.g. Eucharists so-called administered by those who are not priests, and ordinations so-called administered by those who are not bishops, are *invalid* for lack of due authority in the ministrant, *but* they may be *efficacious* in the sense of being the means or occasions of spiritual fellowship with God which is certain to win a blessing.' (W. Bright, *Sylva*, xxiii. No. 25, unpublished MS., quoted by Dr Kidd, *ut supra*.)

CHAPTER III. THE CHURCH OR EKKLESIA

I

OUR word 'church', like the German *kirche*, Dutch *kerk*, Scottish and Northern English *kirk*, comes from the Greek *kuriakon*, and means 'the Lord's' (house), i.e. an actual building of any kind devoted to Christian worship. *Kuriakon* does not occur anywhere in the Bible; until long after the first century Christians possessed no 'church' buildings. It is a curious thing that the same word is also used to translate the *ekklesia* ('Church') of the New Testament, which is no stone structure but a divine society of men, and it adds to the confusion of our names. Dr Hort entitled his well-known book *The Christian Ecclesia* because, as he said, 'The English term "church", now the most familiar representative of *ecclesia* to most of us, carries with it associations derived from the institutions and doctrines of later times, and thus cannot at present without a constant mental effort be made to convey the full and exact force which originally belonged to *ecclesia*'.

II

If we seek to get behind words and names to the simple facts that they denoted in the beginnings of Christian history, we may profitably focus our attention on the New Testament word *ekklesia*, of which 'church' is so unsatisfactory a translation. In actual Greek use, *ekklesia* meant the legislative assembly of the citizens, the nation in its political and corporate character. In the Septuagint, the Greek version of the Old Testament, it was taken as the equivalent of the Hebrew *qāhāl*, the usual name for the congregation of Israel. When St Stephen spoke of Moses 'in the *ekklesia* in the wilderness',[1] his actual spoken word may have been the Hebrew *qāhāl* or the corresponding Aramaic *keneset*. *Qāhāl* (*ekklesia* in the Septuagint) occurs often in the Old Testament, and it is unfortunate that our English version translates there by such words as 'congregation' or 'assembly', but in the New Testament by 'church', because we are apt to miss the close connexion that exists between the Jewish and Christian dispensations.

[1] Acts vii. 38.

The Ekklesia or Church of Israel under the Law was intensely national, although proselytes might be admitted with circumcision, which was regarded as a spiritual as well as a physical rite of admission.[1] The 'Church' was one great people, great not so much politically as in a religious sense, united by the blood-relationship of common descent from Abraham, Isaac and Jacob, by a unique history of divine guidance and protection, by a divinely appointed system of religious observance and worship. The divine character of the 'Church' of Israel is the constant theme of the Old Testament: *My people Israel, Israel whom I have chosen;*[2] *The assembly of the Lord, the Congregation of the Lord.*[3]

Now all of this is full of significance for us, because the Christian *ekklesia* or 'Church' of the New Testament is the renewed Church of Israel. The new Israel is no longer confined to the Children of Jacob after the flesh. Jews and Gentiles are now united within it: *Ye that once were far off are made nigh in the blood of Christ. For He... brake down the middle wall of partition,* i.e. the old racial division of Jew and Gentile.[4] The new Ekklesia of the Gospel is open to all, Greek or Jew, barbarian and Scythian, yet it is a continuance and succession of the old Ekklesia and, like that, it is a definite assembly, body, or community. Its Gospel rite of admission is the sacrament of Baptism. The New Testament shows clearly that the apostolic society were fully conscious of themselves as the true Israel. This can be seen in many passages where an Old Testament reference to the Israelite nation is applied to the Christian community.*[5] Thus St Peter, when he says *Ye are an elect race, a royal priesthood, a holy nation,* is applying to the new Israel, the Christian Church, words from the book of Exodus, originally spoken of the Old Israel.[6]

III

In the New Testament, *ekklesia* is also frequently used in the sense of a local group or congregation of members of the great Ekklesia, and again it is loosely rendered in English as 'church'. Such congregations are named in many towns or districts, or identified as meeting together in private houses such as those of Prisca, Philemon, or Nymphas. Although the group is thus referred to, the descrip-

---

[1] Lev. xxvi. 41; Deut. x. 16, xxx. 6; Jer. ix. 26; Ezek. xliv. 7, 9.
[2] Is. xliv. 1.   [3] Num. xvi. 3, xxvii. 17.   [4] Eph. ii. 13, 14.
[5] Note A. *The Christian Ekklesia as the Church of Israel* (p. 19).
[6] I Pet. ii. 9; Ex. xix. 6.

tion simply implies that its members belong to the great Ekklesia of the faithful, *continuing stedfastly in the apostles' teaching and fellowship*, and controlled by their authoritative guidance. It is referred to as the ekklesia in, not of, Ephesus, or Corinth, or Philemon's house. (It is interesting to find that the original meaning of *paroikia*, the word from which 'parish' is derived, is 'the Ekklesia sojourning or lodging locally'.)*[1] This use of ekklesia or church denoted an unbroken unity,*[2] and it is utterly different from the modern usage which denotes separation in doctrine or fellowship. An incipient tendency to denominationalism was sternly rebuked by St Paul. Those who disregarded the apostolic injunctions were *fallen away from grace*.[3] Later on, when another trace of sectarianism appears, those who are described in the Apocalypse as Nicolaitans are sharply distinguished from the Ekklesia;[4] in conventional modern language, they would be called 'the Nicolaitan Church of Ephesus', but it would be contrary to the thought and language of the New Testament to apply the name of ekklesia or church to any dissident or separated group.

IV

The modern use of 'Church' to describe a denomination or sect has no scriptural authority or precedent whatever. The name is now commonly given to any religious association or society that is distinguished by some particular divergence from the doctrine or worship of other Christians. It has come to imply separation instead of unity. In the words of Dr Headlam,[5] 'It is difficult to conceive of anything more fundamentally alien to the whole spirit of the New Testament than this'. Thus the Wesleyans, until they were more and more estranged from the fellowship of the Church in England by the cold stupidity of its leaders, were called a 'Connexion'. After they seceded altogether, they became known as a 'Church', to mark the tragedy of separation. The dangerous advantage of secular establishment carries with it the title of the Church 'of' the country where it predominates, irrespective of its tenets. If the Nicolaitan Christians survived and were established to-day at Ephesus they would be called 'the Church of Ephesus'. Unitarians, Mormons, Christian Scientists, and Spiritists all describe themselves

---

[1] Note B. *The Church 'sojourning'* (p. 20).
[2] Note C. *Local ekklesia part of the one Ekklesia* (p. 20).
[3] I Cor. i. 12 *seq.*; Gal. v. 4.   [4] Rev. ii. 6.   [5] Headlam, p. 78.

as Churches. If Buddhists or Mohammedans chose to adopt the name, no one could forbid them.

On the other hand, there are associations of devout Christians, holding fast to evangelical truth, that do not adopt the name of Churches, such for instance as the Society of Friends and the Salvation Army. They are highly esteemed; their piety and good works cannot be hid under any bushel. No one can 'un-church' them, who do not 'church' themselves. In the same way, it implies no disparagement of the faith and works, or other essential Christian graces, apparent among the members of any Christian denomination or society, to say that the word 'church' in the New Testament sense is not appropriate to it as a society.

The sacrament of Holy Baptism is the admission into membership of the Catholic Church, the Ekklesia of the New Testament, not into any 'national' Church or denomination or society. As regards all individual adherents of such societies who have been baptized, they have received membership of the Catholic Church, the Ekklesia of the New Testament, whether or not they remain loyal members of it, and notwithstanding that their society holds itself apart from that fellowship. Baptized persons can 'un-church' themselves by deserting the fellowship of the Church, but they cannot be 'un-churched'. 'It would be quite impossible to make those who have once been baptized to be other than members of the Church.'*[1]

[1] Note D. ‘*To un-church*’ (p. 20).

NOTES TO CHAPTER III

A. THE CHRISTIAN EKKLESIA AS THE CHURCH OF ISRAEL

Many New Testament passages identify the Church of the New Covenant, the Christian Ekklesia, with the Church of the Old Covenant. See Acts iii. 23, xv. 14–17; Rom. xv. 10; I Cor. x. 1–4; II Cor. vi. 16–18; Gal. vi. 16; Heb. iv. 7–11, viii. 10, x. 15–17; I Pet. ii. 9.

‘The first Christians did not regard themselves as a new society, but as the ancient "People of God", that is, as that portion of the Church of the Patriarchs and Prophets which had not, by rejecting the Messiah, forfeited the birthright and cut itself off from the "promises of Israel". Many of the prophets had proclaimed that only a "remnant" of Israel after the flesh would repent and be saved; others had foretold that in the Messianic age Gentiles also would be brought to share the religious privileges of Israel. The Christian position was that, by recognizing Jesus as Messiah, they and they alone understood the prophets aright. The

number of Jews who had rejected the Messiah was larger than might have
been expected, so also was the number of Gentiles who had accepted Him;
but that did not in any way alter the fundamental position that only the
community of those who did accept Him could claim to be the "Israel
of God".' (Streeter, p. 47.)

B. The Church 'sojourning'

παροικία, from which *parochia* and parish, originally applied to what
we now call a diocese, is in fact a shortened form of ἡ ἐκκλησία ἡ παροικοῦσα 'the Church which sojourns' or lodges, in such-and-such a place.
(Wordsworth, p. 145; see also Bright, pp. 51-3.)

C. Local ekklesia part of the one Ekklesia

'The very word "ekklesia" forbids us to think of any mere local community; the *ekklesia* in a place is *the one race* as existing in that place, e.g.
the "ecclesia" at Corinth is the one called-out race of God which exists
in Corinth as in many other places. The one race existed first, precedes
the local ecclesia and is represented by it.' (A. M. Ramsey, *The Gospel
and the Catholic Church*, p. 47.)

D. 'To un-church'

The baptized cannot be 'un-churched'. 'One must protest against the
use of the expression "to un-church". It would be quite impossible to
make those who have once been baptized to be other than members of
the Church.' (Hamilton, II. p. 207.)

CHAPTER IV. CHRIST & THE EKKLESIA

I

THERE are good people who cry out against theology and creed because they fail to see them in the Gospels. They regard theology as an excrescence upon religion, marring the 'simplicity' of the Gospel story. But only those who do not think could speak of 'the simplicity of the Gospels'. To the thoughtful they bristle with questions demanding answers. For example, take our Lord's saying, *Come unto me...and I will give you rest,* and think what they mean. Who was the speaker? Is He alive now or dead? Was He speaking to His contemporaries or to us as well? Ignore such questions, and you treat the Gospel as only a surpassingly beautiful biography of a uniquely noble man. But the first recorded creed was spoken by St Peter, *Thou art the Christ, the Son of the living God.* All Catholic theology is a following-out of that brief confession to its profound implications. On that creed or confession, our Lord said that He would build His Ekklesia.*[1] Christians who seek to uphold the ethical teaching of the Gospels detached from a theological basis evade the question *Who say ye that I am?*

The same people who decry theology and creed stand aloof from the ancient Church and protest against what they speak of as 'organization' in religion. Here also it is failure to see the necessary implications of the Gospel that leads them to think of the Ekklesia in the world as a kind of abstraction, independent of any visible social framework, a 'society' independent of the organic links that join individuals in a recognizable group, a 'society' without visible marks of association. Just as to think lightly of doctrine is to ignore the implications of our Lord's words about Himself, so also to think lightly of the organism of the divine Society that He founded is to ignore the implications of what He said regarding it.

The Law and the Prophets are the constant background of His teaching; He came not to destroy but to fulfil. The parable of the vineyard and the husbandmen describes the old Ekklesia of Israel and its officers, the chief priests and scribes and elders, as indeed they themselves clearly perceived;[2] the lord of the vineyard *will come and*

---

[1] Note A. *St Peter's confession, and the Ekklesia* (p. 27).
[2] Mark xii. 12; cp. Matt. xxi. 45; Luke xx. 19.

destroy the husbandmen, and will give the vineyard to others. These *others* were, in the first instance, the chosen Twelve, to whom He appointed *a kingdom* and symbolic *thrones.*[1] Their special authority *to bind and to loose*[2] was expressed in the familiar Rabbinic terms for the power of the doctors of the Law to 'pronounce forbidden' or 'pronounce permitted' some action about which a question has arisen. The *keys* of the kingdom include the *key of knowledge* which the scribes of Israel had taken away, entering not in themselves, and hindering them that were entering in,[3] thus shutting the kingdom of heaven against men.[4] The apostles were the appointed husbandmen of the restored Ekklesia, the new Israel.

II

The new Ekklesia of the Lord, thus rebuilt upon the old Ekklesia of Israel, is to be a society recognizable in the world both collectively and individually. Its members should *all be one, that the world may believe.*[5] The unity of the members of the Ekklesia is to be more than mystical and spiritual, it is to be such as can be perceived★[6] by those who are still outside it, such as will draw them in by its attraction, *until they shall become one flock, one shepherd.*[7]

Again, the kingdom of heaven is like unto a net, that was cast into the sea, and gathered of every kind, good and bad.[8] This parable of the kingdom of heaven describes not the ideal kingdom of perfection that shall be when all things are accomplished, but only the Ekklesia as the kingdom of heaven temporarily in the world. In modern times there has grown up a conception of the Ekklesia as a society composed of individuals who are members of it in virtue of being 'good', a society to which the 'bad' cannot belong, a society that is invisible except in so far as its members are visible because they are 'good'. The parable gives no support to such a conception of the Ekklesia, indeed it rules it out. The drag-net which is the Ekklesia in the world contains bad as well as good; the sorting-out shall not be until the end of the world.[9] The members of the Ekklesia are visibly members of it not because they are 'good', but because they have been visibly received into it, as if into the drag-net.

[1] Luke xxii. 29, 30; cp. Matt. xix. 28.
[2] Matt. xviii. 18.   [3] Luke xi. 52.
[4] Matt. xxiii. 13.   [5] John xvii. 21.
[6] Note B. *A visible unity* (p. 27).   [7] John x. 16.
[8] Matt. xiii. 47.   [9] Matt. xiii. 49.

The short parable of the man *having left his house, and given authority to his servants, to each one his work,*[1] seems to refer particularly to apostolic authority; for when St Peter asked whether this parable was spoken to the apostles, *or even unto all,* in reply, *the Lord said, Who then is the faithful and wise steward, whom his lord shall set over his household, to give them their portion of food in due season?*[2]

For how many years, or thousands of years, was the new Ekklesia to endure in the world? During His earthly life, our Lord said that He did not know; after the Resurrection, He said it was not for the apostles to know the times and seasons.[3] There is, indeed, a strong indication that it is to endure for a long tract of world time. *The end is not yet. The gospel must first be preached unto all the nations.*[4] This *gospel of the kingdom shall be preached in the whole inhabited earth for a testimony unto all the nations; and then shall the end come.*[5] The end is not yet. But unless all things were to be accomplished in the lifetime of the apostles, it was necessary that these stewards of the household, so solemnly chosen and commissioned, must as solemnly hand on to others who should come after them their stewardship and keys, and due measure of their authority; otherwise the Ekklesia would cease to possess the stewardship appointed for it by the Founder. The principle of succession in the stewardship seems to be implied in our Lord's dispositions and directions, although not (so far at least as they are recorded)★[6] the methods to be followed in securing its continuance.

III

Nowadays we spell 'Apostle' with a capital letter, and treat it as a title. It is worth while to notice that in the Gospels it is a description rather than a title. It means, of course, one who is sent forth, and is closely equivalent to 'missionary'. (There are, unfortunately, far too many of us who do not realize that we profess in the Creed our belief in the Holy Missionary Church.) The word 'apostle' occurs once only in each of the first and second Gospels. In the fourth Gospel, although the Twelve are never referred to as apostles, the same meaning is clearly brought out: *As the Father hath sent me, even so send I you.*[7] This announces a world mission that, in some way, must be carried on until 'the end', the same mission, manifestly

---

[1] Mark xiii. 34; cp. Luke xii. 35 *seq.*   [2] Luke xii. 41, 42.
[3] Matt. xxiv. 36; Mark xiii. 32; Acts i. 7, 8.   [4] Mark xiii. 7, 10.
[5] Matt. xxiv. 14.   [6] Note C. *Our Lord's directions* (p. 27).
[7] John xx. 21; see also xvii. 18.

'sent forth' from the one original impulse. The Founder of the Ekklesia will not be sent to the world a second time on a second mission. There will be no sending of a new apostolate. If the divine mission-impulse has not been imparted to the Ekklesia of to-day and to-morrow, so that its chosen representatives are still 'sent forth' with the force and authority of the prime impulse, that impulse must have ceased. But the end is not yet.

The implications of Holy Communion as the great sacrament of the Ekklesia are profound and far reaching. For the present it must suffice to notice that they involve (a) a close and manifest unity of those who partake of it, (b) the appointment of a presiding officer who shall break the Bread and bless the Cup of which all partake. Further (c) it is the social sacrament of the whole Ekklesia; the presiding officer does not represent only the particular members who are present, and his stewardship in this office should have authority of a universal kind.★[1]

Any study of our Lord's provisions for His Ekklesia must include His promise for its continued after-guidance by the Holy Spirit. *He shall teach you all things. He shall guide you into all the truth...and He shall declare unto you the things that are to come.*[2] The Gospel records of our Lord's indications and directions for His Ekklesia, although they are vivid and illuminating, are parabolic and general; what completes them is the promise that He Himself will continue the building of the Ekklesia, *I will not leave you desolate: I come unto you. Lo, I am with you alway, even unto the end of the world.*[3]

The Ekklesia of the New Testament, *which is His Body*,[4] is a living Body, with the Lord its Head continually present. It is no man-made society, and its guidance has not been limited entirely to those words of our Lord that were recorded in the Gospels. If therefore the New Testament reveals to us the institution of the stewardship we shall look beyond the New Testament to see how it was continued by the first stewards and by those whom they taught and appointed to come after them. Unless we can suppose that the stewardship ordained by our Lord ceased with the deaths of those who knew Him in the flesh, we must further seek to perceive how it has persisted, and what is the principle of its continuance.

There has sometimes been a rather fruitless dispute as to whether

---

[1] Note D. *Holy Communion of the whole Ekklesia* (p. 27).
[2] John xiv. 26, xvi. 13.   [3] John xiv. 18; Matt. xxviii. 20.
[4] Eph. i. 22; Col. i. 24.

the Church came before the Gospel, or the Gospel came first,[1] and there is even some confusion between the Good News and the four written Evangels. The truth is that the two are indissolubly linked; the Church is part of the Gospel, and it is also the herald of the Gospel. It has been well said that our Lord came not so much to preach the Gospel as in order that there might be a Gospel to preach. He did not so much found 'a religion' as found a divine society to proclaim the Good News to all the world. For a generation or more before His sayings had been written in our Scriptures, that society, the Ekklesia or New Israel, had been carrying out its missionary work.

It is plain that the early Christians, believing that the Messiah had appeared in the person of Jesus, were fully conscious of themselves as the true post-messianic Israel. As has been already noted, Old Testament sayings, originally spoken to or of the Israelitish nation, are applied again and again to the Christian community. Baptized Christians are no longer Gentiles but Israelites, the Christian Ekklesia being *the Israel of God,*[2] *the people of God.*[3] Previously they were *separate from Christ, alienated from the commonwealth of Israel, and strangers from the covenants of the promise,* but now they are *no more strangers and sojourners, but fellow-citizens with the saints, and of the household of God.*[4] The apostolic band 'could no more think of themselves as an invisible body, as a society whose real limits were known to God alone, than they could think of the nation of Israel as being without clearly defined marks and limits to distinguish it from all other religious organizations'.*[5]

The need that was felt for restoring the initial ministry of the new Ekklesia to its appointed number of twelve is shown by the putting forward of two names, those of Barsabbas and Matthias. This solemn appointment to apostleship furnishes the Church for ever with guidance on the principle underlying all ordination. There are devout minds that have not understood the transmission of ministerial office and its integral part in the organism of the Church. The office of the apostle, it has been said,[6] 'could not be transmitted'. To those who have not grasped the principle of succession in apostolic authority, it seems almost meaningless, 'a mysterious kind of quality which is supposed to be essential for a valid ministry'; 'a mysterious, indescribable "quality" derived from the Apostles'.[7] Yet Barsabbas

---

[1] See Manning, pp. 72, 73.   [2] Gal. vi. 16.   [3] Heb. iv. 9.
[4] Eph. ii. 12, 19.   [5] Note E. *The apostolic society visible* (p. 28).
[6] Macgregor, p. 187.   [7] Ainslie, pp. 199, 249.

and Matthias were equally well qualified as faithful disciples, and as witnesses of the Resurrection. One only was appointed to *this ministry and apostleship*,[1] and his appointment was a definite transmission of the ministerial office then to be filled. It should also clear away any confusion of thought regarding the 'mysterious kind of quality' supposed to attach to ministerial succession; it is just the difference between a ministry of apostolic authority (and therefore universal authority) which Matthias received, and such unauthoritative ministries as may be exercised by other members of the household, among whom Barsabbas remained, as far as we know.

The Lord's reference to the stewards of His Ekklesia seems to have been strongly impressed upon the apostolic band. St Paul speaks several times of his stewardship and says that an overseer *must be blameless as God's steward*.[2]

We get a glimpse of the apostolic authority of 'binding and loosing' in operation at the Council of Jerusalem, and the narrative shows, at the same time, how vivid was the sense of direct guidance given by the Holy Spirit.[3]

As soon as occasion arose for the work of an auxiliary ministry in the Ekklesia, even for duties that at first were simple and menial, the Seven were appointed to the *diakonia* or 'service' by a solemn act signifying the imparting of authority, the laying on of the apostles' hands[4] in accordance with the solemn rites of the old Ekklesia.

Thus all indications we possess of the early apostolic conception of the Ekklesia are in accordance with the underlying principles of our Lord's sayings. They are not immediately carried into operation in the form of a fully developed ministerial system. Such traces as we have of the early development of the ministry show that the stewardship was delegated and handed on only step by step, and only as the original stewards or apostles, continuing under divine guidance, felt that this was becoming necessary.

Very early in the history of a new mission, the apostles who founded it appointed local overseers who could preside at the weekly Breaking of the Bread; but there is no indication anywhere that they provided for or authorized the subsequent ordination of additional overseers or presbyters in the absence of the itinerant missionaries,

---

[1] Acts i. 25.   [2] I Cor. ix. 17; Eph. iii. 2; Col. i. 25; Tit. i. 7.
[3] Acts xv. 28: *It seemed good to the Holy Ghost, and to us, to lay upon you no greater burden than these necessary things....*
[4] Acts vi. 6.

the apostles and 'apostolic men', who had the care of the Churches. The Second Coming was thought to be near at hand; the need for providing for an enduring continuance and replacement of the stewards and servants of the household could not be seen at first.

NOTES TO CHAPTER IV

A. St Peter's confession, and the Ekklesia

Matt. xvi. 18. 'If we may venture for a moment to substitute the name Israel and read the words as "on this rock I will build my Israel", we gain an impression which supplies at least an approximation to the probable sense. The Ecclesia of the ancient Israel was the Ecclesia of God; and now, having been confessed to be God's Messiah, nay His Son, He could to such hearers without risk of grave misunderstanding claim that Ecclesia as His own.' (Hort, p. 11.)

B. A visible unity

'The central text of John xvii. 21, provides no argument for any particular scheme of church order: yet it speaks of a visible unity so expressed as to be discernible not only to the spiritual but to "the world" with the eyes of flesh. It is to be a unity manifested in terms understandable by the man in the street.' (Hugh Martin, *Christian Reunion: a Plea for Action*, p. 67.)

C. Our Lord's directions

The Gospels mention that their record is not exhaustive, and during the forty days, our Lord was *speaking the things concerning the kingdom of God unto the apostles whom He had chosen* (Acts i. 2, 3; cp. John xxi. 25). Clement of Rome, who knew St Paul and St Peter (see chapter xvi), says that 'our apostles knew through our Lord Jesus Christ that there would be strife over the name of the bishop's office'. (Clem. *ad Cor.* 44.)

D. Holy Communion of the whole Ekklesia

'The very nature of the sacrament seems to look beyond the group to the whole Church; and since one cannot get rid of the corporate or representative element without altering the nature of what Jesus instituted, it would seem that the president ought to receive authority, not from the local group, but from the whole body throughout the world.

'Furthermore, if it is from the local Church alone that authority is derived to break the bread, then the separation of this company of believers from all others is thereby emphasized; for if the breaking of the bread is the act of this local group alone, then this group thereby becomes itself a corporate whole and the Church universal is divided into so many constantly changing local entities. But surely if there is a unity and a fellowship to be symbolized by and realized in this sacrament, it is the unity and fellowship of all believers in the Messiah, the great truth that in Christ Jesus all are brethren united in one world-wide communion and fellowship. But such a truth cannot find its proper expression unless the president of each local gathering derives his right to act, not from the local body, but from the whole Church throughout the world.

'The Holy Communion, then, as a function of the Church's life, seems to differ from all other functions in this, that it requires for its proper discharge an organ constructed after a certain definite principle—that of authorization from the whole body.' (Hamilton, II. p. 201.)

E. THE APOSTOLIC SOCIETY VISIBLE

Hamilton II. p. 28. See also R. Sohm, quoted Harnack, p. 224: 'The people of Israel, the people of God (qāhāl, ecclesia), really was in the old covenant an entity visible to everyone. The Christians considered themselves to be the new, the true, people of Israel. Hence it was inevitable that men should think of the new people of God involuntarily as of an outward visible society.'

CHAPTER V. THE EKKLESIA VISIBLE ON EARTH

A THEORY of a Church that is in the world, and yet is invisible, has caused some confusion of thought for which closer attention to Scripture is the best remedy. The word 'church'—*ekklesia*—occurs a hundred and ten times in the New Testament; it carries the meaning of an invisible Church only once, and there the reference is to the heavenly Church, the New Jerusalem.[1] Elsewhere, the Ekklesia is a visible fellowship or society, a community that *continued stedfastly in the apostles' fellowship*. Those who are its members can be known with certainty; they have been admitted by Holy Baptism which is outward and visible, as every sacrament must be, as well as inward and spiritual. The other great sacrament is central to the common life of the fellowship, is the normal sustenance of its life and the primary purpose of its assemblies; and, though later developments have tended to lay stress on other aspects of the Eucharist, the original principle always remains true.

We find this society already endowed by its Founder with stewards who derive from Him an office of authority throughout the whole society. Very early in its life, we see that these stewards impart a measure of their authority to others whom it will be enough at the moment to refer to as under-stewards, for we are not now considering their precise functions. While it is still possible, those who are appointed to office for the whole society are chosen by the voice of the whole society, *the whole multitude*.[2] During the short period of the life of the society covered by the New Testament records, we see this process extending, and the imparting of authority to other stewards in varying measure.

Day by day *those that were being saved* were added to the fellowship, but its members, the 'saints', were imperfect saints, still in the process of being saved; how sadly imperfect sometimes appears from St Paul's plain speaking to his flock. It is no invisible company of the elect, known only to God, that the New Testament portrays. In the words of a distinguished Presbyterian theologian, Dr T. M. Lindsay, 'The New Testament Church is fellowship with Jesus and with the brethren through Him; this fellowship is permeated with a sense of unity; this united fellowship is to manifest itself in a visible

[1] Hebrews xii. 23.   [2] Acts vi. 5.

society; this visible society has bestowed upon it by our Lord a divine authority; and it is to be a sacerdotal society. These appear to be the five outstanding elements in the New Testament conception of the Church of Christ.'[1]

Among those who hold the theory of an invisible Church in the world, a well-known modern writer has said: 'The Church is invisible in the sense that we do not see it; we cannot absolutely identify the empirical organization with the real community of those who are truly united to the Body of Christ....From the first, the Church has lived and moved in history, as a *coetus fidelium* which becomes an institution as it develops the aims and object of its fellowship.'[2] This line of thought does not tally with that of the New Testament. We can 'absolutely identify' the community in its membership of baptized persons. An 'institution' is an epithet that would better fit a society of human establishment, such as that, perhaps, of 'Christian Science', but if the Church is an institution in any sense, it was so from the first, it cannot 'become' one. The essential organism of the Church, too, its sacraments and ministry, is not empirical or experimental, but is its divine endowment. Organization of every kind is subject to change and modification as centuries pass and circumstances alter; but the organism of the Church belongs to its identity, and must always remain.

No one, of course, would deny that the Church 'appears before us as an external phenomenon of history and social organization', in the words of the same author, and he says that 'the Church is both visible and invisible'. Now this conceals a great truth, because the visible Church in the world is sacramental. It is as true, and exactly in the same way, of the great sacraments of the Gospel. Thus Holy Baptism is a visible occurrence in the material sphere, by appointed audible words and the appointed material element of water. Yet unless it were also unseen, if it were not also an inner and spiritual event in the realm of the invisible, it would not be a sacrament at all. Nevertheless, until we are pure spirits, when we shall no longer need sacraments, our participation in them must be visible, and so must be our membership and life in the outward fellowship of the divine and sacramental society. And in order *that the world may believe*, the unity of the society must be such as 'the world' of ordinary men can see and recognize. Individuals or groups without organic and *visible* unity cannot carry out the mission of the Ekklesia.

[1] Lindsay, pp. 5, 6.   [2] Moffatt, p. 97.

CHAPTER VI. THE EKKLESIA IS SACRAMENTAL

I

IF we believe in the reality of sacraments, we shall hold them necessary; but the reality of a sacrament depends upon the operation of
the Holy Spirit, and to Him the outward sacrament is not necessary.
So a true understanding of the nature of sacraments leads to something like a paradox; they are both necessary and unnecessary. This
is just the old theological truth that 'God is not tied to His sacraments, but we are'.

The Ekklesia or Church to which the sacraments have been given
is itself sacramental. The organism which is its outward endowment—
its divinely appointed stewardship, its Gospel sacraments—is all
essential or 'unessential' according as it is considered in relation
to its human constituents, or to the infinite grace of God. Because
this truth has often been forgotten in Protestant thought,·the Church
and its nature have not received the place of importance that New
Testament teaching allots to it. There is a common tendency to
regard the visible Church as a mere aggregation of believers and
groups of believers, a sort of loose and fickle federation, set up by
Christians for their mutual edification and improvement. The New
Testament teaching is very different from this. The society it tells of
is of divine, not human, foundation. Its individual members are
figured as stones built together into a house, a temple, a habitation
of God, or fellow-citizens in a city,[1] or particles of flour kneaded
into one loaf.[2] From the variety of these scriptural metaphors the
essential corporate unity of the Ekklesia stands out clearly as a central
thought.

II

Most often, and most emphatically, St Paul teaches that, in a spiritual
and therefore in a very real sense, the Church is the Body of our
Lord Himself. *Ye are the body of Christ, and severally members thereof,*[3]
and again, *Even as we have many members in one body, and all the
members have not the same office: so we, who are many, are one body in*

---

[1] I Pet. ii. 5; Eph. ii. 21, 22.   [2] I Cor. x. 17.
[3] I Cor. xii. 27; also Eph. i. 22, v. 30-32; Col. i. 18, 24.

Christ, and severally members one of another.[1] We cannot doubt or deny the truly sacramental nature of the Church without rejecting some of the New Testament's most definite teaching.

In order to grasp the principle underlying this scriptural figure, one must consider the organic principle of a living physical body. A living body is something essentially distinct from the cells and corpuscles that compose it. It is the interrelations and functions of these that make them a body. Crush a body under a steam hammer, and the particles that composed it will no longer be a body. So long as the body lives and endures, on the other hand, it remains an entity, although in the course of time all its original particles have disappeared and have been replaced by others (a process which, it is said, takes about seven years).

Any permanent human society must possess an identity of its own, analogous and comparable to that of an organic physical body. In the span of about seventy years all its members have disappeared and have been replaced, but the society itself may persist unaltered.

One principle then, clearly involved in the New Testament doctrine of the Church, is that it is a living entity, like a physical body, with the same faculty of continuing endurance, of a continuity that can persist throughout all the changes in composition that are experienced alike by a human body and the 'body' of a human society.

III

In a physical human body the most striking parts are the features, the lips and tongue, the hands and fingers. The body has the vital power of self-renewal without loss of identity, or any break in its continuity as a body. Throughout many seven-year renewals of cells, the features remain, even the marking of the finger-prints remains unmistakable. Moreover, these special features are requisite to the bodily life and activities, the tongue to speak, the fingers to handle, although they are only members of the body, and apart from the rest of the body they would be dead flesh. In other words, the organism is integral to the body, yet no organic feature can live or act apart from the body.

Now hath God set the members each one of them in the body, even as it pleased him. And if they were all one member, where were the body? But now they are many members, but one body. And the eye cannot say

---

[1] Rom. xii. 4, 5.

to the hand, I have no need of thee: or again the head to the feet, I have
no need of you....Now ye are the body of Christ, and severally members
thereof.[1]

In the mystical Body of the Church, visible in the world, are not
the permanent features, the lips and fingers (so to speak), those
members that are appointed to do its specialized work, those who
are appointed to the functions of ministry? The correspondence is
striking. The tongue and fingers are nothing apart from the body;
if they were cut away, they would be dead flesh. So also, apart from
the Body which is the Church, its ministers are nothing of themselves. That is the true corrective of so-called clericalism. The physical
members of a body must be organically part of it, the tongue speaks
and the fingers handle as actions with which the whole physical body
is identified. In just the same way the ministry of the Church can
rightly exercise the priestly office (which is the office of the priestly
Church) only in acts that are acts of the whole Body of the Church.
They can do this only if they are truly identified with the whole
Body, just as the tongue and fingers are identified with the physical
body.

IV

From time to time there has been erroneous thinking which a closer
following-out of the New Testament doctrine would have corrected,
concerning the stewardship or ministry in its relation to the Church.
Thus in the Eucharist, the giving of thanks and the blessing of the
Bread and the Cup are the priestly acts of the whole Body, not
merely of the priest who is its appointed organ, its tongue or its
hand, as it were. Again, the distinction between clergy and laity
has often been misconceived. The hand is of like flesh with the rest
of the body; priest and layman are alike members of the Body. In
both cases the contrast is one of function, not of nature, although it
is easy to fall into the opposite error and to regard too lightly the
difference of function.

V

Sometimes, too, there has been faulty thought and language concerning the 'apostolic succession' of the stewardship. The replacement of steward by steward down the centuries, the transmission
of office from the ordained to those who are to come after them,

[1] I Cor. xii. 18–27.

has too often been spoken of in figurative language suggesting the independent life of an order *by itself*, apart from the rest of the Church. Expressions such as 'a golden chain' of ministry, or 'a conduit-pipe down from the apostles', have been used. Such conceptions do not accord with the New Testament doctrine of the organic unity of the Church, as figured by a physical body. This writer's hand, which is penning these words, is composed of cells entirely different from the cells that composed it when it was a child's hand. They have many times been changed, but the organic succession has always been a function of the whole body of which the hand forms part. The hand has not been continued *by itself*, although it has always been an essential instrument, vehicle, or 'minister', of its own continuity. In the same way, the continuance of the stewardship of the Church in organic continuity may be truly figured as an organic function of the whole Body, although it requires the immediate participation of those ministers themselves who are its ministers of ordination.

VI

A human body retains its identity throughout all the changes of its life; its features remain recognizably its own. In the same way the Body of the Church, throughout the changes of the centuries, retains its characteristic features in its apostolically appointed ministry.

The teaching of the New Testament not only insists on the unity of the Church, *The body is one, and hath many members, and all the members of the body, being many, are one body,*[1] but also implies its continuity. Unity and continuity go together. The sacramental doctrine of the Church reveals the apostolic ministry as its organism, as no human development, no mere human organization, but part of its very nature and endowment, just as is the physical organism of the human body.

But a hand may be palsied, or it may become infected and fester. It needs to be healed and cleansed. Amputation is maiming. That organ of the Church which is its ministry is not immune from disease. Medieval ills of the Church were especially grievous when they appeared in clerical corruption. They led to Reformations which, in many lands, unnecessarily severed all organic continuity with the past. The result was maiming, separation, discontinuity.

[1] I Cor. xii. 12.

VII

As the Church is holy, so ought ideally all its members to be holy.
But 'there is a very large mixture of hypocrites, of ambitious,
avaricious, envious, evil-speaking men, some also of impurer lives'.[1]
This evident fact has always presented a problem. In modern times
a theory[2] has been put forward of an invisible Church in the world
that includes none but the elect, who are known only to God. The
New Testament gives no support to that theory and, indeed, is at
variance with it. 'The Apostolic Scriptures know but one great
Christian Society, including all the baptized, good or evil, sincere
or insincere, who have not been cut off from the communion of
the Church or cut themselves off by open apostasy. The True Vine
has branches in it that bear no fruit and are practically dead; yet
until the Husbandman sees fit to take them away, they remain in
the Vine.'[3] The parable of the drag-net, gathering of every kind,
good and bad,[4] embodies the same teaching. Zwingli's invisible
Church theory cannot therefore be the true solution of the problem.

The sacramental doctrine of the Church supplies a key to the
problem. It is recognized that man can set a barrier to the grace of
sacraments.[5] That is universally true. Of those who came in contact
with the Incarnate Lord Himself, it was to the faithful that virtue
went out. A most solemn warning is given to anyone who receives
the sacrament of Holy Communion 'unworthily', that he obtains
no grace, but a judgement.[6] In the same way, an unrepentant evil
liver does not receive grace from membership in the sacramental
Church.*[7] We are still to come to the sacraments of the Church for
grace although some may come 'unworthily', receiving none. So
also we are to be faithful members of the visible Church, although
some who are outwardly members are secretly unfaithful.

The problem is further answered by the first principle of all sacraments, viz. that God is not tied to His sacraments—but we are.[8]
He has appointed Holy Communion for us, and although He is able
to impart grace through other channels we are not presumptuously

---

[1] Calvin, *Inst.* IV. i. 7.
[2] Ulric Zwingli of Zürich (1484–1531) appears to have been the true author of
this theory.
[3] H. B. Swete, *The Holy Catholic Church*, p. 52.   [4] Matt. xiii. 47–50.
[5] *Homo potest sacramentorum gratiis obicem ponere* is the theologians' maxim.
[6] I Cor. xi. 27–30.   [7] See note D on p. 6.
[8] See chapter I, section III.

to reject that sacrament. He has given us the ark of the Church, and although He can save us otherwise,*[1] knowingly to leave it or refuse to enter it is to 'tempt' Him.

VIII

The Gospel sacraments, for their due observance, require outward parts which, together with accompanying prayer, are their credentials and the recognizable promise of the grace bestowed with them and through them.

The organic stewardship of the Church is a visible *office*, similarly demanding, for its due exercise, certainty of recognition. Now although the Son of God in the world was, and is for ever, *a priest after the order of Melchizedek*,[2] for whose credentials no authority or commission imparted through men was needed, outward credentials are needed for the apostles and stewards whom He has sent. Their whole authority and commission is that they are sent by Him,[3] and the first stewards received visible commission from our Lord Himself. What are the credentials of their successors? A steward 'after the order of Melchizedek' could only be recognized by reason of some manifest and unusual outpouring of the Spirit upon him, and, even so, recognition would always be doubtful. From the earliest times it has been the belief of the Church that the first generation of stewards, under divine guidance, appointed other stewards to come after them. From the earliest times of which any clear record of the way of the Church survives, the stewards of each generation have so appointed their successors, with the visible and recognizable commission of the laying on of hands with prayer.*[4] They have done so not as representing their own order, but as the representative organ of the whole undivided Church.

Christians of some modern denominations have thought it right to make variations in the outward parts of the Gospel sacraments, either in the elements appointed for Holy Communion, or even in that of Baptism. One sect, it is said, baptizes with flowers instead of with water.[5] An earnest Congregationalist writes of Baptism that 'Some of us seem prepared to treat lightly and frivolously this most

---

[1] See note D on p. 6.
[2] Hebrews, chapters v, vi, vii.   [3] John xx. 21, xvii. 18.
[4] Note. *The outward and visible part of ordination* (p. 37).
[5] Archbishop W. Temple, *Christus Veritas*, p. 236: 'Christ might have so appointed; but He did not.'

venerable part of our Christian heritage, and to substitute for it some dedication services for infants and for new members which we have hastily concocted for ourselves after the pattern shown to us by our fancies'.[1] St Augustine mentioned a sect called Aquarians from their strange custom of offering water in the Eucharist instead of wine. In certain denominations to-day the sacraments are wholly discontinued.

The abandonment by many Christians of the organic life and fellowship of the Church and its stewardship is a thing of the same kind. The unity of the Church is grievously impaired by all these desertions of appointed channels of grace, yet always it remains true that God is not tied to them. We are not to judge those who neglect them, much less assert that the free grace of God is not often bestowed upon those.

'Now, a little before them, there was on the left hand of the road a meadow, and a stile to go over into it, and that meadow is called By-path Meadow. Then said Christian to his fellow, "If this meadow lieth along by our wayside, let us go over into it". Then he went to the stile to see, and behold a path lay along by the way on the other side of the fence. "'Tis according to my wish," said Christian. "Here is the easiest going; come, good Hopeful, and let us go over."'

Bunyan's pilgrims had to endure dreadful afflictions, but the parable cannot rightly be applied to the Church highway, and the bypaths of to-day, without two vital qualifications. Many, alas, have been turned off the highway by the misconduct of those upon it, and, for another thing, the bypaths have been trodden out so smooth and broad that pilgrims can in all good faith mistake them for the road. We believe that the King's protection and blessing still follows them even in By-path Meadow.

But the pilgrims will not be a united band until they trudge the highway together again.

NOTE TO CHAPTER VI

THE OUTWARD AND VISIBLE PART OF ORDINATION

'That the laying on of hands was regarded as conferring the charisma necessary to the office is obvious from the passages in Timothy, and it is improbable that these express only a later idea. The laying on of hands was thus certainly "sacramental", but what old or newly created rites were not sacramental in a community which had the Holy Spirit giving practical proof of His presence in its midst?' (Harnack, p. 26.)

[1] Manning, p. 151.

CHAPTER VII. THE BODILY FRAME

IF then the Body of Christ in the world is outward and visible, as well as inward and spiritual, we must seek to know its outward marks, the structure and features that distinguish it in the world as an organic society. It is a society, although a unique one, a society of men and women in the world, although not of the world. Where must the identity and continuity of any definite human society be found? It will not be in its name or its by-laws, for these may be varied from time to time, not in its precise membership, for in every long-lived society the membership must change altogether as the generations pass by. This very problem has, in fact, arisen with regard to the continued identity in 1900 of a religious society, a Church in the modern sense, founded in 1843, and it is interesting to study the arguments that were advanced. 'The Church', it was said in reference to this particular religious society, 'is like an organism; the organism parts with every part of its material every few years, but its identity consists in this, that it assimilates and parts during the period of its life with the old material and takes in fresh material; so the Church does not consist in the identity of its members. The materials may change, and there may be metabolism of every item of which it consists, and yet the Church goes on preserving its organic life through the medium of its system of Church government. The Church could not do any act which puts an end to the identity of its organization. The mark of distinction is to be found in the continuity of the organism, in the continued existence of the governing body.'*[1]

'Government', indeed, in an ordinary secular sense, does not suitably describe the divinely appointed organism of the Ekklesia. Its 'great ones' are to be its servants, not to lord it or to exercise an authority like that of worldly rulers.[2] 'Ministry is the general term for all office of dignity in the Church, and after many divagations of ambition the proudest of prelates desires to be called *servus servorum Dei*.'[3] 'The Church is not like civil society, having rulers and subjects: it has only members, like a living body, and they have

---

[1] Note A. *Identity of an organism* (p. 42).   [2] Matt. xx. 25–27; I Pet. v. 3.
[3] T. A. Lacey, *The One Body and the One Spirit*, p. 90.

no bond but that of a living spiritual solidarity and of mutual love.'[1]
Yet the shepherds of the flock, the stewards of the household, must
have a special duty of guidance and management. Moreover, they
supply an organic connexion for the locally scattered membership
of the Body. Thus in the thought of St Cyprian of Carthage in the
third century, the mutual concord or communion of bishops, expressing the mutual charity in which stands the unity of the Catholic
Church, is the cement or *gluten* that holds all together.*[2]

The identity of the Ekklesia is certainly not to be found in its
name, for which expressions such as the Way, or the Brotherhood,
sufficed at first, nor in the names of its ministers, which have not
always been the same, nor even in the precise allocation of all their
duties. It is a familiar axiom that unity does not lie in uniformity.
Much that is conspicuous in everyday Church affairs is no part of
its real organism, although it may be useful as *organization* in its own
time and place. Many things in the modern ecclesiastical vocabulary,
such as deaneries, chapters, canons and prebendaries, archdeacons
(who are not deacons and have nothing particular to do with them),
stipendiary niceties of rectory and vicarage, and countless other
ecclesiasticisms, belong to mere systems of organization, and are
unessential. Some accustomed things may be no longer beneficial
or useful. Some accretions are relics of a degeneracy now happily
bygone, like the medieval style of 'palace' for the pastoral residence.
Some are merely ridiculous, like the eighteenth-century pretence of
riding costume, worn by clerical dignitaries in England. Among the
most important of adventitious things is the doubtful privilege of
State establishment, which many now believe to be, on balance,
a hindrance rather than a help to the work of the Church. Whether
or not it is desirable, it is certainly not essential to the community
life of the saints on earth, of which the Ekklesia was more fully
conscious in the early centuries than after it came to be established
in the Roman Empire. It seems unlikely that establishment could
be retained in any wide reunion of Christianity.

Reunion of the organic society which is the Church will involve
the possession by all its membership and parts of a share in an organism
that is common to the whole Body. On the other hand, it will not
involve uniformity in matters of mere organization, which are no
necessary parts of that organism. Such practical things as endow-

[1] M. J. Congar, *Divided Christendom*, p. 210.
[2] Note B.   *Bishops, and unity of the Church* (p. 42).

ments, sustentation funds, parsonages, manses, pension funds, are all of this kind. Different countries or provinces will probably always be independent of each other in all matters such as these; they are only implements used in the work of the Church, not part of the organic life which is its unique endowment. The catalogue of unessentials might be lengthened indefinitely, but the problem in hand is to discern what is integral and essential.

It is the corporate character of the Christian fellowship that distinguishes the Church in the world ever since its Pentecostal beginning. Corporate life is central to it. We are not only the Lord's sheep; we are, or we should be, a fold or flock. We are His household, for which He has appointed stewards.[1]* St Paul in four of his epistles takes the organism of a physical body to teach the same truth concerning the Church in the world. 'The paradox, if paradox it be, of a visible body with an invisible head belongs to the Old Testament as to the New.'[2]

In *The People of God* Dr H. F. Hamilton has written[3] of the relationship between the sacrament of Holy Communion, the ministry of the historic Church, and the unity of the Church: 'The breaking and the blessing are acts in which every individual who has a right to partake has an equal interest and share; they are therefore, in a word, corporate acts, the acts of the whole Church as a corporate body.' If one loaf is to be broken and one cup blessed, only one person at a time can act, and not by any right belonging to himself personally, but only in virtue of some authorization given to him by the whole Church, by means of which he is set apart to act as the organ or instrument of the whole. As the faith spreads throughout the world it will be impossible for all to meet together in one place, and yet the very nature of the sacrament seems to look beyond the group—the local eucharistic gathering—to the whole Church. 'It would seem that the president ought to receive authority, not from the local group, but from the whole body throughout the world...for if the breaking of the bread is the act of this local group alone, then this group thereby becomes itself a corporate whole and the Church universal is divided into so many constantly changing local unities.'

'The Eucharist is the great central fact in the origin and develop-

---

[1] Note C. *Stewardship and the household of God* (p. 43).
[2] H. L. Goudge in *Anglo-Russ. Sym.* p. 39. He cites Judg. viii. 22, 23; I Sam. xii. 12; Is. xxxiii. 22.
[3] Hamilton, vol. II, chapter XIII, esp. pp. 199–209.

ment of the Christian ministry.' We find two organs to act for the whole Church: (1) an organ which acts for the whole Church in bestowing this representative character upon individuals; (2) an organ which acts as the representative of the whole Church to break the Bread at the Eucharist; the one condition to which all must conform is the due transmission of authority from the whole body. Dr Hamilton's full and careful study cannot, of course, carry its proper weight in summary or brief quotation, but the central principles contended for by him receive striking endorsation in a resolution adopted by the World Conference of 1937 on Faith and Order, viz.: 'We believe that every Sacrament should be so ordered that all may recognize in it an act performed on behalf of the universal Church. To this end there is need of an ordained ministry recognized by all to act on behalf of the universal Church in the administration of the Sacraments.'

Dr Hamilton proceeds to consider how far these needs have been met by new ministries parallel to the older ministry: 'Certain Christians, feeling themselves unable to continue under the ancient ministry, went apart from it and broke their bread in memory of the Lord Jesus under conditions of their own choosing. But here again, the essentially social nature of the sacrament is such that new ministries*[1] were developed from these departures, new ministries which are representative of, and authorized by, the particular groups which separated themselves from the rest of the Church....These new ministries are parallel to the older ministry; but there is this difference. The older ministry is representative of the whole Church in precisely the same sense as the new ministries are the representatives each of a particular group of Christians....The more clearly the particular ministry is derived from a local group, the more emphatic becomes the separation from the Communion of the whole Church.'

The whole world-wide Church in the second and third centuries was one living society of which its common ministry or stewardship was unmistakably a part. The commission of its stewards was plainly of world-wide operation, they were stewards of the whole household; the bestowal of that commission in new ordinations was also recognizably of universal authority; in the case of the head stewards this was demonstrated by the participation of not less than three of that order of ministry. In the nature of things, when the whole

[1] Note D. *New ministries* (p. 43).

Ekklesia could no longer be assembled in Jerusalem or any other single centre, commission representative of the whole Ekklesia could be conferred only through those individuals on whom this representative character had previously been conferred, that is to say the head stewards themselves; thus organic continuity of the household and its stewardship was preserved and maintained.

Notwithstanding the divisions that have rent the Ekklesia, this representative organic ministry persists in unbroken continuity from the undivided Ekklesia of the second century and its universal ministry;[1] this continuity is not broken by schism alone. Thus, to take only the leading instance, in spite of the schism of East and West, neither the Eastern Orthodox Church nor the Roman Catholic Church denies the other's possession of a ministry in unbroken organic continuity with that of the undivided Church.

NOTES TO CHAPTER VII

A. IDENTITY OF AN ORGANISM

The Free Church of Scotland Appeals, 1903–4, ed. by R. L. Orr, pp. 479, 514–17. In 1843 a great part of the (Presbyterian) Church of Scotland seceded and formed a new body under the name of the Free Church of Scotland. In 1900 its General Assembly, consisting of ministers and elders, decided by an overwhelming majority to unite with another independent Presbyterian body, adding the word 'United' to its name. The United Free Church claimed that it had preserved its identity with the Free Church of 1843, and it strenuously maintained the principles here quoted in the text.

B. BISHOPS, AND UNITY OF THE CHURCH

St Cyprian, *Ep.* lxvi. 6: 'The catholic church is one and cannot be divided, but is connected together by the cement of her bishops, closely and intimately adhering to each other.' Similarly in *Ep.* lxviii. 2. With this it is interesting to compare the recent declaration of a Congregational theologian 'that the local congregation is the Church Catholic in a particular place and cannot fulfil its true nature without holding communion with other Churches, and that the office of the Ministry is the organ of the Church's unity'. (Daniel T. Jenkins, *The Nature of Catholicity*, pp. 109, 110.)

[1] Continuity from the second century only is here referred to because it is indisputable. The subject of continuity from the first to the second century remains for consideration later, when reasons will be advanced for regarding it also as not doubtful.

C. STEWARDSHIP AND THE HOUSEHOLD OF GOD

Matt. xxiv. 45; Luke xii. 41–48; Eph. ii. 19; I Cor. iv. 1, 2; Tit. i. 7; I Pet. iv. 10. The great Swiss Presbyterian scholar, F. Godet, commenting on Luke xii. 41–48, says: 'This saying seems to assume that the apostolate will be perpetuated till the return of Christ; and the figure employed does indisputably prove that there will subsist in the Church to the very end a ministry of the word established by Christ. Of this the Apostles were so well aware, that when they were themselves leaving the earth, they took care to establish ministers of the word to fill their places in the Church.' (Commentary on St Luke's Gospel, Eng. trans. by E. W. Shalders, II. p. 108.)

D. NEW MINISTRIES

As Dr A. Dakin, President of Bristol College, says (Calvinism, p. 129): 'Since the Reformation by implication of its theories was bound to dispense with the Roman Catholic hierarchy, all the Reformers were faced with the necessity of creating a new Church order.' Dr J. L. Ainslie has shown how completely and deliberately in every country the Churches of the Calvinist Reformation severed all organic continuity with the unreformed Church and its ministry. (Ainslie, chapter VII. See also infra, chapter XX.)

A curious acknowledgement of the origins of the ancient and modern ministries is to be seen in what is in itself a comparatively trifling thing, viz. the traditional dress of their ministers. At the times of these origins, clergy and laity wore garments of the same kind, which was their 'Sunday best'. Conservatism has preserved the original styles of vesture for the ministry throughout centuries of changing fashions for the laity. Thus, as Dr Ainslie has observed (p. 37, citing S. M. Jackson, Huldreich Zwingli, pp. 290, 291), the black gown preferred by ministers of most Protestant denominations is a survival of the ordinary gala dress of central Europe in the sixteenth century. In the same way, every vestment now worn by a priest or presbyter of the Church represents an article of ordinary dress such as was worn universally throughout the Roman Empire in the infancy of the Christian Ekklesia. (Adrian Fortescue, The Vestments of the Roman Rite, p. 6.)

CHAPTER VIII. 'WE ARE NOT DIVIDED'

AT the World Conference on Faith and Order held in Edinburgh in 1937, it was finely said[1] that 'though the purpose of our meeting is to consider the causes of our divisions, yet what makes possible our meeting is our unity. Those who have nothing in common do not deplore their estrangement.'

But the divisions of Christians are manifest, sad, and disastrous. Is the Body of Christ divided? Roman Catholics and Protestants agree in denying it. The teaching of Rome is attractively simple. There is only one, united, Church: 'All who do not acknowledge the Roman Pontiff as their Head do not belong to the Church of Jesus Christ.'[2] The Bull *Unam Sanctam* of Pope Boniface VIII in 1303 declared and defined 'that for every human creature it is altogether necessary to salvation that he be subject to the Roman Pontiff'. Some modification of that doctrine is now generally admitted in regard to those who are outside the Roman Church 'from ignorance and in good faith',[3] but the cardinal assertion remains. The Church is not divided, and it cannot be divided, simply because any Christian who does not acknowledge the papal claim is not in the Church. A recent convert to Rome has recorded the conclusion he drew from our Lord's prayer *that all may be one*. 'It is impossible to doubt', he says, 'that Christ's prayer was answered; consequently not only was the unity of His Society in His intention; it was realized; it remains realized to-day.' He fails to remember that part of the same prayer, *that the world may believe*, is not yet realized. The assertion that the Roman Church is the undivided Body of Christ, and that all who are out of communion with its pope are heretics and schismatics, cannot of course be accepted by any who are unable to accept the modern papal claims. Moreover the theory that 'schismatics' are outside of the one Church is contradicted in the practice of the Roman Church.*[4]

[1] By the chairman of the conference, Dr W. Temple, then Archbishop of York.
[2] Larger Catechism prescribed by Pope Pius X for all dioceses in the province of Rome, p. 51.
[3] Otto Karrer, *Religions of Mankind*, trans. by E. I. Watkin, London, 1936 (with imprimatur), chapter XIII, 'Salvation outside the visible Church', esp. p. 255.
[4] Note A. '*Schismatics*' *and the Roman Church: contradictory theory and practice* (p. 49).

In sharp contrast with the Roman theory stands the so-called Protestant conception. 'It is the state of Faith and not the belonging to the visible Church which distinguishes the Faithful from the rest of mankind.... It is obvious, therefore, that here on earth the Church remains unseen, its exact bounds are known to God alone, and the visible organizations of Christians commonly called "Churches" are only shadows of the true Church, for they contain not only the elect, but also sinners, who in reality do not belong to the Body of Christ.' Protestants then, like the Roman Church, evade the responsibility for division, but in a wholly different way, by preaching the doctrine of the invisible Church, which they infer can never be divided. 'In the meantime, all the earthly conflicts among Christians are described by them as having a strictly secondary importance.'[1]

> We are not divided,
> All one body we,

is sung vigorously in a popular hymn. 'All one body we' may be truthfully said or sung by all baptized, even if they are gathered from separate confessions or communions. But that 'we are not divided' has no fullness of truth except for those who accept either the Roman claim to universality, or else the theory that the only true Church is an invisible Church of the elect only, which cannot be seen or known, and which *ex hypothesi* cannot be divided. It is coming more and more to be perceived that the Ekklesia has been divided and still is divided. Thus the Orthodox theologian, Dr Nicholas M. Zernov, writes: 'Christians to-day have at last to accept and to bear the reality that the One, Holy, Catholic and Apostolic Church has been divided through the sins of her earthly members, and that as God has allowed sinful men to crucify the Lord of Glory, His Only-begotten Son, so also has He allowed the members of the Church to divide and torture the living Body of Christ in the world.'[2] Anglican theology too is coming to realize more clearly that the One Church is divided.[3]

The possibility of calamitous divisions is not ruled out by the scriptural figures of the Ekklesia. A flock of sheep may scatter into groups, even if every sheep is recognizably marked as a member of the flock. A family may separate into bitterly hostile sections, but

[1] N. M. Zernov in *Anglo-Russ. Sym.* pp. 212, 222, 223.   [2] *Ibid.* p. 223.
[3] O. C. Quick, *The Christian Sacraments*, chapter VII, 'The Church, Orders and Unity', esp. pp. 143-47.

the fact remains that it is one family. A household may divide into sections holding no converse with each other, or with the stewards of other sections, although all remain members of the household. The Body of St Paul's teaching is not subject to the dissolution and death that serious division would cause to a physical body. Division occurs in both. There is division whenever one living cell is separated from a body; there is division whenever one baptized Christian secedes from the common life of the Body. If enough cells were parted from a body, it would die, but the Body cannot die. Even if its limbs are severed, it survives, weakened; limbs that in separation still retain their living organic structure may continue to live as separated parts of the organic Body.

On the other hand, individual cells, however numerous, that have not only separated from the Body but have also lost the common organic structure which before united them in the Body, do not merely by a new assemblage become reconstituted as a part of the Body. That is a figurative expression of the truth that an association or group, although formed entirely of professing Christians, is not necessarily a part of the one Church. Even if all its members are members of the Church, the group or association or 'denomination' composed by them is not, as a group, necessarily a 'Church', is not as a group part of the one Ekklesia. Thus the Salvation Army and the Church Army, the Society of Jesus and the Society of Friends, have, in various ways, manifestly been used as instruments of divine grace, but none of them is a Church in the New Testament sense; that is to say none of these *societies* is a part of the Body. The members of two of them have never been baptized into the Ekklesia. All the members of the other two societies have been so baptized, and it is that baptism which makes them individual members of the Ekklesia, not the fact that they happen to be members of these societies.

There is a constant wastage from the membership of the Church because of the lapse of individuals from its fellowship, but that evil does not present the same problem that the collective divisions of Christians present. These collective divisions are of two types.

1. In one type of division the divided parts of the Body retain the organic structure that they formerly possessed in the undivided Body; the outstanding examples of this type are derived from the great Schism of East and West. Both halves of the Catholic Church, the Orthodox and the Roman, then retained all the sacramental life

of the undivided Ekklesia, and also the ministry necessary for that sacramental life, a ministry in organic continuity with the original, divinely appointed, stewardship of the household. This was so and has remained so, notwithstanding grave differences of doctrine and observance, and notwithstanding that East and West each denied that the other continued to be part of the true Church. There are other communions of this type, among them the Anglican Communion, which claims to have retained in unbroken and organic continuity the ministry of the undivided Church.

2. Another type of division arises where geographical or other associations of baptized Christians secede and form new societies to satisfy their conscience and religious desires. Some societies of this character are methodically organized according to various systems that more or less resemble the ancient organism of the one Body; some are organized very loosely, some hardly at all. Some retain and strictly honour the two great Gospel sacraments; some do not. Some are called Churches (in the modern sense),[1] some prefer other collective names.

The distinction between these two types of division is perfectly clear in principle, but it is much less so in its practical application to the many communions and confessions of to-day. It is partly hidden by reason that abounding divine grace overflows all boundaries of the visible Church. It is even difficult for separated Christians to examine it together in brotherly harmony; any discussion of these boundaries is apt to become embittered, because to maintain their importance is often wrongly understood as an assertion that they set a limit to grace. The truth is that *Deus non alligatur*, God giveth not the Spirit by measure. The declaration of the bishops assembled at Lambeth in 1920, and again in 1930, thankfully acknowledging that the ministries of these communions which do not possess the Episcopate have been manifestly blessed and owned by the Holy Spirit as effective means of grace, has been of great value in the assuaging of this former bitterness.

But why, it may well be asked, in the light of that truth, should so much importance be attached to preserving the organic continuity of the visible Church? The answer to that question is found in the sacramental principle, and a consideration of the sacraments themselves best explains it.

The sacraments were not given to us to be abandoned because we

[1] See chapter III, section IV, also chapter II.

have come to know that *Deus non alligatur*. Some sincere Christians deny the need for the outward and visible parts of the sacraments; yet we are bound to hold to these although God is not bound. Just in the same way, the members of some Christian denominations fail to see the need for the one visible Church in its organic continuity; yet the same principle shows that we should be loyal and constant to the one Church, while thankfully acknowledging that divine grace flows over its limits. Many who have not felt the force of this principle have now been led by more pragmatic reasoning to see something of the same necessity. Thus the Faith and Order Conference of 1937 resolved that 'It is essential to a united Church that it should have a ministry universally recognized'. It is difficult to imagine any ministry not in some recognizable organic continuity with the ancient ministry that could claim or obtain such recognition. Even ten years earlier, at the Lausanne Conference of 1927, one of the things that came out most clearly was the 'recognition of the fact that a reunited Church was inconceivable except on the basis of an Episcopal Ministry'; the phrase was that of the leading representative of the Congregational Churches of America.[1] A general reunion of Christians cannot well be hoped for in a near future. The mere form of 'episcopacy', regarded as a system of presidential 'government', would afford no firm basis. 'It is really useless to press for reunion in outward order by methods which, when examined, seem to imply that matters of outward order are spiritually unimportant.'[2] When Christians of the scattered denominations have regained belief in the reality of the Church as a visible divine society in the world, and only then, they will come to see the need for universal recognition of its ancient ministry, not as 'episcopal' but as maintaining the organic continuity of the divinely given stewardship in the household. A distinguished Methodist theologian[3] has truly said that 'There is only one great Christian doctrine, that of the nature of the Church, which really divides the different communions from one another...it is a mistake to set the divisive subject of the Christian ministry in the central arena of debate, unless the prior question has been faced: What is the nature of that Body to which the various ministries belong, and which its ministers serve? How is the Ecclesia constituted, and what makes it one, in spite of all severances?'*[4]

---

[1] E. S. Woods, *Lausanne*, 1927, p. 93.   [2] O. C. Quick, *op. cit.* p. 153.
[3] Dr Newton Flew.   [4] Note B.   *Dr Newton Flew on Church and Ministry* (p. 49).

NOTES TO CHAPTER VIII

A. 'SCHISMATICS' AND THE ROMAN CHURCH: CONTRADICTORY THEORY AND PRACTICE

Although schism and unity are correlative, and (as the encyclical of Leo XIII declares) those who are not in communion with the unity of the Church *non sunt in Ecclesia*, yet (1) 'We find the validity of sacraments administered by schismatics to be completely acknowledged, with partial exceptions only in respect of marriage and the sacrament of penance....It will hardly be contended that sacramental ministrations are not activities of the Body of Christ, which are thus made to extend beyond the supposed unity of the Church.' (T. A. Lacey, *Unity and Schism*, pp. 60, 61; Bull *Apostolicae Curae* of Pope Leo XIII, 1896, para. 9.) (2) Although a person excommunicate is obviously not in communion with the Roman Pontiff, and is therefore *ex hypothesi* not 'in the Church', yet an excommunicate cardinal is allowed to take part in the election of a pope. For this purpose, then, he is allowed to act as if within the Roman Church. (*Ibid.* p. 61, citing Lucius Lector, *Le Conclave*, pp. 98, 120, 131.) (3) Although the decree *Ne Temere* of 1907 does not apply to *acatholici* in general, it operates on 'all who have been baptized in the Catholic Church and all who have been converted to it from heresy or schism, even though they may afterwards have broken away from the same'. Those who have once been within the Roman Church are not, by subsequent schism, removed from its jurisdiction or thrust entirely outside. (4) The Great Schism of the West, which lasted thirty-seven years, produced three rival popes, each of whom excommunicated his rivals and their cardinals, as well as a fourth group which was out of communion with them all. The Council of Constance, which solved the deadlock, was composed of four groups, in theory and practice schismatically separated from each other. It procured a vacancy by resignations and a deposition, and then ordered all three colleges of cardinals—two of which were *ex hypothesi* schismatic—to meet together for a new election. (See T. A. Lacey, *The Universal Church*, pp. 44–9.)

B. DR NEWTON FLEW ON CHURCH AND MINISTRY

Flew, pp. 9, 10. In his illuminating study of the New Testament Ekklesia, the Principal of Wesley House, Cambridge, shows the Church to be a definite community of divine establishment, 'the ecclesia, the people of God, Israel as God intended Israel to be' (p. 122). He sees the episcopal ministry, however, as a form of *government* rather than as integral to the *continuity* of the community itself; 'the emergence of the episcopal office' accordingly seems to him to present an authoritative claim of a kind different from that of the Twelve, so that 'that development in the second century, by which episcopacy became universal', should not 'be regarded as a divine provision binding all parts of the universal Ecclesia for all time' (p. 258). So he concludes that the most hopeful approach to unity is for all 'to acknowledge one another gladly and frankly as within the one Ecclesia of God on earth, to refrain from any condemnation of the ministries and sacraments which are regarded by any modern Church as God's gift, and to join repeatedly, and as fully as may be, in united worship' (p. 260).

Part Two

Continuity in the organic life of the Church through the centuries

❖

A. CONTINUITY UNAFFECTED BY DIVERSITY OF CIRCUMSTANCE AND METHOD

CHAPTER IX. CONTINUOUS VARIETY

I

IN the previous chapters, some reasons have been put forward for thinking that the Church possesses and must continue to possess as part of its endowment an authoritative stewardship, a visible office with recognizable credentials, as an organism common to the whole Body. It has been suggested that this is necessary as a framework and unitive medium of the divine society in the world; it has been shown how a ministry of universally recognized authority is coming to be more widely perceived to be a necessity for Christian reunion. But it must be said quite clearly that this essential organism cannot simply be identified with episcopacy as many understand it, that is to say as a cut-and-dried system of 'government'. A great deal of controversial debate has been neatly summarized in the question whether episcopacy is necessary to the being of the Church or only to its well-being, to the *esse* or the *bene esse*. It must be admitted, then, that administrative 'government' by bishops, in any exclusive sense, is not of the *esse*. Although some supporters of episcopacy might dissent from this, it seems to follow from the historical fact that diocesan episcopacy has not prevailed always and everywhere. The differing arrangements obtaining within the apostolic ministry during the nineteen centuries of the life of the Ekklesia would form a large and interesting chapter of history. A rapid survey of the principal variations will be attempted here in order to justify what has been said and, at the same time, to make clear the continuity that persists through all superficial changes of custom and method. These include a wide range of variation in the powers and duties of bishops, in the manner of their election or selection, in the size and importance of the districts and populations entrusted to individual bishops, in the grouping of bishops under the presidency of 'metropolitan' bishops and patriarchs, and also in the secular dignity accorded to the office at different times. There have also been changes in the sphere of work of presbyters and deacons.

II

Mon-episcopacy, which best describes the local presidency of a single member of the episcopal order, often rather misleadingly called 'monarchical episcopacy', was a settled system in Syria and Asia Minor at all events by the beginning of the second century. The well-known epistles of St Ignatius show this clearly, but they portray the three orders of bishop, presbyters and deacons as the necessary component parts of one sacred ministry, each in its own order, all in harmonious accord, and entitled to the loyal adherence of the Church as a whole. The bishop is the centre of unity and spiritual leadership, but there is no trace of any unbalanced domination such as in later times has come to be reprehended as 'prelacy'.

The earliest ordination prayers that have been preserved are contained in the *Apostolic Tradition* written by St Hippolytus about A.D. 215 but reflecting the normal practice[1] in his younger days, perhaps thirty or even fifty years earlier.[2] A comparison of the prayers at the ordinations of a bishop and a presbyter is interesting, and a little surprising. 'From the modern point of view it is almost as though the two prayers had been mixed up and the bishop's had got attached to the presbyter, and *vice-versa*.'[3] The power of the Holy Spirit is asked for the bishop 'to feed Thy holy flock and to serve Thee as thine high-priest, blamelessly liturgizing by night and day...to offer to Thee the gifts of Thy Holy Church and by the high-priestly spirit to have authority to forgive sins according to Thy command, to ordain[4] according to Thy bidding, to loose every bond according to the authority which Thou didst give to the

---

[1] Although this work reflects the outlook and customs of Rome, 'this Roman polity may, in many regards, be accepted as the polity held everywhere'. (A. Harnack, *Theologische Literaturzeitung*, 1920, col. 225.)

[2] B. S. Easton, *The Apostolic Tradition of Hippolytus* (1934), p. 25.

[3] G. Dix, O.S.B., 'Jurisdiction, Episcopal and Papal, in the Early Church', in *Laudate*, xv. p. 104 (June 1937).

[4] διδόναι κλήρους, literally 'to give lots'.

Apostles'. For the presbyter the corresponding prayer is 'fill him with the spirit of grace and counsel that he may share in the presbyterate and govern Thy people in a pure heart',[1] which seems to echo the duties of local administration that rested upon the presbyters in the early days when the apostles were itinerant, and the presbyters in the Gentile churches were actually local overseers.

In another 'Church order' dating about the fourth century, 'once more the bishop is the liturgical and doctrinal authority in his Church. But the only requirements for him beyond age and moral probity are that he should be "capable of giving instruction and able to interpret the Scriptures. But if he be unlettered, let him be meek and abounding in charity to all, lest ever the bishop be found rebuked by everyone concerning anything." Clearly this nice old gentleman was not expected to lord it over the household of God! On the other hand the presbyters are to "give praise and blame for whatever needs it", to "have the care of the Church", and, as a body, to "punish wrongdoers".'[2] Harnack comments, on the evidence of the *Church Orders* and the *Shepherd* of Hermas, that 'The bishops preside over the worship and distribution of gifts, but the presbyters exercise control even over the bishops'.[3]

The Celtic Church, in Ireland and Scotland, never became organized in dioceses. Long after diocesan 'mon-episcopacy' prevailed throughout the rest of the Church, it retained a monastic organization under the rule of abbots, who might belong to the episcopal order but might be only presbyters. Bishops were comparatively numerous, no monastery was without them. They were held in special honour, a bishop celebrated the Holy Mysteries alone, priests by concelebration; no priest might celebrate in a bishop's presence without his permission. Only a bishop could ordain, but theirs was a spiritual rank, they were not burdened with the cares of administration.[4]

Suffragan bishops have been appointed as need required from a date at least as early as the beginning of the fourth century, when they were known as *chorepiscopi*, i.e. 'country bishops', ordained to supervise the scattered flock in rural districts. Canon law forbade

[1] G. Dix, *op. cit.* p. 103.

[2] *Ibid.* p. 105, quoting from the *Apostolic Church Order*, 16, 18.

[3] A. Harnack, 'On the Origin of the Christian Ministry', in *Expositor*, May 1887, v. p. 336.

[4] *History of the Church of Ireland*, ed. W. A. Phillips, 1933, vol. I, chapter v, by J. L. Gough Meissner, pp. 159–61, 359–60.

them to exercise their office of ordaining presbyters or deacons without the express permission of the diocesan bishop.[1] In modern times, suffragan and assistant bishops have been appointed to an increased extent; they are equal in order with the diocesan bishops, but they exercise jurisdiction only so far as that has been delegated to them.

The authority of a diocesan bishop within his jurisdiction has varied considerably; in this respect the personality of the individual bishop is naturally an important factor. The bishop, like the rest of the ministry, and like the laity, is subject both to the accepted rules of the universal Church and also to the domestic canons of the province.

III

According to Catholic tradition, the whole people of the Church should have a voice in choosing him who is to be ordained as their bishop. Ordinations of bishops should be performed in the presence and with the privity of the people; 'the ordination may proceed regularly and fairly which hath first received the approbation of the whole body'.[2] When the Novatian schism occurred at Rome, St Cyprian of Carthage supported Cornelius as Bishop of Rome as approved by 'the unanimous testimony of almost all the clergy, by the concurring suffrages of the laity then present, and by the college of those ancient and worthy bishops who were upon the spot';[3] Cornelius had been duly ordained 'by the choice of clergy and people'.[4] Sometimes, as in the famous instances of SS. Cyprian and Ambrose, nothing but the insistent voice of the people was heard. In England, the chapter of a cathedral formerly chose the bishop, but even before the Reformation the right of nomination was being usurped by kings and popes, who were rivals for it. Election of the Prime Minister's nominee by an English cathedral chapter survives to-day as a piece of solemn mockery. Throughout the eighteenth century, and sometimes since, the fruits of this Erastianism have been enough to give point to Liddon's well-known *mot*, that episcopacy is of the *esse* of the Church but not of its *bene esse*. In Ireland, Wales, Scotland, and throughout the world where the Anglican

[1] Bright, pp. 29–33; Gore and Turner, p. 330. See also Joseph Bingham (1668–1723), *Antiquities of the Christian Church (Origines Ecclesiasticae)*, II, xiv. 4–15.
[2] Synodical Epistle from Council at Carthage, A.D. 254. Cyprian, *Ep.* lxvii. 2. For a full historical view of the principle, see Bingham, *op. cit.* book IV, chap. ii.
[3] Cyprian, *Ep.* lv. 5.   [4] *Ibid.* lxviii. 1.

Communion is a 'free' Church, its bishops are elected by the Church. Both clergy and laity of the diocese have a voice, and the constitution of the Church in Wales gives a voice to the other dioceses of the province; since the bishops of a province have a collective responsibility extending throughout its dioceses, this seems to give effect to a sound principle. It only remains to add that nowhere, even when secular influences have been most powerful, has it ever been thought or suggested that anyone could become a bishop without due ordination by other bishops of the apostolic order.

IV

There have been, and still are, extremely wide differences between different countries as to the numbers of their bishops and the corresponding size of their dioceses. Thus there were at one time fifty-five bishops in Palestine, an area smaller than Wales which has five.[1] The fifth-century historian Sozomen observes that 'there are many cities in Syria which possess but one bishop between them; whereas, in other nations, a bishop is appointed even over a village, as I have myself observed in Arabia, and in Cyprus, and among the Novatians and Montanists of Phrygia'.[2] Eighty-seven bishops met at an African council convoked by Cyprian. He mentions a council held before his time when ninety bishops assembled. A few centuries later, there were as many as six hundred and ninety sees in 'Africa', i.e. its northern coastal area.[3] In the Celtic Church bishops were numerous. When St Columba went to Scotland, he took with him twenty bishops, forty priests, and thirty deacons.[4] There were some four hundred bishops in Asia Minor. In South Italy to the present day almost every little town has a bishopric. In North Italy they are comparatively few.[5] The very large dioceses usual in North Europe make it impossible that the chief pastors should be fathers to their flocks in the intimate way of the earlier bishops elsewhere. 'In the Netherlands, as in the rest of Northern Europe, there were in the later Middle Ages too few bishops, and out of those few many had become great secular princes. The bishops had become remote from

---

[1] Story, p. 29, referring to the map of Palestine by Le Quien in *Oriens Christianus*, Paris, 1740.

[2] Sozomen, *Eccl. Hist.* book VII, cap. xix. See also Bingham, *op. cit.* II. xii, 2, 3.

[3] Lightfoot, *Christian Ministry*, p. 225.

[4] *History of the Church of Ireland* (cit.), I, p. 160, citing *Vita Columbae* in *Lismore Lives*, ed. Whitley Stokes, p. 178.

[5] Wordsworth, p. 145.

the ordinary life of the people, and this corruption of the episcopal system was one of the main causes of the Reformation. Bishops had so long neglected their real duties that the reformers could see no value in episcopacy. Up to 1560 there was only one bishop in the territory now called Holland, and that one had been until 1528 a "prince-bishop" with secular sovereignty, usually performing his spiritual duties by deputy.'[1]

V

After the chief pastors of the Church had ceased to be itinerant and had become a settled ministry, for convenience' sake the authority of each was restricted normally to a particular sphere. Each 'bishop', as he came to be called, became in most cases the bishop of a city and the surrounding district; it was convenient and natural to follow the boundaries of the civil organization. His authority was restricted normally to this sphere, yet he retained his authority as a bishop of the universal Church. Occasions were bound to arise when the intervention of neighbouring bishops was necessary, as for example when a bishop died, or in case of disputes: it was convenient therefore to federate the bishops of any neighbourhood into a formal group. For such areas as these also the civil lines were followed; the bishoprics were grouped for ecclesiastical purposes into a province exactly as the districts were for civil purposes. Just as each province had its chief city or metropolis for its civil government, so the bishop of that mother city came to be the president of the group; the group was formally called a province and he the metropolitan bishop. As president of the provincial synod, the 'metropolitan' came to have considerable duties, especially with regard to the consecration to vacant sees in the province and with regard to legal appeals.

It was thus that the Church became organized into provinces. The patriarchates of Jerusalem, Antioch, Rome, Alexandria, and Constantinople came into existence much in the same way, provinces being federated into these larger groups for the sake of unity, on similar lines to what the Emperors Diocletian and Constantine had been doing on the civil side. These five patriarchates embraced the main part of the Roman Empire, but not the whole of Christendom. A patriarch came thus to have rights over and duties towards the provinces and metropolitans under him.

[1] C. B. Moss in *Episcopacy A. & M.* p. 335.

The foregoing account is an abbreviation of a paper by the late bishop of Truro. He emphasizes the distinction between the essential organism and the convenient federal groupings of bishoprics. 'We must distinguish between organization and doctrine.' The episcopate is absolutely essential, the divinely appointed centre of unity of the Church, 'but the rest is all a matter of convenience'.[1] The responsibilities that rest upon an archbishop, or a patriarch, and the influence he possesses do not alter the fact that he is a bishop by order, *primus inter pares*. In some provinces of the Anglican Communion this is recognized in the title accorded to the metropolitan as 'presiding bishop', or 'primus'. St Cyprian is sometimes accused of extreme language in maintaining the complete equality of bishops, and that the bishop of a Numidian townlet was in all respects equal to Cornelius of Rome (with whom St Cyprian was upon most cordial terms), but Cyprian, who himself was primate of Africa, was no simpleton. The equality lies in the equal membership of the episcopal order, not in the spheres of jurisdiction of its individual members.

VI

The standing of bishops in worldly estimation has ranged between extremes of lowliness and grandeur. Before and after the establishment of the Christian religion in the Roman Empire the contrast is startling; on the one hand the martyr bishop, thrown to the beasts as a criminal, on the other, St Ambrose as bishop of Milan forcing the Emperor Theodosius to do public penance for his fault. The greatness of a bishop such as St Augustine of Hippo owed nothing to secular pomp or power. His biography shows how, living a life of apostolic simplicity and zeal, he was the centre of everything in the community of the faithful. 'It is not the dignity of his see, nor social prestige, nor wealth, nor political influence in secular affairs which gives him the position. These things, which were the snare of the typical mediaeval bishop, and as embodied in all that is commonly understood by "prelacy" and continued down to the early part of the Nineteenth century are the ground of much of the modern prejudice against episcopacy, Augustine neither had nor desired to possess.'[2] One harmful consequence of establishment in course of

[1] W. H. Frere, *Collection of Papers* (posthumous, 1940), pp. 1–3. On the whole subject, see Bingham, *op. cit.* book II, chaps. xvi–xviii.
[2] C. Jenkins in *Episcopacy A. & M.* p. 70; cp. Manning, p. 207: 'It is sometimes hard for a Free Churchman to be sure whether what he dissents from in England is Establishment or Episcopacy.'

time was to bring the chief pastors of the Church into false positions of worldly power and grandeur. The danger did not come unnoticed, and the General Council of Chalcedon in A.D. 451, by its 7th canon, decided that 'persons who had once been numbered among the clergy...must not enter on the public service or any secular dignity'. Clerics disobeying this who 'do not repent and turn again to what they once chose for God's sake are to be anathematized'.[1] But this expression of the mind of the united Church was persistently ignored and, under medieval conditions of Western Church life, a combination of ecclesiastical and secular functions became familiar in the stately forms of prince-bishop, chancellor-bishop, or regent-abbot. The history of our own land is full of such quasi-clerical potentates, and the greater sees of England have lingered in something of their semi-regal state down to modern times. The bishops of Durham, for example, were princes-palatine and kings in all but name, with their own civil and criminal courts, armed forces, peerage, parliament, and vast revenues. Until a little more than a century ago, bishops of Durham reigned from a great Norman castle. Even in times since then, when the true pastor has displaced the potentate, such a see remains too large to admit of real intimacy of the chief pastor with his flock. Great contrasts still persist. The pioneer missionary bishop, threading African jungles or voyaging between the islands of Melanesia, is outwardly unlike his brother bishop in England, a peer of Parliament perhaps, and his life work is very different; it bears more resemblance to that of a scriptural apostle. Yet the order and office of both are the same, although they are exercised so differently.

The greatest bishop of Durham of last century was Dr J. B. Lightfoot. He adopted the theory that the early diocesan bishops of the Church were only presbyters in order who, becoming chairmen or presidents over their brother presbyters, had somehow or other expanded into a higher order. This theory disregards the immemorial and universal belief of the Church that these early diocesan bishops were the successors of the apostles, not of the presbyters, but Dr Lightfoot's great eminence as a scholar gave it weight. It is interesting, therefore, on analysing the reasons that led him to this view, to find that he was largely influenced by the contrast between the functions of the itinerant and the settled ministries. 'In fact', he says, 'the functions of the Apostle and the bishop differed widely. The Apostle, like the prophet or evangelist, held no *local* office. He

[1] Bright, pp. 148-50.

was essentially, as his name denotes, a missionary, moving about from place to place, founding and confirming new brotherhoods.'[1] Yet the same might be said of the missionary bishop of to-day, who is every whit as much a bishop as the diocesan of any settled see in Europe.

VII

The foregoing brief sketch is enough to indicate the wide range of variety in the dignity and administrative powers of bishops at different times and places. These great variations of organization are in striking contrast with the settled principle that ordination must be administered by a bishop. We know this principle to have been recognized from the earliest times to which our exact knowledge stretches back, that is to say to the latter half of the second century. It is an organic principle because upon it depends the continuity of the divine society and its stewardship. The chameleon-like character of what is commonly called 'episcopacy' gives all the more significance to the strict preservation of the essential principle that underlies it.

VIII

A word may be given here to some changes of organization or custom that have affected the two lower orders of presbyters and deacons. Presbyters at first were not parsons or parish priests, there were then no parishes. In each Church was a body of presbyters, as a kind of council supporting the bishop, very much as the letters of St Ignatius picture at the beginning of the second century. As the Church grew, and its whole local membership could no longer assemble in congregation with the bishop, the presbyters were gradually dispersed, and individual presbyters were put in charge of 'parishes' in and near great cities like Rome, Carthage and Alexandria. In this way, from the third century onwards, the parochial system gradually developed.[2] It is a marked change of organization comparable to the earlier change of the chief pastors from itinerancy to diocesan residence.

Deacons, in the Churches of the West, have undergone a great displacement, which seems to have come about gradually during the Middle Ages. In the undivided Church everywhere in the early

[1] Lightfoot, *Christian Ministry*, p. 196.
[2] *Essays on Early Hist.*, W. H. Frere, pp. 302, 303; F. E. Brightman, p. 387.

centuries, and still to-day in the Churches of the East, the diaconate
is a numerous and active body of ministers who perform their own
distinctive and important duties without any general expectation of
passing on to be priests. In the Church of Rome, the diaconate
gradually dwindled in importance until it became a mere stepping-
stone order for the priesthood;[1] the Anglican Communion has in-
herited this degeneracy from Rome, and still tolerates it. There is
much to be said for a restoration of deacons in the West to be again
an active and distinctive order, as in the East and formerly in the
universal Church; but it would be out of place here to go into the
merits of that proposal.[2]

[1] 'In modern times the diaconate has been so entirely regarded as a stage of preparation for the priesthood that interest no longer attaches to its precise duties and privileges' (*Catholic Encyclopedia*, 1908, IV. p. 651, s.v. 'Deacon'.)
[2] The new ministry of 'ruling elders' set up in the Reformed Churches bears a
striking resemblance to the Catholic order of deacons, in its intermediate position
and its practical merits, although not in its theory, which is obscure and still remains
unsettled (see note E to chapter XII). Can there have been an instinctive sense of the
need for a type of ministry which belonged to apostolic and Catholic order, but
which in the Western Church had dropped out of its due place?

B. KNOWN CONTINUITY FROM THE SECOND CENTURY ONWARD

CHAPTER X. CONTINUITY SINCE THE SECOND CENTURY

I

WHERE then is to be found the continuity of the Church as an organism, a living society? A short survey of the varieties of its organization has shown that continuity is not to be looked for in any stereotyped code of 'government' or administration; indeed it is perfectly plain that it could not be. Organization has varied greatly since the first century. Then there was no resident chief pastorate (except at Jerusalem and later, perhaps, at Rome) although presbyters were appointed 'in every church', and the pastoral epistles indicate that the order of deacons also was represented everywhere. There were no dioceses or fixed areas of jurisdiction for the chief pastors, that is to say the Twelve and St Paul, together with a growing number of their colleagues and coadjutors such as Barnabas, Silvanus, and Timothy; all of them were itinerant evangelists, although in the latest glimpse that Scripture affords, Timothy and Titus are seen in Ephesus and Crete in temporary charges of a quasi-diocesan kind.

If by an effort of imagination we suppose that the whole of Christendom now agreed to restore these scriptural arrangements of Church life, each local group possessing its local presbyters and deacons, all of them acknowledging the direction and the authoritative guiding hand of itinerant chief pastors, that of itself would amount to no more than a reconstruction of the primitive arrangements; it could not create continuity, because there has not in fact been a continuance of these arrangements since the first century. Mere restoration of what has become obsolete, whether or not it is in itself possible or desirable, is only another change, another discontinuity. Thus Presbyterianism and Independency (the forerunner of Congregationalism and other vigorous Christian movements) were sixteenth-century attempts to reconstruct the local Churches of the scriptural period; it has been said of them that they were both antiquarian reconstructions of the Apostolic Age without the apostles.[1] We need not pause here to weigh the justice of that comment: on the assumption that they did effect a reproduction of the primitive congregations, no continuity could be claimed for it, for the very reason of its being a re-production, a re-construction, of what had been discontinued.

In the quest for continuity we must begin with the known. Our exact knowledge of organic Church life from contemporary documents begins in the latter half of the second century; for the present that will be taken as a starting point. From that time until now the life-process of the Church can be reviewed in perspective and in ample detail. If this inquiry should disclose no principle of organic life continuing unbroken through these seventeen or eighteen centuries, the whole conception of the Church would be affected; the Church in the world could not well then be one visible organic society. If, on the other hand, the Church can be seen to possess, from the second century until now, a distinctive, unbroken, organic life-principle, the inquiry must afterwards be carried farther back to the more obscure period that begins at the close of the New Testament history; but consideration of the first century and the apostolic era must in the meantime be postponed.

II

Through all the vicissitudes and vagaries of the centuries from the second onward, one principle seems to endure unchanged. It is to be found in the structure that distinguishes the society as an organic body, the stewardship which is at once an organ of its sacramental fellowship and of its continuing endurance. In the society, the precise arrangements of what the world calls 'government' have been changed or modified from time to time; continuity does not depend upon them, important though they are. Government in the worldly sense cannot be of the essence of its stewardship in that household whose stewards are never to lord it over their charge, the greatest of whom is to be servant of all.

Not in a legalistic aspect, therefore, is the ministry or stewardship of the second-century Church to be regarded. No doubt the same threefold order of bishop, presbyters and deacons was then universally recognized, and known by the same names; but too much reliance must not be placed upon names. No doubt too, diocesan organiza-

---

[1] W. K. Lowther Clarke in *Episcopacy A. & M.* p. 43.

tion had generally been adopted by the latter part of the second century, so that the chief pastors were settled singly in 'mon-episcopacy' and had ceased to be roving evangelists; but as we have seen, the episcopal ministry has at times been, and sometimes still is, dissociated from any diocesan jurisdiction. The intimate relation of the stewardship to the sacramental life of the household has been traced clearly in the work of Dr H. F. Hamilton, passages from which have already been quoted.[1] In his words: 'The Eucharist is the great central fact in the origin and development of the Christian ministry. The presbyters or priests are those who possess the authority of the whole Church to represent it at the breaking of the bread; the bishops are those who possess the authority of the whole Church to confer this representative character upon others; the deacons are Christian ministers who lack just this representative capacity. This fundamental relation of the three orders to each other has never varied, because the relation of each to the Eucharist has never varied'.[2] Leaving aside all legalism then, and looking only to the primary character of the stewardship, the second century displays it in these three ranks, classes, or orders standing in that fundamental relationship to each other and to the whole household of which they are stewards, that is to say servants—ministers—with particular responsibilities and powers.

III

This threefold stewardship has been preserved in the household of the Church down to the present day in unbroken continuity notwithstanding the sad divisions that have rent the Church.

In the Orthodox Churches of the East, auxiliary or minor orders of Subdeacon and Reader are in use to assist in the work of the Church without affecting or in any way encroaching upon the three Holy Orders, which are what they always have been.

The Anglican Communion in all its provinces claims to 'retain inviolate in the sacred ministry the three orders of Bishops, Priests and Deacons as of Divine Institution'.[3] Their fundamental relationship is exactly what it was in the Church of the second century. Minor orders are not in use; 'readers' are laymen, not ordained to that office. The denials by the Roman Church of the validity of Anglican orders are an interesting side issue only to the present

---

[1] *Vide supra*, pp. 40, 41.   [2] Hamilton, II. p. 205.
[3] Canon I of the Episcopal Church in Scotland.

inquiry.*[1] The Old Catholic Churches, which are in communion with the ancient see of Utrecht, have about fourteen bishops; the validity of their orders is admitted even by Rome.

The threefold stewardship of bishops, priests, and deacons, in their constant and ancient relationship, has been preserved by the Roman Church, only partly obscured by some peculiarities. The gradual aggrandizement of the bishop of Rome into universal bishop led inevitably to a corresponding depression of all bishops who sub-mitted to his claims, and to their being thought of as forming only a higher grade of the priesthood: this tendency received monastic support because of the desire of the Regular orders for freedom from diocesan control, and there were two other contributory causes.*[2] Nevertheless in Rome, as in the Orthodox and Anglican Churches, the orders of presbyters and bishops preserve unchanged the funda-mental character they have always had, in the words of Dr Hamilton already quoted, an organ which acts as the representative of the whole Church to break the bread at the Eucharist, and an organ which acts for the whole Church in bestowing this representative character upon individuals. That intrinsic character remains wholly unaffected by the rather confused enumeration of orders peculiar to Rome.

IV

In controversial discussion of Church and ministry, it is sometimes contended that an actual historical continuity of the ministry cannot be proved, or that it is unlikely to have been preserved through the centuries. It is said, for example, 'that the records in the early centuries are scanty and uncertain'.[3] Such doubts attach themselves naturally to mistaken ideas of the nature of continuity in the Church, for which some blame must rest on those who have most strenuously contended for ministerial continuity. The ancient and historic ministry has been likened, in picturesque but misleading metaphors, to a golden pipe or chain passing down from the apostles to the present day. The fallacy of these lies in a failure to see clearly that the ministry or stewardship is inseparably part of the society or household, and that its continuity does not stand alone, but partakes reciprocally of the continuity of the whole society.

Continuity is concerned with two main periods; the first includes

---

[1] Note A.   *Rome's denials of Anglican orders* (p. 68).
[2] Note B.   *Lowered status of bishops in the developed Roman system* (p. 70).
[3] Ainslie, p. 205.

the days of the New Testament and the following century in which detailed records of Church life are certainly scanty. That century is the subject of the next chapter. The second period extends to the present time. As will presently be seen, our knowledge of this period is full enough to give assurance of the continuity of the stewardship in accordance with the organic principle of ordination that is still in operation.

In later chapters, reasons will be given for believing that this same organic principle has from the beginning received the same expression, but it must be freely admitted that this cannot be proved by positive evidence. Is the continuity of the stewardship throughout the first period therefore doubtful? Not at all, for reasons that can be shortly stated in the words of a distinguished Presbyterian theologian. It is the Church which ordains, acting through duly authorized persons.[1] Dr Carnegie Simpson later points out that the continuity of the living Church from apostolic days 'is beyond any historical cavil'.[2]

When the obscurity of the first period clears away then, the living Church and its stewardship are seen, together and inseparable, in a continuity of life beyond all question. We know, at all events, how the continuity of the stewardship was receiving expression then, in a manner recognized throughout the whole Ekklesia. The principle has received that expression ever since, in a known manner that leaves no room for doubt. From the earliest times it has been the custom of the Church for at least three bishops to join in ordaining a bishop. There is reason for thinking that this custom was observed from the beginning; as the result of study it appears (1) that in ordaining by the laying on of hands the Church was perpetuating what, in the first century, was the custom of the Church of Israel, and (2) there is striking evidence of a contemporary Jewish rule requiring three ordainers of a presbyter or rabbi.*[3] In the Christian Ekklesia, the primary and conscious purpose of this ancient requirement of not less than three ordainers has always been to prevent clandestine ordinations and to be a guarantee of provincial recognition, to give some security that the ministers of ordination, those recognized representatives of the whole Church, shall not abuse their representative authority. 'The idea of thereby securing validity (in case one of the bishops was, by some accidental omission of a

---

[1] Carnegie Simpson, pp. 153, 154, 157.   [2] Ibid. pp. 157, 158.
[3] Note C. *Jewish ordination by three ordainers* (p. 70).

necessary rite, no real bishop at all) is perhaps too materialistic to have entered into the mind of the early Church. When things were duly done according to Christ's ordinance, they were regarded as certainly having His certificate.'[1] But when, under a misconception of this kind, the organic continuity of the ancient ministry is called in question, the challenge is easily repelled. The credentials of a bishop as an accredited chief steward of the household depend not on any single 'chain' of descent. but on myriads of interlacing lines of spiritual 'ancestry'. A challenge of this legalistic kind fails entirely, for if, by vast antiquarian industry, the 'line' of consecrators of any bishop of to-day could be ascertained and written out in full, his episcopal 'ancestors' of, say, a thousand years ago, would be found to include practically all the contemporary bishops of the whole Church.★[2]

In truth all such questioning and answering belong to a mistaken conception of the relationship of the ministry and the Church, for which false metaphor, such as the 'golden chain', is largely responsible. When that relationship is thought of in its true nature as that of an organic body and its organs, it is seen at once that any possible accidental flaw, such as has been imagined, is comparable only to some microscopic lesion in a physical body that does not affect the solidarity of the tissues and is quickly re-knit.

V

In the search for the principle of the organic continuity of the Church as a living society, the household of God in the world, reasons have been found for believing that its stewardship embodies that principle, and supplies the medium of continuity. If so, the due continuance of that stewardship must be a vital necessity. The Gospels depict the Twelve chosen disciples as the first to hold the stewardship. The short parable of the man *having left his house, and given authority to his servants, to each one his work*,[3] seems to refer particularly to them; for when St Peter asked whether this parable was spoken unto them *or even unto all*, in reply, *the Lord said, Who then is the faithful and wise steward, whom his lord shall set over his household, to give them their portion of food in due season?*[4] The comparison of the Church and its ministry to a household and stewardship occurs repeatedly in the Epistles of St Paul and St Peter, showing how firmly it was im-

---

[1] Gore and Turner, p. 94.   [2] Note D.   *Suggested 'flaws' in succession* (p. 71).
[3] Mark xiii. 34; cp. Luke xii. 35 *seq.*   [4] Luke xii. 41, 42.

pressed.[1] If that stewardship is to continue in the household through the centuries, later generations of stewards must receive their office in some manner that will make it unmistakably recognizable throughout the household. It seems necessary, therefore, that a steward of to-day must have received an authority recognizably imparted to him through the stewards of yesterday; *through*, not *by*, for they are not the household but only its representatives. It is because they are the *representatives* of the household that their instrumentality is essential.

Out of all the thought and discussion concerning Christian ministry, no suggestion has emerged of any other method of appointment to it that will confer a recognizable authority wider in its scope than that of a particular group. Those denominations which reject the organic continuity of the ministry within the Church quite logically deny that the Church possesses any continuing office of stewardship.★[2]

VI

Ever since the latter part of the second century, then, the Church has possessed the same stewardship of three orders or classes which might fitly be described as chief stewards, stewards, and understewards, standing in the same unchanging relation to each other and to the rest of the Church. But that is only one stage of the inquiry. Either that continuity has remained unbroken from the very beginning, or the visible Church can hardly be said to have had a continuity of organic life: inquiry must therefore be carried back to the apostolic period and the hundred years that succeeded it. The history of the Church during that time is obscure, and is largely a matter of inference from the fragmentary information which is all that has come down to us.

We are now coming to the arena of a four-hundred-years-old controversy. What was the organic life of the Church through the hundred years after St Paul's death? What was the relationship between the ministry of his time and that of a century later? What exactly was the transition, and did the pastorate of the bishop really carry on the pastorate of the apostles or secondary apostles? In the next seven chapters the known facts are collected. They afford some

[1] Gal. vi. 10; Eph. ii. 19; I Pet. iv. 10; I Cor. iv. 1, 2; Tit. i. 7.
[2] Note E. *A continuing stewardship denied* (p. 71).

positive evidence that the ministry remained identical in substance, with some change of nomenclature; they afford strong evidence that there was never any revolution or break in the organic life of the Church.

What is set out in the first part of this book, especially in chapters VI and VII, may point over and beyond the incomplete historical evidence of the obscure period to grounds for believing that the organism of the Church has been, and will continue to be, divinely guarded from being broken and lost. No candid student claims that the early evidence is conclusive in favour of any one exact historical interpretation, but assurance of the unbroken continuity of the Church through the period does not depend upon the establishment of one or other exact historical theory.

NOTES TO CHAPTER X

A. ROME'S DENIALS OF ANGLICAN ORDERS

As is well known, the Roman Church asserts that Anglican orders of ministry are invalid. The reasons that have been assigned for this are less well known, so that it may be of interest here to enumerate them.

(1) The *Nag's Head Fable* was a grotesque tale published by one John Holywood in 1604, alleging that Archbishop Matthew Parker received no consecration but a mockery, conducted by an apostate monk in a tavern called the 'Nag's Head'. Actually, he was duly consecrated in the chapel of Lambeth Palace on 17 December 1559, by three bishops, Barlow, Coverdale and Hodgkins. There is complete extant evidence of this, as well as of the formal preliminary stages (congé d'élire, election, and confirmation). This ground of attack has for a long time been abandoned.

(2) The episcopal status was challenged of Bishop Barlow, formerly of Bath and Wells and then elect of Chichester, who was the principal of the three consecrating bishops. Documentary evidence of his original consecration in 1536 is lacking. Much documentary evidence of the consecration of other bishops is also lacking, and there is no reason to suppose that he could have entered into his bishopric under Henry VIII and Cranmer without due consecration. In any case (*a*) the orders of the other two consecrators of Archbishop Parker are unquestionable, and (*b*) Anglican orders do not depend on the 'line of succession' through him; Italian and Irish lines of 'valid succession' met less than a century later in Archbishop Laud. This line of attack also is not now much relied upon.

(3)   In the Roman Church at the time of the Reformation a rite of delivery of a Chalice and Paten had come to be included in the ordination of a priest. The rite was omitted from the English Ordinal as revised in 1549, and this was claimed as demonstrating the palpable invalidity of English orders; no ordination without the *porrectio* or *traditio instrumentorum*, it was confidently said, could possibly be valid. But it was afterwards discovered that this *traditio* (which had never been adopted by the Church in the East) had not been used or known even in the West before the eleventh century, so that the supposed defect would have condemned as invalid the orders of all the Roman popes and ministry. This attack was abandoned.

(4)   In 1896 Pope Leo XIII issued his Bull *Apostolicae Curae*: 'We pronounce and declare that Ordinations carried out according to the Anglican rite have been and are absolutely null and utterly void.' A contrary opinion had been widely held among Roman Catholic scholars. Infallibility is not claimed for this Bull (although it is declared to be irreformable in perpetuity!), but in virtue of the papal *magisterium* it must receive implicit acceptance from all in the Roman obedience.

It is argued that the English Ordinal in use between 1549 and 1661 was defective in form and in intention. The Preface to the Ordinal explicitly states the 'intent' to 'continue and reverently to use' these Orders of Ministry in Christ's Church, Bishops, Priests, and Deacons 'which from the Apostles' time there hath been'. The Bull wholly ignores this. 'The Form of Ordering Priests' then four times names the order or office of Priesthood before the prayer at the laying on of hands:— 'Receive the Holy Ghost; whose sins thou dost forgive, they are forgiven, and whose sins thou dost retain, they are retained : and be thou a faithful dispenser of the Word of God and of His holy Sacraments. In the Name...' The Ordinal was (a) defective in form, so argues the Bull, because the words of that prayer do not once more name the Order that is being conferred, and 'do not in the least definitely express the Sacred Order of Priesthood, or its grace and power, which is chiefly the power of consecrating and of offering the true Body and Blood of the Lord.' The divergencies from the Ordinal in contemporary Roman use show, it is also argued, (b) a 'defect of intention', i.e. 'the manifest intention of introducing another rite not approved by the [Roman] Church.' Therefore it was not the intention to ordain a 'Priest' in the Catholic sense.

The words that the Bull claims as essential are absent from some surviving early Ordination forms, and since 1896, a MS. collection of fourth-century prayers has been found at Mount Athos, which shows that in the prayer used in the ordination of a priest at that period no reference was made either to priesthood or the power of sacrifice. Dr Headlam remarks on this (p. 253) that 'It has seldom happened that the utterance of a Pope or any other controversialist has been so decisively proved to be wrong by future discoveries as that of Leo XIII'. Nevertheless, most Roman Catholics find the combined effect of arguments (a) and (b) convincing; whether or no, they are all bound by the Bull. It all turns upon the infallibility of Roman doctrine, and the claim that the Roman Church is the whole Catholic Church. As Mr C. G. Mortimer says, in *Anglican Orders*—published by the (Roman) Catholic Truth Society—at p. 24: 'The question resolves itself back into a simple one—What after all is the Church?' Every Christian who comes to believe in the truth of the Roman claim ought at once to seek admission to the Roman Church; he need then have no further concern for non-Roman ministerial orders. For all others, the Bull and the arguments used to support it are valueless.

B. LOWERED STATUS OF BISHOPS IN THE DEVELOPED ROMAN SYSTEM

In addition to the primary causes mentioned in the text, two others contributed:

(1) In relation to the high service of the altar in the Eucharist, the presbyter was all but equal to the bishop. As St Jerome asked rhetorically (*Ep. cxlvi, Ad Evangelum*): 'What function, excepting ordination, belongs to a bishop that does not also belong to a presbyter?'

(2) Of the various subordinate Church offices or minor orders, Roman practice ultimately adopted five, viz. Doorkeeper, Exorcist, Reader, Acolyte, Subdeacon (but not the Healer or the Interpreter). In veneration for sacred numbers, it came to be reckoned that there are seven orders of which three pertain to the altar and are 'Holy', the others being 'minor'. Although the Subdiaconate admittedly was not a major order originally in its nature, Pope Innocent III at the beginning of the thirteenth century ordered that it should be counted among the major orders. Accordingly, in the modern Roman computation, the three major or sacred orders are Subdeacon, Deacon, and Priest and Bishop reckoned in this connexion as one. Yet Rome still remembers that 'Three orders are of Divine institution, the episcopate, the priesthood and the diaconate....The remaining orders are of ecclesiastical institution'. (*The New Catholic Dictionary*, 1929, with imprimatur, p. 707.)

C. JEWISH ORDINATION BY THREE ORDAINERS

'In the Babylonian Talmud we are told, "There is a *Baraitha*: To laying the hand upon the elders...three are needed. What does this mean? R. Johanan said: Laying the hand upon the elders means to ordain one a rabbi."' (Lockton, p. 26.) 'It is plain that the rule that ordination must be performed by the laying on of the hands of three persisted until the time of R. Jehoshua and R. Akiba....Ordination by the laying on of the hands of three would thus be the rule of the Jewish Church in the days of our Lord and His apostles, and throughout the whole period of the inauguration of the Christian Church.' (*Ibid.* p. 41.) See also W. K. Lowther Clarke in *Episcopacy A. & M.* p. 7: 'The later practice [after A.D. 133] is given by Tosefta Sanhedrin (i. 1), "The *semikha* is to be decided by three and the laying on of the elders' hands by three"'; see also G. Dix in *Laudate*, xv. p. 107: 'The evidence is obscure except for the period *c.* A.D. 75–150. The laying on of hands probably existed in Judaism before this. It seems to have died out later on.'

D. Suggested 'flaws' in succession

On a mistaken supposition that succession in the apostolic ministry of the Church must be something tactual, tenuous, mechanical, and therefore exposed to a constant possibility of dislocation, some writers (e.g. Ainslie, p. 205) suppose it to be doubtful that it has been 'carried out correctly and without a break throughout all the centuries'. It is suggested that there may have been 'ordinations carried out under heretical prelates', overlooking what became the settled doctrine of the whole Church, that a sacrament performed by a duly ordained minister is 'valid' notwithstanding his own mortal sin, or his heresy. Thus even Rome recognizes as valid ordinations by the bishops of the Eastern Churches, who in the view of Rome are schismatical and heretical.

The baselessness of any fear of a 'break in the succession' owing to some informality in ordination was shown by W. E. Gladstone (*Church Principles considered in their results*, pp. 235, 236): 'The probability of a flaw affecting the present orders of the clergy is indefinitely minute; and is not increased but diminished at each new transmission of the ordaining power.' The effect of the ancient rule requiring three consecrators of a bishop 'is to multiply to the third degree the chances in favour of continuity'. Even on the extravagant assumption that, at some time, the consecration of one bishop out of twenty had been incomplete or informal through accident or neglect the chances would be 8000 to 1 against three such 'bishops' collaborating in a new consecration, and 512,000,000 to 1 against a repetition in the succeeding 'generation' of consecrators. 'But enough', he concludes, 'of this rather unworthy discussion, which can only justify the attention given to it from the fact that men of note and name have been misled by the fallacy in question.'

E. A continuing stewardship denied

'The Apostles appointed no canonical successors. They could not.... The Apostles could not send as they had been sent by Christ.... The strict successor of the Apostles is the New Testament as containing the precipitate of their standard preaching. It is not the ministry that is the successor of the Apostolate, but the ministry *plus* the true Apostolic legacy of the Bible—the ministry *of the Word*.' (Forsyth, pp. 128, 129. Dr Forsyth was the Principal of the Congregational Theological College at Hampstead and had been Chairman of the Congregational Union of England and Wales.)

C. CONTINUITY FROM PENTECOST TO THE SECOND CENTURY

CHAPTER XI. THE TUNNEL

FROM the Day of Pentecost until the latter part of the second century, about A.D. 170, when Hippolytus was young, the definite evidence of the ways and customs of the Church is so scanty that much room is left for inference and conjecture. The New Testament is our earliest source; it covers the period to the martyrdom of St Paul on the Ostian Way at Rome, about A.D. 68. Incidental references in the Acts of the Apostles, and in some of St Paul's epistles, give a little information. When the New Testament ceases to throw light upon the organism of the Church, history enters on a hundred years of obscurity which Dr Salmon, in a well-known metaphor, compared to a tunnel.*[1]

The Church enters this tunnel as one great society, spread throughout the Old World, having as its local ministers everywhere presbyters and deacons, as its chief pastors itinerant evangelists generally described as apostles. It is being edified too, and to some extent directed, by prophets, who may or may not hold specific ministerial office. It emerges from the tunnel as beyond doubt the same great worldwide society. Everywhere still it has presbyters and deacons in its local ministry, but its chief pastors are no longer mobile evangelists. They are settled in residence, usually one by one, as single individuals to whom the description of 'the bishop' is now applied. Diocesan organization has not been fully developed; although 'the bishop' is settled as chief pastor in most cities, the territorial dioceses are not everywhere determined.*[2] Prophets are not now found.

In nomenclature there is a notable change. The presbyters, who in the Gentile Churches in the first century were overseers in fact, and were often so called, i.e. 'bishops', are not now or ever again called bishops. Although the chief pastors of the first century were never called bishops, the chief pastor is known as 'the bishop' now that he is a settled resident. This exchange of names was in progress between A.D. 95 and 110, the years intervening between the epistle of Clement to Corinth and the epistles of Ignatius to the Churches

---

[1] Note A. *Salmon on the 'tunnel' period* (p. 79).
[2] Note B. *Diocesan system a development* (p. 80).

of Asia Minor. The tunnel, to keep to the metaphor, is not all dark. There are shafts of illumination; these epistles give some valuable light.

The laying on of hands in ordination is recorded by St Luke on the occasion of the first ordination, the only one he describes,[1] when it was administered by the chief pastors, the Twelve. It is found in universal observance when the Church emerges from the 'tunnel', and it is still administered for the Church by its chief pastors. There is no express mention of it in the surviving documents of the hundred years; but there is nothing whatever to suggest that it had ever been discontinued.[2] In respect to continuity, the Church possesses the same stewardship or ministry, subject to the change already noticed in the labours of the chief pastor, from that of roving evangelist to that of resident overseer. There is no trace of any question or controversy either about this change or about ordination and the laying on of hands by the chief pastors. That is very significant, because the human generations during the period of obscurity, in the ordinary course of nature, mingle and overlap. The force of this is easily seen when the approximate life-periods of a few notable leaders of the Church are compared, of whom short descriptive notes follow here. These known lives are, of course, examples of countless other linkings of the generations individually unknown, which together weave the lives of Christians of the whole period into a seamless web.

St Peter is believed to have been crucified about A.D. 64, St Paul to have been beheaded on the Ostian Way at Rome about A.D. 68. St John, according to the Asiatic tradition recorded by Irenaeus, lived 'till the times of Trajan' (A.D. 98–117), latterly at Ephesus.

CLEMENT OF ROME, a Hellenist Jew, who was chief pastor of the Church in Rome from A.D. 92, lived to A.D. 100. The great epistle written by him to the Church in Corinth in 95 or 96 supports by its contents the tradition that he was a disciple of SS. Peter and Paul, to whom also tradition attributes his ordination.[3] This important document is the subject of chapter XVI.

IGNATIUS, bishop of Antioch, an 'apostolic man' in the narrower

[1] Acts vi, the ordination of the Seven.
[2] 'The universal prevalence in later times implies the continuity of the custom.' (Headlam, p. 83.)
[3] Lightfoot, *Clement*, I. pp. 4, 59, 61, 73, 342, 343. 'The date of his birth, we may suppose, would synchronize roughly with the death of the Saviour.' (*Ibid.* p. 72.)

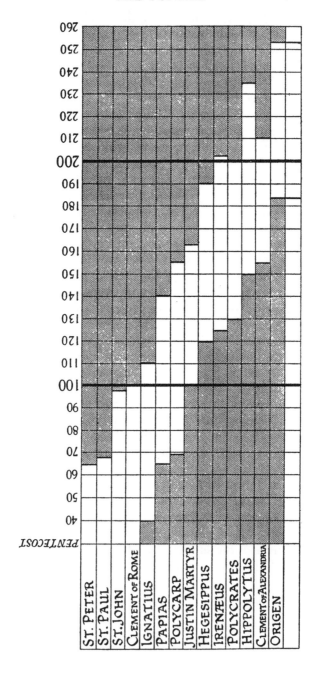

sense of having been ordained by one of the first apostles,[1] may have been born *c.* A.D. 40. He suffered martyrdom by being thrown to the beasts in the arena at Rome *c.* 110.[2] The seven epistles written by him during his journey to Rome for execution prove that settled 'mon-episcopacy' was then already established throughout Asia Minor.*[3]

PAPIAS, bishop of Hierapolis in Phrygia, 'may have been born *c.* A.D. 60–70 and probably wrote *c.* 130–40'[4] his *Expositions of the Oracles of the Lord*, of which unfortunately very few fragments remain. In the most important of these[5] he tells that he had learned from 'the elders': 'And if ever anyone came who had been a follower of the elders, I would inquire as to the discourses of the elders, what was said by Andrew, or what by Peter, or what by Philip, or what by Thomas or James, or what by John or Matthew or any other of the disciples of the Lord; and the things which Aristion and the elder John, the disciples of the Lord, say.' He seems to make two classes of the sources of his information, viz. Andrew, Peter, and others, of whom he speaks in the past tense, having learned from their 'followers', and Aristion and John the presbyter or elder, of whom he speaks in the present. The statement by Irenaeus that Papias was 'a companion of Polycarp' is probably correct.[6]

POLYCARP, bishop of Smyrna, born A.D. 69, died A.D. 155. St Irenaeus, who had known him, says he 'was appointed by the Apostles for Asia as bishop in the Church at Smyrna'.[7] He suffered martyrdom by burning at Smyrna at the age of eighty-six, in February 155. Only in the previous year he had visited Bishop Anicetus of Rome.

JUSTIN MARTYR, 'a Samaritan by race, the typical apologist of the Church, the champion of the Gospel against Jew and Gentile alike',[8] was converted in youth before A.D. 132, and lived latterly at Rome. Of his many writings there survive only a first and a second *Apologia*, the first dedicated to the Emperor Antoninus in 148, and the *Dialogue with Tryphon the Jew*, the scene of which is laid at Ephesus, where he was staying a few years before his death. He suffered martyrdom with some companions in or shortly after 163.

HEGESIPPUS, a native of Palestine and a Hebrew by birth, was

[1] Lightfoot, *Ignatius*, I. p. 29.   [2] *Ibid.* p. 30; II. p. 472.
[3] Note C. *Early 'mon-episcopacy' in Asia Minor* (p. 80).
[4] Lightfoot, *Clement*, II. p. 494.   [5] Preserved by Eusebius, *Hist. Eccl.* III. 39.
[6] Lightfoot, *Ignatius*, I. p. 442.   [7] *Ibid.* pp. 441, 666; Irenaeus, *Haer.* iii. 3. 4.
[8] Lightfoot, *Ignatius*, I. p. 451.

the earliest historian of Christianity,[1] and a traveller. At Rome he compiled a chronological list of all its bishops down to Anicetus (A.D. 154–65) and he published it in the time of Eleutherus (175–89). St Jerome said, probably inaccurately, that his life had bordered on the apostolic age.

IRENAEUS, born *c.* A.D. 125, probably in Asia Minor, was a presbyter of Lyons for some time before he became bishop of that see in 177. His magnum opus, *Against Heresies*, in five books, was written *c.* 180–85.[2] About 190 he wrote to a former fellow-student, Florinus, who had fallen into heresy, a letter of remonstrance, preserved by Eusebius:[3]

These opinions the elders before us, who also were disciples of the apostles, did not hand down to thee. For I saw thee, when I was still a youth, in lower Asia in the company of Polycarp, while thou wast faring brilliantly in the royal court and endeavouring to win his favour. For I distinctly remember the events of that time better than recent events, for what we learn in childhood grows as the mind grows and becomes part of it; so that I can tell the very place where the blessed Polycarp used to sit when he discoursed, his goings out and his coming in, his manner of life, his personal appearance, the discourses that he held before the multitude, and how he would tell of his intercourse with John and with the others who had seen the Lord, and how he would relate their words; and whatsoever things he had heard from them about the Lord, His mighty works and His teaching, Polycarp, as having received them from the eye-witnesses of the life of the Word, would relate altogether in accordance with the Scriptures. To these things I used to listen attentively then, by the mercy of God which was granted me, noting them down not on paper but in my heart.

He is said to have fallen a victim to the persecution of Severus in 202.

POLYCRATES, bishop of Ephesus in the end of the second century, was probably born *c.* A.D. 130, for there is a letter from him to Bishop Victor of Rome (189–99) on the question of the date of Easter, in which he speaks of his 'hoar head' and 'numbering sixty-five years in the Lord'. In appealing to tradition he adds that he had had seven relatives who were bishops.[4]

HIPPOLYTUS of Rome, a pupil of Irenaeus before A.D. 177,[5] born probably about 150–55, died an old man in exile in Sardinia in 235. A leading scholar and writer; also a bishop.

---

[1] Lightfoot, *Ignatius*, I. p. 451. [2] *Ibid.* pp. 445 *seq.*
[3] Eusebius, *Hist. Eccl.* v, 15, 20. [4] Lightfoot, *Ignatius*, I. pp. 393, 394.
[5] Lightfoot, *Clement*, II. pp. 383, 423, 440; *Ignatius*, I. p. 451.

CLEMENT OF ALEXANDRIA was an Athenian by training if not by birth. One of his teachers was an Ephesian. He was a voluminous author, four of whose books are preserved with fragments of five others, and was head of the catechetical school of Alexandria from A.D. 190 to 203 when the persecution under Severus took place, and he retired from Alexandria. He was born probably between 150 and 160. The date of his death is unknown.

ORIGEN, an Alexandrian of Greek family, was aged sixteen when his father perished at Alexandria in the persecution under Severus A.D. 202, and he died at Tyre aged sixty-nine. He was a pupil of Clement of Alexandria, and he heard Hippolytus preach in Rome; he also visited Athens, Ephesus, etc.; a great scholar and voluminous writer, he made his home at Caesarea from 231 onwards.

Even these few instances exemplify how intimately the generations in the Church were linked, Clement, Ignatius and Polycarp being connected with the first Apostles, Irenaeus learning from Polycarp, Hippolytus from Irenaeus, Origen from Hippolytus.

For the most part, these prominent names are associated with the great cities of the Roman Empire. It is a little astonishing to find how close was the intercourse and correspondence kept up between all these fairly distant places at that period. As Professor C. H. Turner wrote:

Never was intercourse between different churches so vivid and continuous, never was the centripetal tendency so dominant, never was the sense of give and take between the scattered groups which constituted the Christian fellowship so untiringly active, as in the days when formal organization to connect the churches was still in the future. The scanty records of Christian history between S. Clement at the end of the first and S. Irenaeus at the end of the second century consist largely of notices of the epistolary intercourse of different and often distant churches.[1] It would be difficult to find many later parallels to the visit of Polycarp to Rome in A.D. 155. Common means of intercommunication, common use of one language, above all, the common inspiration of a faith and life shared as an exclusive inheritance in the face of a hostile world, made Christian unity a more real thing in the second century than it ever was at any later date. One of the greatest of its fruits was the consensus by which the four Gospels were accepted or 'canonized'.[2]

[1] Such as Rome and Corinth, which were, however, only one week's journey apart. (Lightfoot, *Clement*, I. p. 82.)

[2] C. H. Turner, review of Streeter's *The Four Gospels*, in *Theology*, April 1925, reprinted in posthumous *Collected Papers*, pp. 149, 150. See also Hamilton, II. p. 146; Wordsworth, p. 148; Sir W. Ramsay, *The Church in the Roman Empire*, p. 365.

To the faithful of the two or three generations of the Church, then, these hundred years of the 'tunnel' were no time of obscurity. They showed a common life in full knowledge of all that concerned the brethren throughout the known world. Even to our eyes, at this distance of time, the tunnel is not very dark. Yet the surviving writings throw little light upon the preservation and renewal of the organic life of the Church. We know that this was world-wide and common to all, the sacraments observed everywhere with un-diminished reverence; the same local ministry labouring everywhere; everywhere there were chief pastors held in a position of higher spiritual authority, mobile evangelists when the Church enters the tunnel, resident 'diocesans' when it emerges. How these chief stewards and the other stewards were chosen, how they were com-missioned for their office, is not mentioned, except for one incidental reference in the letter of Clement to the Corinthians about A.D. 95, which calls for attention later. An ordination with the laying on of the chief pastors' hands is one of the earliest episodes recorded in the Acts. At the end of the period we find that same ordination with the laying on of hands of the chief pastors, now called bishops, in universal and unquestioned observance. We have no direct evidence of its continuance during the tunnel period. The silence on this subject is the more marked because of the fullness of record regarding any heresy or other subject of controversy. Even the correct date for the commemoration of Easter was the subject of a prolonged dispute that is amply recorded.

In sharp contrast with these echoes of disagreement is the absence of any trace of diversity of opinion or observance affecting the one-ness of the divine Society, its apostolic ministry, its order of 'bishops' and their spiritual authority, or the continuation and renewal of this stewardship on which the organic continuance of the household depends—with ordination at the hands of the chief stewards. The explanation seems to be that these things were never doubted, were observed without question; it was not until the sixteenth century that they came into prominence, just because for the first time in the history of the Church they had become controversial.

After the divisions of the sixteenth century, a theory was put forward that the episcopate was not truly a chief pastorate repre-senting that of the New Testament, but that it had only developed out of an aggrandizement of presiding presbyters into a new and artificial order, while all other presbyters had, in the same brief period, been depressed into a subordinate rank and had lost the exercise of their primitive powers. In criticism of this theory, Dr Salmon said:

When the Church comes out of the tunnel, of which I spoke, into the full light of history, we find bishops ruling everywhere, and no one having the least suspicion that since the apostles' times any other form of Church government had prevailed. Two things lead me to think that they were not wrong in their belief. If the original form of government had been different, I cannot think that a change would have been universal, or that it could be silent. There would surely be found in some places survivals of the primitive form, and other places where the primitive form had not been changed without a struggle. If domineering or exceptionally gifted men in some places set themselves above their fellows, this would not happen everywhere, and surely the usurpation would in some places be so resisted that we could not help hearing of it. The presumption that the Church of the second century was not mistaken in its belief in the Apostolic origin of an Institution, which in that early age had obtained universal and uncontested acceptance, is confirmed when we turn to the New Testament....[1]

In the human body the breathing muscles are incessantly at work, unnoticed by their possessor except when they are checked, or for some particular reason attention is directed to them. A careful study of all the records of the early Church strongly suggests an analogy to this in the Body of the Church. Its essential organic life, and the manner in which its stewardship was replenished, seem to have depended less upon any conscious organization than upon an original endowment, accepted and carried on continuously, without question and even, perhaps, with little or no conscious thought of its purpose or principle.

The various theories as to what occurred during the period of the tunnel must be examined later, but it is necessary first to go back to scriptural times.

NOTES TO CHAPTER XI

A. SALMON ON THE 'TUNNEL' PERIOD

'Immediately after the Apostolic times Church history, as it were, passes through a tunnel. There is bright light on the history as long as we have the New Testament to guide us, and there is bright light again when we come down to the copious Christian literature which began to

[1] G. Salmon, *Episcopacy and other Sermons*, pp. 18, 19. On this subject, see further in chapter XVIII.

be plentiful towards the end of the second century. But there is a comparatively dark intervening period, of which we have but few records; for the generation that immediately succeeded the apostles does not seem to have included many men of literary ability, and the Church was then pressed by persecution, and eagerly looking forward to the second coming of their Lord. So it has happened that the greater part of the scanty literary remains of the sub-apostolic age is taken up with the controversy with heathenism and Judaism, and tells us little about the internal constitution of the Church.' (G. Salmon, on 'The Historic Claims of Episcopacy', in *Episcopacy and other Sermons*, pp. 15, 16.)

B.   DIOCESAN SYSTEM A DEVELOPMENT

'It is now the received theory of the Christian Church, that a settled Christian land should be covered with sees, conterminous but not overlapping one another; that each is independent of its neighbour;...No doubt when Hippolytus lived, the practice of the later Church had already become general, but it cannot have been universal. Indeed from the very nature of the case, the development of the system must have been more or less gradual; though it was the ideal at which the Church would aim.' (Lightfoot, *Clement*, I. pp. 432, 433.)

C.   EARLY 'MON-EPISCOPACY' IN ASIA MINOR

After the appearance in 1646 of the Greek text of the authentic letters of Ignatius, which show 'mon-episcopacy' to have been a settled institution as early as the beginning of the second century, the opponents of episcopacy, especially the French Presbyterian scholars such as Blondel and Daillé, strove either to post-date the letters by a full century, or to reject them wholly. 'Apparently it did not occur to them to ask whether Ussher's discovery did not require them to reconsider their fundamental position as regards episcopacy.' (Lightfoot, *Ignatius*, I. p. 331.)

CHAPTER XII. VERBAL AMBIGUITIES
AND OBSCURITIES

I

O U R knowledge of the internal life of the Church is limited by the scanty historical records of the New Testament period and the succeeding hundred years, and also by another impediment. Early nomenclature is so undefined and uncritical as to give little help in the study of the organic life of the Church. Even the word 'Christian' was apparently invented by the outside pagan world.[1] In the Acts, the Christians are called the *brethren*,[2] *the believers*,[3] *the disciples*,[4] *the way*,[5] *the saints*,[6] and in I Peter *the elect* or *the brotherhood*.[7]

The names or epithets attached to the different kinds of ministers were never new names, coined for the purpose, but old, everyday words, used descriptively. *Diakonos* merely means a servant, a minister. *Presbuteros* means an elder man; sometimes it is used of office, sometimes of seniority in years. *Episkopos* only means an overseer, *apostolos* a messenger sent forth with authority, which may be purely human or may be divine. Yet the language of Scripture leaves us in no doubt that apostles, presbyters, and deacons were recognized as holding distinct offices. The office comes before the title, even before its precise functions and status have become settled.★[8] At first no need is felt for any title. The Church in Jerusalem was presided over by an apostle[9] (not one of the Twelve), in a position similar to that of the later diocesan bishop; he is sufficiently distinguished as 'James'.[10] 'It is important to remember that the names of Christian ministerial offices were not stereotyped in the Apostolic Age. Many theories have been erroneously built on the supposed identity of offices in different centuries, because of the identity of names.'[11]

[1] Acts xi. 26. (Compare the word 'yankee', originally a derisive epithet.)
[2] Acts i. 15, ix. 30, x. 23, xii. 17, etc.   [3] Acts ii. 44, iv. 32, v. 14.
[4] Acts vi *passim*, ix *passim*, xi. 29, etc.   [5] Acts ix. 2, xix. 9, 23, xxii. 4.
[6] Acts ix. 13, 32, 41.   [7] I Peter i. 1, ii. 17.
[8] Note A. *The office before the title* (p. 88).
[9] Gal. i. 19; I Cor. ix. 5, xv. 7.
[10] Cp. the reference in the *Shepherd* of Hermas to the chief pastor settled at Rome as simply 'Clement'.
[11] Hastings, *Encyclopedia of Religion and Ethics*, VIII. p. 659, s.v. 'Early Christian Ministry', by A. J. Maclean.

As regards deacons, there is little or no uncertainty. The word *diakonos* meant only 'minister' and it had no previous religious associations to colour it. Deacons, who are found in all the local Churches, were always regarded as a rank or order of ministry corresponding with that of 'the Seven' of Acts vi. 1–6.[1] They had special charge of the collection and distribution of alms, and of the visitation of the sick. They had particular duties at the celebration of the Eucharist. They were ordained with the solemn laying on of hands, but it has never been suggested that they had power to pass on their office to others by the laying on of their own hands.

II

'Presbyter' is a word of much less definite meaning. Its literal translation, of course, is simply 'elder', although it is also the parent of various European words such as *prester*, *prêtre*, for the Christian priest. It is ambiguous, because it is used quite indifferently to denote either seniority in age, or an official status. It was probably equivocal even in Greek usage[2] from which it was adopted by the Hellenistic Jews. It was used by the Jews to denote an elder by age without official distinction,[3] but this did not prevent its concurrent use to denote an official class, for it is regularly applied to the official elders of Israel in the Septuagint and the New Testament. The same ambiguity continues in the Christian application of the word in the New Testament. Occasionally it implies mere seniority, e.g. *Likewise, ye younger, be subject unto the elder. Rebuke not an elder, but exhort him as a father; the younger men as brethren*,[4] but in its specific meaning it is used of a definitely appointed minister, e.g. *appointed for them elders in every church; appoint elders in every city*.[5] Some New Testament occurrences of the word admit of being understood in either sense.

During the first two centuries the word is often used in a third sense, as a general term of respect, somewhat in the same way as are modern styles such as 'reverend', 'venerable', or 'eminence'. Thus

---

Because of this, a rule, peculiar to Rome, limited the number of deacons there to seven. (Sozomen, *Eccl. Hist.* book VII, cap. xix.)

[2] Hamilton, II. p. 214.

[3] Gen. xviii. 11, 12, xix. 4, xxiv. 1, xliv. 20; Joshua xiii. 1; II Sam. xix. 32; I Kings i. 1; Luke xv. 25.

[4] I Pet. v. 5; I Tim. v. 1.

[5] Acts xiv. 23; Tit. i. 5. Cp. Clem. *ad Cor.* 54: 'Only let the flock of Christ be at peace with its duly appointed elders.'

Papias, writing about A.D. 130–40, refers to the apostles Andrew, John and Matthew in a general way as 'elders', and separately to 'Aristion and the elder John'.[1] Dr Streeter even conjectures that 'John the elder' of II and III John was head of the Church of Ephesus and that he held a position virtually that of an archbishop in relation to the other Churches of the province.[2] That is only a conjecture; the interesting point is that a minister referred to merely as 'presbyter' may perhaps have been one whose position and functions would in later days be given a higher and more specific title. Even St Peter, it will be remembered, described himself as a 'fellow-presbyter'.[3] Towards the end of the second century, when St Irenaeus speaks of 'the blessed elder' he is speaking of Papias or his own master St Polycarp, both of whom were bishops, and in a letter to Bishop Victor of Rome he refers thrice to the bishops of Rome as 'presbyters'. For long before that date the 'monarchical' episcopal status of the Roman bishops is beyond doubt. The purpose of the letter was to conciliate Victor, but to address him as 'presbyter' would not conciliate him 'unless that were, in this particular instance, an official title', as Dr Streeter suggests,[4] or, much more probably, a generic term of respect. Later still, Hippolytus uses the same expression, 'the blessed elder', of Irenaeus himself and other bishops of the past. Lightfoot says of this use of the word 'presbyter' that 'It does not represent *office*, but it expresses venerable dignity'.[5] It seems open to doubt whether, in the solitary mention in the New Testament of the *presbuterion*, or council of presbyters,[6] St Paul is alluding only to presbyters in order, or whether he uses that word comprehensively, much as 'the reverend synod' is styled in modern ecclesiastical phrase. The early commentator, Theodore of Mopsuestia, understands St Paul to refer here to his own co-operation with other ministers 'who are now called bishops but were then called apostles', calling the assemblage *presbuterion* 'out of respect'.[7]

Although, therefore, there are many places where the precise meaning is obscure, there is general agreement on all sides that the term 'presbyter' denotes a definite class or order of ministers,

---

[1] Eusebius, *Hist. Eccl.* III. 39; quoted above at p. 75.
[2] Streeter, pp. 84, 88, 260.   [3] I Peter v. 1.
[4] Streeter, p. 222. Damasus, bishop of Rome 366–84, is referred to by a contemporary as at present 'Rector' of the Church. Wace and Piercy, *Dict. of Christian Biog.* s.v. 'Ambrosiaster'.
[5] Lightfoot, *Clement*, II. p. 435.   [6] I Tim. iv. 14.
[7] Theodore of Mopsuestia on I Tim. iii. 8, iv. 14, ἀπὸ τοῦ ἐντίμου.

definitely appointed to office. 'It is clear then', says Lightfoot, 'that at the close of the apostolic age, the two lower orders of the threefold ministry were firmly and widely established.'[1]

III

Episkopos, shortened by us into 'bishop', means simply an 'overseer'. It was an ordinary word among the Greeks for officials and inspectors. It is common in the Septuagint, where it is used, for example, for the foremen artificers at the rebuilding of the Temple.[2] In order to appreciate its use in the New Testament, it is necessary to clear one's mind of ideas of grandeur that have since become attached to the later office of bishop; the name as used there implied responsibility but little of dignity.

In the second century, and ever since then, 'bishop' has been the designation of a minister superior to the presbyters and usually (not universally, as has already been noticed),[3] presiding singly over the Church of a city, or later of a diocese. But it was not applied to the chief pastors of the first century. In the New Testament it occurs as a description of the presbyters of the Gentile Churches at Philippi,[4] in Asia Minor,[5] and in Crete,[6] yet without displacing their primary description of 'presbyters'.[7] The two descriptions seem to be applied indifferently to the same ministers, and the same thing is found in the last decade of the century in the epistle of Clement to the Corinthian Church.[8] It has been suggested that, while all overseers were elders, not all elders were overseers.[9] This is possible, just as to-day not all presbyters are parsons, although the majority are; but the generally accepted view ★[10] is that the two descriptions were used synonymously in the first century; this has been pointed out by commentators from the fourth century onwards.[11]

Since the end of the first century, no clear instance occurs of the term *episkopos* or overseer being used as the description of presbyters.

---

[1] Lightfoot, *Christian Ministry*, p. 195.
[2] II Chron. xxxiv. 12–17; Neh. xi. 9, 14, 22.
[3] *Vide supra*, chapter IX, section II.   [4] Phil. i. 1.
[5] Acts xx. 28; I Tim. iii. 1, 2; cp. I Pet. v. 2.   [6] Tit. i. 7.
[7] Acts xx. 17; I Tim. v. 17; Tit. i. 5; I Pet. v. 1.
[8] Clem. *ad Cor.* 42, 44; Lightfoot, *Clement*, I. p. 129 n.
[9] G. Edmundson, *The Church in Rome in the First Century*, p. 183; cp. Harnack, pp. 70, 71.
[10] Note B. *Presbyters called 'overseers'* (p. 88).
[11] By the fourth century, Hilary 'Ambrosiaster', Chrysostom, Pelagius, Theodore of Mopsuestia, Jerome.

In second-century documents, the earliest of which are the Epistles of St Ignatius, about A.D. 110, 'the bishop' is the chief pastor of a Church, superior in order to the presbyters and deacons. The subject of ordination does not come into mention. Actually, these chief pastors, now called bishops and locally settled in charge of particular Churches, exercised as residents the same kind of spiritual control that the apostles and 'apostolic men' had exercised in the first century as itinerants. It is clear that, in some sense at least, they succeeded to the ministry and authority of the apostolic mobile chief pastors. To what extent were they really successors? How did the chief pastorate cease to be mobile and become a resident ministry? How did the description of 'the bishop' come to be transferred to the chief pastor? Theodore, bishop of Mopsuestia (near Tarsus) at the end of the fourth century, gives an explanation in an antiquarian excursus to his commentary on one of St Paul's Epistles.[1] Richard Bentley (1662–1742), 'England's supreme classical scholar of all time', thus refers to the fact of transference:

> Those bishops, with all Christian Antiquity, never thought themselves and their order to succeed the Scripture *episkopoi*, but the Scripture *apostoloi*:...Though new institutions are formed, new words are not coined for them, but old ones borrowed and applied. *Episkopos*, whose general idea is *overseer*, was a word in use long before Christianity; a word of universal relation to œconomical, civil, military, naval, judicial, and religious matters. The word was assumed to denote the governing and presiding persons of the Church, as *Diakonos* (another word of vulgar and diffused use) to denote the ministerial....It was agreed, therefore, over all Christendom at once, in the very next generation after the Apostles, to assign and appropriate to them the word *Episkopos*, or Bishop. From that time to this, that appellation, which before included a *Presbyter*, has been restrained to a superior order. And here's nothing in all this but what has happened in all languages and communities in the world. See the *Notitia* of the *Roman* and *Greek* Empires, and you'll scarce find one name of any state employment, that in course of time did not vary from its primitive signification. The time has been when a commander even of a single regiment was called *Imperator*: and must every such now-a-days, set up to be *Emperors*?[2]

The subject of ordination is not mentioned by the earlier writers. All that can definitely be asserted is that, when it is first again noticed,

---

[1] *Vide infra*, chapter XVII, section IV.
[2] Richard Bentley, *Remarks upon a late Discourse of Freethinking*, ed. 1743, pp. 136, 137.

the chief pastor, now 'the bishop', is the essential minister, and there
is no evidence that ordination was ever at any time conferred by
presbyters without the co-operation, at least, of a chief pastor.

IV

A minor ambiguity occurs in reference to ordination or appointment of ministers, and the laying on of hands. Sometimes, in the
New Testament, the laying on of hands is expressly mentioned, as
in the ordination of the Seven, and the charge to lay hands hastily
on no man;[1] sometimes the appointment of presbyters is spoken of
without specifying the manner of it.[2] Three words are used for
'appointment' in the New Testament and early Christian writers.
One of them means primarily only election, another has more
emphatic reference to the imposition of hands, but they were confused and interchanged, and both became technical words of ordination.*[3] Accordingly the references to admission to ministry often
do not precisely describe ordination. A writer does not pause to
describe matters that he supposes to be familiar to his readers; even
a modern historian may mention that so-and-so was 'made a bishop'
by Queen Victoria or one of her prime ministers, without meaning
to suggest that the Queen or Lord Palmerston had usurped the episcopal function, or that the bishop's consecration was omitted.

V

It would be a mistake to assume from all this vagueness of nomenclature that there were not, from the earliest times, fundamental
distinctions of ministerial order and function. The same indifference
to the use of exact titles persisted much later, when the threefold
ministry, differentiated just as it is to-day, was established in immemorial operation; as late as the fourth century, unspecific language is common. Eusebius, bishop of Caesarea, wrote his great
History of the Church in ten books during the period A.D. 305–15.
They are written as chronological annals from the beginning of the
Christian era; he records the succession of bishops, as they followed
one another, in several of the most ancient 'apostolic sees', such as
Antioch, Alexandria, Jerusalem, and Rome. He is quite indifferent
to the use of technical language. The succession of bishops at Alex-

---

[1] Acts vi. 6; I Tim. v. 22.   [2] Acts xiv. 23; Tit. i. 5.
[3] Note C.   *Technical words for ordination* (p. 88).

andria, for example, is recorded here and there in the course of books II to VII, written during a period of several years. 'Annianus succeeded, first after Mark the evangelist, to the ministry of the community at Alexandria' (A.D. 63). 'Annianus the first of the community at Alexandria died...and Avilius succeeded him as second' (A.D. 85). 'Cerdon was the third who presided over the people of that place' (A.D. 99). 'The bishop of the community at Alexandria whom we mentioned departed this life and Primus, the fourth from the apostles, was appointed to the ministry of the people there' (A.D. 110). And so he continues through six books. The office of bishop, which Eusebius knew only in the fully developed sense that had become universal long before his day, is referred to by him indifferently as 'presidency', 'episcopate', 'ministry', 'pastor', 'first of the community', 'the episcopal office'.[1] A similar untechnical indifference of language in earlier Christian writers affords no safe ground therefore for inferences sometimes drawn from it, that the orders of the primitive ministry were fluid or indefinite, or that ordination by the chief pastors of the ministry was ever treated as unnecessary.

VI

The transference of the name of 'overseer' which took place about the end of the first century or the beginning of the second, is a historical fact. The explanation of it is a central problem of early Church history. It is of great importance, because the basis of the Calvinist and Presbyterian theory of the ministry is the fact that the same epithet was applied to first-century presbyters as has ever afterwards been applied to the chief pastor, *the* 'bishop'. Thus, at the Edinburgh Conference on Faith and Order in 1937, the following declaration was recorded: 'Presbyterian delegates desire to have it noted that the conception of the ministry held by their Churches is founded on the identity of "bishops and presbyters" in the New Testament.' The argument is a simple one. From the second century onwards, overseers, i.e. 'bishops', have been the ministers of ordination. Therefore those ministers who were referred to in the first century as overseers must have been ministers of ordination. Reasons have already been suggested for caution in interpreting early verbal usage; nevertheless there are many to whom that argument seems so cogent that they still devote effort to show the 'identity of bishops

---

[1] Eusebius, *Hist. Eccl.* II. 24; III. 14, 21; IV. 1, 4, 11; V. 9, 26; VI. 35; VII. 28.

and presbyters in the New Testament', forgetful that it has been a commonplace observation of commentators from the fourth century onwards; there are some who even suppose that the fact has been overlooked by scholars.★ [1]

The weight of inference that is made to rest upon this basis of supposed verbal exactitude and nominal identification seems insecure, the more so when it is set alongside of the ministerial nomenclature of communions whose systems are built upon that basis. Although that nomenclature was deliberately chosen, it is not exact or consistent, and would not, of itself, furnish safe support for any distinct principle.★ [2]

[1] Note D. *Supposed novelty of a hackneyed observation* (p. 88).
[2] Note E. *Nomenclature of reformed ministries* (p. 89).

NOTES TO CHAPTER XII

A. THE OFFICE BEFORE THE TITLE

Great Britain had no Prime Minister officially so called until 1905. Lord Salisbury, for example, was Foreign Secretary, or was sufficiently distinguished by his personal title. Yet we can truly say that Pitt was Prime Minister in his day.

B. PRESBYTERS CALLED 'OVERSEERS'

A contrary view has been maintained. Dr W. Lowrie (*The Church and its Organization in Primitive Catholic Times* (1904), p. 96) says that 'it was the chief service of Mr Edwin Hatch's *Organization of the Early Christian Churches* that he finally discredited the notion which so long persisted of the original identity of presbyters and bishops'.

C. TECHNICAL WORDS FOR ORDINATION

χειροτονεῖν originally meant election by a show of hands, then merely election, and it came to be a general word of appointment to clerical office. χειροθετεῖν has more particular reference to the laying on of the hand. Their meanings became confused and both words became technical terms of ordination, the imposition of hands being implicit. A third term, καθιστάναι, is used of appointment, whether election or ordination or both. See A. J. Maclean at p. 48 in *Episcopacy A. & M.*, W. H. Frere at pp. 265, 266, and C. H. Turner at p. 177 in *Essays on Early Hist.*

D. SUPPOSED NOVELTY OF A HACKNEYED OBSERVATION

Thus Dr Ainslie (at p. 202) astonishingly supposes that 'Gore would not agree with the conclusion accepted by so many scholars that "episkopos" and "presbuteros" were different designations of the same office in the Apostolic Age', and 'appears to have left out of account the probable fact'. Whereas in *The Church and the Ministry* Bishop Gore treats the fact as unchallenged and devotes considerable attention to its bearing on the development of the ministry, e.g. pp. 217, 219, 220, 362.

E.   NOMENCLATURE OF REFORMED MINISTRIES

Calvin discovered two orders of presbyters or elders in Scripture (I Tim. v. 17), the ruling-elder and the teaching-elder. In the *Westminster Form of Church Government*, adopted in 1645 and still retained, the teaching-elder is indifferently referred to as *elder, pastor, preaching-presbyter, preaching-elder, minister, minister of the gospel, minister of the word.* 'The teacher or doctor is also a minister of the word as well as the pastor, and hath power of administration of the sacraments' (but the provisions for ordination do not seem to include him). There are '*other church governors* which officers reformed churches commonly call *elders*': '*elders* are also called *ruling-elders, lay-elders* or *overseers*' (Ainslie, p. 91)—and *overseers* are presumably *bishops.* The elder (ruling-elder) is solemnly ordained without imposition of hands, which is given in the ordination of the minister (preaching-elder). Whether ruling- and preaching-elders are one order or two has never been settled; the latter view is prevalent, but a recent Moderator of the Church of Scotland declared his belief that they are all members of one order. The expression 'lay-elder' has been objected to; on the other hand, some Presbyterian theologians have repudiated any distinction of clergy and laity as 'Popish and anti-Christian'. The scriptural order of deacons is not retained. The word *diakonos* means 'minister', and deacons were certainly ordained. Some Reformed congregations appoint 'deacons' as almoners, but they are not ordained even in name (like the ruling-elders) and their office is not even quasi-ministerial like theirs. It is interesting to notice that Calvin also discovered two orders of deacons in Scripture (*Inst.* IV. iii. 9, citing Rom. xii. 8), but the Reformed Churches have not followed his teaching on this point.

It can be seen that the names of the Reformed ministry, deliberately chosen by leading divines of the seventeenth century in conclave, reveal some ambiguity. This suggests that the important inference drawn from the unsystematic nomenclature preserved in first-century documents is a precarious one. The foregoing observations, however, are directed solely to this aspect; I have the highest respect for the actual excellences of the Presbyterian system, in particular for its rich possession of the subordinate ministry of 'ruling-elders'. In fact, though not in theory or in name, they supply a class of ministry somewhat resembling that of the ordained deacons in the early Church, which has always been preserved by the Churches of the East although the Churches of the West have let it fall into virtual disuse except as a mere grade for apprentice priests. Where it exists, it contributes to the ideal of the Ekklesia as 'a true body politic, in which different functions were assigned tò different members, and a share of responsibility rested upon the members at large, each and all' (Flew, p. 195, endorsing Hort, p. 52). The diaconate, intermediate between priests or presbyters and laity, emphasizes the homogeneity of the whole priestly Ekklesia and the ministry of every member of it: *All the body fitly framed and knit together...according to the working in due measure of each several part* (Eph. iv. 16).

CHAPTER XIII. APOSTLES, EVANGELISTS, AND PROPHETS

I

WHAT is meant by 'apostles' in the language of the New Testament? In a common modern understanding, the word is understood to mean only the twelve disciples chosen by our Lord for His inner circle, with the addition of St Matthias and St Paul. But 'neither the Canonical Scriptures nor the early Christian writings afford sufficient ground for any such limitation of the apostolate'.[1]

The actual word 'apostle' is rarely used in the Gospels. The Greek *apostolos* signifies one who is 'sent forth', and it has this quite general meaning and is so translated in the only place where it occurs in the Fourth Gospel, *a servant is not greater than his lord; neither one that is sent greater than he that sent him*.[2] It is the substantive corresponding to the verb *apostello*; there is no substantive in English corresponding thus to the verb 'to send'. In order to bring out the close relation between the verb *apostello* and the noun *apostolos* in the original language of the New Testament, it is almost necessary in English to coin a verb 'to apostell'.

St Mark's Gospel, probably the earliest of the four, often speaks simply of 'the Twelve'[3] or of 'the Eleven'.[4] The noun 'apostle' occurs only once, the verb 'to apostell' four times: *As in Isaiah... behold I apostell my messenger before thy face;*[5] *And he called unto him the twelve, and began to apostell them by two and two...and the apostles gather themselves together unto Jesus; and they told him all things, whatsoever they had done.*[6] *Whosoever receiveth me, receiveth not me, but him that apostelled me.*[7] *Then shall he apostell the angels, and shall gather together his elect.*[8]

St Matthew's Gospel refers four times to *the twelve disciples*, twice to *the twelve*, and once to *the eleven*. There are four instances of the verb 'to apostell', and only a single instance of the noun, all in one chapter. *Now the names of the twelve apostles are these...these twelve Jesus apostelled...behold, I apostell you as sheep in the midst of wolves...*

---

[1] Lightfoot, *Apostle*, p. 94.   [2] John xiii. 16.
[3] Mark iii. 14, iv. 10, vi. 7, ix. 35, x. 32, xi. 11, xiv. 17, 20.
[4] Mark xvi. 14.   [5] Mark i. 2.   [6] Mark vi. 7–30.
[7] Mark ix. 37.   [8] Mark xiii. 27.

he that receiveth you receiveth me, and he that receiveth me receiveth him that apostelled me.[1]

St Luke's Gospel speaks four times of *the twelve* and twice of *the eleven*. The noun *apostolos* and the corresponding verb occur only as follows: *He called his disciples: and he chose from them twelve, whom also he named apostles.*[2] *And he called the twelve together...and he apostelled them to preach the kingdom of God, and to heal the sick...and the apostles, when they were returned, declared unto him what things they had done.*[3] *Now after these things the Lord appointed seventy others, and apostelled them two and two before his face.*[4] *I will apostell unto them prophets and apostles; and some of them they shall kill and persecute.*[5] *And the apostles said unto the Lord, Increase our faith.*[6] *When the hour was come, he sat down, and the apostles with him.*[7] *They returned from the tomb, and...told these things unto the apostles.*[8]

In the Fourth Gospel, *the twelve* are mentioned four times, but they are usually referred to merely as *the disciples*. 'Apostle' occurs once only, as already noted, in a general sense without any direct reference to the Twelve. The verb 'to apostell' is used very often, e.g. *As the living Father apostelled me; As thou didst apostell me into the world, even so apostelled I them into the world; As the Father hath apostelled me, even so apostell I you.*[9] There is no special sanctity in the word 'apostell' itself, it is used for ordinary sendings,[10] and, moreover, an alternative Greek word for sending occurs frequently even in sacred connexions.[11]

II

In the Gospels, then, it appears that the inner circle of twelve, although they are sometimes alluded to as *the apostles*, or *the disciples*, are more particularly described as *the Twelve* or *the Eleven*. They are called apostles only once in each of the first two Gospels and never in the Fourth Gospel. There is an obvious and close connexion too between the description 'apostles', where it occurs, and the fact of their being 'apostelled' by our Lord.[12] In St Luke's Gospel, the Seventy are also said to be apostelled, and in the early Church they were counted as

---

[1] Matt. x. 2, 5, 16, 40. [2] Luke vi. 13. [3] Luke ix. 1, 2, 10.
[4] Luke x. 1. [5] Luke xi. 49. [6] Luke xvii. 5.
[7] Luke xxii. 14. [8] Luke xxiv. 10. [9] John vi. 57, xvii. 18, xx. 21.
[10] E.g. John i. 19–24, so also Mark iii. 31, vi. 27, xii. 13.
[11] E.g. John v. 23, 24, ix. 4.
[12] See Mark vi. 7, 30; Matt. x. 2, 5, 16; Luke ix. 1, 10.

apostles. 'After the twelve apostles our Lord is found to have sent forth seventy others';[1] 'Seventy other apostles'.[2]

In the Acts of the Apostles, the Twelve or the Eleven are spoken of thrice;[3] 'the apostles', which occurs often up to xvi. 4, refers usually to the Twelve, but twice to Barnabas and Paul.[4]

In the Epistles, St Peter describes himself as *an apostle of Jesus Christ*,[5] and the Epistle of Jude refers to *the words which have been spoken before by the apostles of our Lord Jesus Christ*.[6] Outside the Pauline Epistles, which call for a fuller study, no further light is thrown by Scripture on the primitive use of the word.

St Paul uses the word 'apostle' twice in its commonplace sense of a messenger,[7] but thirty-two times in the distinct sense of 'the apostles' or 'apostles of Christ'. It is only incidentally that we learn the names of some of those whom he intends to describe in this way. Thus he ranks St James of Jerusalem with 'the apostles', and apparently the other 'brethren of the Lord' also.[8] Andronicus, and Junias or Junianus,[9] St Paul's kinsmen or fellow-countrymen, who were in Christ before him, are also said to be *of note among the apostles*.[10] He groups both Silvanus and Timothy with himself as *apostles of Christ*;[11] by implication only does St Paul call Barnabas an apostle[12] although 'the apostleship of Barnabas is beyond all question'.[13] Even in speaking of the Church before Pentecost, St Paul 'seems in one passage to distinguish between "the Twelve" and "all the apostles" as if the latter were the more comprehensive term'.[14]

St Paul refers to some of his fellow-workers, fellow-servants, or fellow-soldiers, as he variously calls them, without expressly calling them apostles. Timothy and Titus are often named, both in the letters addressed to them and in those to Rome, Corinth, and Philippi, in terms that indicate their high standing and authority as missionary evangelists. St Paul aimed at preaching *not where Christ was already named, that I might not build upon another man's foundation*,[15] and there are indications that others whose names have not been recorded were

[1] Irenaeus, *Haer.* ii. xxi. 1.   [2] Tertullian, *adv. Marc.* iv. 24.
[3] Acts vi. 2, i. 26, ii. 14.   [4] Acts xiv. 4, 14.
[5] I Pet. i. 1.   [6] Jude 17.
[7] *Messengers of the churches. Epaphroditus your messenger.* II Cor. viii. 23; Philip. ii. 25.
[8] Gal. i. 19; I Cor. ix. 5, xv. 7; see Lightfoot, *Apostle*, p. 92; Hort, p. 77.
[9] Lightfoot, *op. cit.* p. 96.   [10] Rom. xvi. 7; see Lightfoot, *op. cit.* p. 96.
[11] I Thess. i. 1, ii. 6.   [12] I Cor. ix. 5, 6.
[13] Lightfoot, *op. cit.* p. 96; Acts xiii. 2, 3, xiv. 4, 14.
[14] Lightfoot, *op. cit.* p. 95; I Cor. xv. 5, 7.   [15] Rom. xv. 20.

at work in the mission field. From St Paul's letter to Colossae, we learn that he was not the founder of the Church there. Epaphras, who was himself a Colossian, seems to have been its pioneer missionary,[1] and he may be one of the chief pastors and evangelists whom St Paul elsewhere refers to as apostles. In the same letter he mentions Archippus, whom elsewhere he calls the fellow-soldier of himself and Timothy, *Say to Archippus, Take heed to the ministry which thou hast received in the Lord, that thou fulfil it* (iv. 17). Professor Harnack says of Archippus, 'His ministry can relate only to the whole community, and if St Paul calls him his own and Timothy's fellow-soldier it must have been considerable....It is, moreover, worthy of note that the ministry was conferred upon Archippus by a solemn religious service, for this can be the only meaning of the words "which thou hast received in the Lord". Comparison should therefore be made with Acts xiv. 23.'[2] Another fellow-worker, Sosthenes, is mentioned only once, but St Paul's language seems to include him with himself as 'apostles'.[3] There are references here and there to a number of other fellow-workers of St Paul whose office and authority is not clearly stated, but seems to have been similar to that of Timothy and Titus.★[4]

From these incidental references it may be inferred that there were many, probably far more than those whose names have been preserved, who were accounted fellow-workers of St Paul and the Twelve. As to the manner of their appointment, and the scope of their ministry and authority, we are left with next to no contemporary record. If any question ever arose on these matters in scriptural times, it has left no trace. Indeed it is probably due to the occurrence of disorder at Corinth that we have St Paul's account of the Lord's Supper and his teaching concerning it, and only a rare occurrence of ministerial disorder at the end of the first century gave us the valuable Epistle of Clement.★[5]

III

It is clear at least that many, who may be called minor apostles, were added to the Twelve and St Paul. In the instances of Barnabas and Timothy, and perhaps of Archippus, at least an allusion to their ordination has been preserved. It is a reasonable conjecture that

[1] Col. i. 7, iv. 12.   [2] Harnack, p. 56.
[3] I Cor. i. 1, iv. 9, ix. 5.   [4] Note A.   *Minor apostles* (p. 99).
[5] Note B.   *Unquestioned things unrecorded* (p. 99).

ordination to apostolic work was bestowed also on those others with regard to whom no record has been preserved. Although they were 'brothers' and 'fellow-workers' of St Paul and the Twelve, they could not possess the same outstanding personal position; they were apostles of the second generation. St Paul seems to claim precedence over them for himself and *them which were apostles before me.* He is *an apostle not from men, neither through man, but through Jesus Christ.*[1] Those others who had been added to the apostolate were *through man,* apostles of the second generation.

A somewhat obscure problem is presented by the filling of the vacant place of Judas by the choice of Matthias, when we contrast it with the absence of any indication that the number of the Twelve was again restored when Herod *killed James the brother of John with the sword.*[2] St Luke gives no explanation. Had it come already by then to be recognized that the Twelve were really the nucleus of an apostolate that must become world-wide?

Towards the end of the first century, we hear of persons falsely pretending to be apostles, at Ephesus.[3] It might hardly be expected that the apostolate should have become numerous enough for this in St Paul's time, thirty or forty years earlier, yet he too speaks to the Church in Corinth of false apostles, masquerading as apostles of Christ.[4] In the same epistle he asks ironically if he needs *epistles of commendation* to them,[5] which suggests that those who had been appointed to this itinerant ministry may sometimes have been given testimonials, resembling the modern 'letters commendatory', to carry with them on their visits to distant Churches.

IV

While the name of 'apostle' was extended thus to those itinerant 'fellow-workers', missionaries who established Churches and visited and guided them, it can be observed that the word is always used of this office more as a description than as an exact title. As has already been noticed, the precise use of titles of ministry was slow in developing. We might expect, therefore, to find that this extended order of apostles, *apostles through man,* was sometimes described in some other phrase. There is reason to think that this was so, and that these mobile missionary leaders of Churches, whose labours

[1] Gal. i. 1, 17.   [2] Acts xii. 2.   [3] Rev. ii. 2; cp. *Didache,* xi. 9.
[4] II Cor. xi. 13.   [5] II Cor. iii. 1.

much resemble those of a modern 'missionary bishop', were sometimes described as 'Evangelists'. St Paul appoints Timothy to *the
work of an evangelist*.[1] Eusebius refers to those who 'occupied the
first step in the succession from the apostles' as 'evangelists'.[2]
Dr Salmon suggested that at one time 'evangelist' was a specific
title for the office of minor apostles such as Timothy and Titus.★[3]
It was the opinion of Calvin that evangelists were 'those who, while
inferior in rank to the apostles, were next them in office, and even
acted as their substitutes. Such were Luke, Timothy, Titus and the
like; perhaps also the seventy disciples whom our Saviour appointed
in the second place to the apostles'.[4] Professor Turner regarded the
office of evangelist as a transitional phase between the functions of
an apostle and of a bishop.★[5] It has already been noticed how Eusebius, writing at the beginning of the fourth century, reproduced
the fluid nomenclature of the early days of which he wrote; he
speaks of Clement of Rome and Ignatius as evangelists.[6] This
description of St Clement of Rome is an interesting variant. In his
own day, his office as chief pastor of the Church in Rome was not
yet distinguished by the name of 'bishop', for his own Epistle to the
Corinthians refers to presbyters as *episkopoi*, just as do the New Testament Scriptures. A later generation spoke of him as bishop of Rome,
because it was believed that he had held the position to which the
name of 'bishop' had since been appropriated. A hundred years
after his time, Clement of Alexandria calls him apostle.[7] Evangelist—
bishop—apostle; the conjunction is interesting. It is also remarkable
that Eusebius should call St Ignatius an 'Evangelist', for, though he
was 'in the first succession from the apostles', or nearly so, he was
most certainly a bishop and was so known in his own day.

That there was an order of ministers superior to the local elders
(*episkopoi*) and deacons is obvious in I Timothy and Titus. Timothy
is to apportion praise and blame to elders. *Rebuke not an elder, but
exhort him as a father....Let the elders that rule well be counted worthy
of double honour....Against an elder receive not an accusation, except
at the mouth of two or three witnesses. Them that sin reprove in the sight
of all, that the rest also may be in fear.* He is to give authoritative

---

[1] II Tim. iv. 5.   [2] Eusebius, *Hist. Eccl.* III. 37.
[3] Note C. *The office of evangelist* (p. 99).
[4] Calvin, *Inst.* IV. iii. 4. Lindsay, p. 80 n., thinks that 'there is really no distinction
between a wider use of the term *apostle* and the *evangelist*'.
[5] Note D. *Apostle—evangelist—bishop* (p. 100).
[6] Eusebius, *Hist. Eccl.* III. 37.   [7] *Strom.* IV. 17. 105.

instruction with regard to what is to be taught, *That thou mightest charge certain men not to teach a different doctrine, neither to give heed to fables and endless genealogies.* He is to ordain local elders (*episkopoi*), or deacons, in the traditional way: *Lay hands hastily on no man.* His position is to be one of supreme authority, *These things command and teach.*[1]

The position of Titus is practically identical. He is to govern the Church and ordain, *For this cause left I thee in Crete, that thou shouldest set in order the things that were wanting, and appoint elders in every city.* He is to deal with false teachers, *Reprove them sharply, that they may be sound in the faith.* He is to speak authoritatively the things which befit sound doctrine to 'aged men', to 'aged women', and to 'the younger men'. *These things speak and exhort and reprove with all authority.* He is to rebuke heretics and excommunicate them, *A man that is heretical, after a first and second admonition refuse.*[2]

Timothy's office of ministry 'is clearly regarded as permanent, the result of ordination, not merely a temporary delegation from St Paul'.[3] Lancelot Andrewes, referring to Timothy and Titus and others in their position, was expressing the immemorial belief of the Church when he said: 'These were they whom posterity called bishops; but in the beginning regard was not had to distinction of names; the authority and power was ever distinct, the name not restrained, either in this or other.'[4]

Prophets are frequently mentioned in close association with apostles, especially in the writings of St Paul, who was himself a prophet.[5] They 'seem to have been closely allied to each other in the nature of their spiritual gifts, though the apostle was superior in rank, and had administrative functions which were wanting to the prophet'.[6] But it does not appear that prophecy, as we read of it in the New Testament, was ever an 'office', or that these latter-day prophets were an order to which admittance or appointment could be given. *Desire earnestly spiritual gifts, but rather that ye may prophesy....I would have you all speak with tongues, but rather that ye should prophesy.*[7] Praying and prophesying alike are possible to *every man, every woman.*[8] Prophecy is a spiritual gift or talent; some

---

[1] I Tim. v. 1, 17, 19, 20, i. 3, 4, v. 22, iv. 11.
[2] Tit. i. 5, 13, ii. 1–15, iii. 10.
[3] Lockton, p. 118. I am indebted to this work of Mr Lockton for the foregoing catena of texts on the position of Timothy and Titus.
[4] *Minor Works*, ed. 1846, p. 359.   [5] Eph. ii. 20, iii. 5, iv. 11; I Cor. xii. 28.
[6] Lightfoot, *Apostle*, p. 98.   [7] I Cor. xiv. 1, 5.   [8] I Cor. xi. 4, 5.

apostles, at all events, were recognized as possessing it, among them Barnabas and Paul, whom St Luke describes as prophets until their setting apart at Antioch for the mission-field.[1] Lightfoot observes that hitherto both alike were styled only 'prophets'. From this point onward both alike are 'apostles'.[2] In a parallel illustration suggested by Dr H. F. Hamilton, many statesmen have been distinguished in the sphere of letters, but their eminence in that sphere is quite distinct from their constitutional office.*[3]

The work of a prophet, to which everyone was urged to aspire, was to speak unto men edification, and comfort, and consolation, and to edify the Church.[4] In accordance with these words of St Paul, we find that *Judas and Silas, being themselves also prophets, exhorted the brethren with many words and confirmed* (strengthened) *them.*[5] A prophet might be inspired to speak of things to come, as was Agabus,[6] and just as the 'multitude' of the faithful selected the first deacons, it appears that 'prophecy' had marked Timothy for his higher ministry. *This charge I commit unto thee, my child Timothy, according to the prophecies which went before on thee....Neglect not the gift that is in thee by prophecy, with the laying on of the hands of the presbytery.*[7] It does not appear that the actual ministry of ordination was performed by prophets, but rather that it was sometimes they who discerned and chose those who should be ordained to important ministerial office. (The Church of England at present acquiesces in the exercise of this choice not by prophets but by the Prime Minister.)[8]

After New Testament times, prophets cease to be mentioned as a recognized class, but prophecies have never wholly been 'done away'. Prophetic gifts are manifested here and there in members of all Christian communions. Prophecy is still a grace bestowed, without other credentials than the fact of its possession, and needing none. Just as in New Testament times it was distinct from the organic ministry of apostles or evangelists, presbyters and deacons, so to-day it is distinct from the ministry of their successors, and is sometimes found outside their ranks.

---

[1] Acts xiii. 2.   [2] Lightfoot, *op. cit.* p. 98.
[3] Note E. *Prophecy distinct from ministry* (p. 100).
[4] I Cor. xiv. 3, 4.   [5] Acts xv. 32.
[6] Acts xi. 28, xxi. 11.   [7] I Tim. i. 18, iv. 14.
[8] Bishops picked by Caesar are not authentic spokesmen of the mind of the Church. Caesar's choice tends to reflect favour towards Caesar's policies—in England, towards the prevalent statecraft of the day.

NOTES TO CHAPTER XIII

A. MINOR APOSTLES

'Perhaps Tychicus and Artemas may also have been Apostles in the wider sense. One of them, presumably Artemas, was to be sent to Crete, apparently to carry on Titus' work (Tit. iii. 12); and at a later date Tychicus was sent to Ephesus, when Timothy was bidden to come to be with St Paul at Rome (II Tim. iv. 9–13). Titus, when he left Crete, was to join St Paul at Nicopolis in Epirus (Tit. iii. 12); and later, he went up the eastern coast of the Adriatic to Dalmatia, presumably on a mission similar to the one which he had carried out in Crete. As Titus' mission to Dalmatia is coupled with that of Crescens to Galatia (II Tim. iv. 10, Galatia possibly means Gaul in this passage), it is not impossible that Crescens may also have been a minor Apostle. These are merely suggestions, which however have, all of them, in my opinion, some foundation. If there is any truth in them, they tend to show that other members of St Paul's staff, besides Timothy and Titus, were Apostolic Evangelists empowered to ordain.' (F. W. Puller, *Essays and Letters on Orders and Jurisdiction*, pp. 34, 35.)

B. UNQUESTIONED THINGS UNRECORDED

'The fact is not enough recognized that St Paul's letters are nearly all controversial, that is, they deal with specific questions which had been asked or specific difficulties which had arisen. The only two writings in which he at all approaches to the compiling of a regular treatise are *Romans* and *Ephesians*....Accordingly it is entirely reasonable to be prepared for the conclusion that the things of which he does not speak in any given Epistle are the things which he is happily able to take for granted.' (S. C. Carpenter, *What mean ye by this Service?* p. 23 n.) On the Epistle of Clement to *Corinth*, *vide infra*, chapter XVI.

C. THE OFFICE OF EVANGELIST

'A few words may be said as to the cases of Timothy and Titus. It is clear that Timothy was not a mere delegate of Paul, but that he held an office which had been conferred on him in the face of the Church by solemn ordination (I Tim. iv. 14). But what was the office? It must have been higher than that of the presbyters, over whom Timothy exercised authority. Was it not then that of bishop, as the ancients held, who inferred that Timothy was first bishop of Ephesus, Titus of Crete? We are here in the region of conjecture, and since no one is entitled to make a positive affirmation, I shall venture to add my guess. In the list of Church officers (Eph. iv. 11), after the inspired "pastors and teachers", we read of an office not mentioned in the Epistle to the Corinthians, evangelists.

The only other places in the New Testament where the name occurs is that Philip is called the evangelist (Acts xxi. 8), and that Timothy is exhorted to do the work of an evangelist (II Tim. iv. 5). My guess is that "evangelist" was an office created in the later apostolic Church, when with the growth of the Church the Apostles no longer sufficed for its missionary needs, and that the work of an evangelist included the planting new Churches, the appointing their ministers, and the exercising apostolic authority over them.' (G. Salmon, in *The Expositor*, 1887, VI. p. 26.)

D. APOSTLE—EVANGELIST—BISHOP

'In Eusebius (iii. 37) the "Evangelists", or they and the Pastors, are named as the first successors of the Apostles. Timothy is bidden to "do the work of an Evangelist" (II Tim. iv. 5) at the same moment that the Apostle is predicting his own immediate death. Their office, in fact, stands midway between the functions of an Apostle and of a bishop." (C. H. Turner, *Studies in Early Church History*, p. 28.)

E. PROPHECY DISTINCT FROM MINISTRY

'The difference between a prophet and an elder is analogous to that between a distinguished novelist or poet and a Secretary of State. The one receives his title from his peculiar gifts and abilities, the other from his work or office. The two titles exist on different planes, belong to different relations of life. Hence, just as a Secretary of State may be also a great novelist, so a bishop or presbyter might be, and probably often was, also a prophet or teacher.' (*The People of God*, II. p. 94.) In the *Shepherd* of Hermas prophets are mentioned, not as holding any ministerial office; but it is said to be one of the marks of a false prophet that he covets the 'chief seat' of the presbyters (see chapter XVII, section VII).

CHAPTER XIV. MISSION AND AUTHORITY

THE Greek word 'apostolos', as an adjective, means 'despatched' or 'sent forth'. As a noun, it denotes more than a mere messenger, an *angelos*. The apostle is a delegate; he is entrusted with a mission, has powers entrusted to him.[*1] In the 'sending forth' of Christ's apostle, a double meaning can be perceived. In the primary and higher sense he is sent forth by the divine authority and command of our Lord to preach the Gospel, to feed and lead the flock, to baptize into the Name, all without thought of locality. In a secondary sense, the original sending forth was also geographical, expeditionary, propulsive. The Seventy were 'sent forth' through Palestine two and two. The Twelve were to preach, and baptize all nations, beginning from Jerusalem; they were to radiate from Jerusalem throughout the known world, and in fact they did so. This roving, geographical phase of the sending forth was bound to remain prominent as long as the Faith was being carried to fresh lands, and local Churches were still being founded; it is still the inspiration of the mission-field. Only when this task had been largely accomplished for the known Old World, when Christianity was becoming necessarily more static, and when those who guided and governed local Churches as chief pastors had ceased to be itinerant and had become resident with their flocks, do we find that they had ceased to be known as apostles, or even as 'evangelists', and were accorded the distinguishing name of overseer or bishop which had formerly been applied to the local presbyters.

The conception of apostleship as derived from divine impulse is, of course, paramount and fundamental.[*2]

This principle of mission, of a communicated authority, is maintained in the functions delegated or entrusted to the subordinate ministries. The original Seven were ordained for a specific and comparatively humble task; the deacons too, of whom they were the prototypes, received a limited authority. Although the scope of their office is not defined in the New Testament, there is no doubt that it was specially connected with the administration of alms and the visitation of the sick. Authority of a different kind was delegated

---

[1] Note A. *'Apostle' in Jewish usage* (p. 104).
[2] Note B. *Apostolic mission* (p. 104).

to the presbyters, whom the Acts of the Apostles show to have been appointed not only in the mother-church of Jerusalem[1] but also *in every church* founded by apostles in their missionary tours.[2] It is hardly open to doubt that these presbyters received authority from their apostolic pastors to celebrate the Eucharist themselves in the absence of an apostle or 'evangelist'.[3] In writing to the newly formed congregation at Thessalonica, St Paul urges them *to know them that labour among you, and are over you in the Lord, and to esteem them exceeding highly in love for their work's sake*;[4] these seem to have been presbyters, and the nature of the duties alluded to here made it natural to refer to them descriptively as *episkopoi*, overseers. At the same time, the New Testament writings give no support to certain modern theories, that such local congregations were self-sufficient and autonomous, or that the local presbyters, the original *episkopoi*, were ever at any time empowered to ordain others to their special ministry, by their own authority, and without the presence and co-operation of an apostle, *apostolikos* or evangelist. The immemorial custom that presbyters join with the bishop in the ordination of new presbyters strongly suggests that the primitive presbyters in the same way joined in ordaining to the presbyterate with the apostle or evangelist who was visiting the local Church; but it does not seem likely that independent authority to ordain was conferred upon the raw converts who were ordained presbyters in the new Churches,[5] and there is no evidence whatever to suggest that it was.

In Christ's Ekklesia, the apostles replaced the leaders of the old Ekklesia of Israel. Their authority 'to bind and to loose' was expressed in the Rabbinic terms for the authority under the Old Law to 'pronounce forbidden' or 'pronounce permitted' in doubtful matters. The 'keys' referred to the 'key of knowledge' abused by the scribes and Levites of Israel.[6] But the fullness of apostolic authority implied in the tremendous words of commission *As the Father hath apostelled me, even so apostell I you*[7] is greater and higher. 'The form of the fulfilment of Christ's mission was now to be changed, but the mission itself was still continued and still effective. The apostles were commissioned to carry on Christ's work, and not to begin a new one. Their office was an application of His office

[1] Acts xv. 2, 4, 6, 22.
[2] Acts xiv. 23.
[3] *Supra*, chapter XIII, section IV.
[4] I Thess. v. 12, 13.
[5] Acts xiv. 23.
[6] Luke xi. 52; Matt. xxiii. 13.
[7] John xx. 21, xvii. 18.

according to the needs of men.'[1] God has given unto us, says St Paul, *the ministry of reconciliation*, has *committed unto us the word of reconciliation, we are ambassadors therefore on behalf of Christ, as though God were intreating by us*.[2]

Of the exercise of apostolic authority the New Testament tells us little except with regard to St Paul and one or two evangelists whom he mentions, or to whom he writes. St Paul himself sometimes speaks *not by way of commandment*,[3] but there is no mistaking the authority that he claims and exercises: it is summarized thus by Dr P. W. Schmiedel of Zürich:

He commands (I Cor. xi. 17–34, xiv. 26–40, xvi. 1), and that very definitely, precisely where institutions are concerned. He makes very short work with contumacy (I Cor. vii. 40, xi. 16, xiv. 37 ff.), partisanship on behalf of individual teachers he sets down (I Cor. iii. 3 ff.) to carnal-mindedness, disregard of his authority to arrogance (I Cor. iv. 18). He disclaims judgement of himself with a clearness that leaves nothing to be desired. Against the Judaizing teachers he declares himself in II Cor. xi. 13–15; Gal. i. 7–9, v. 10–12 with the greatest asperity. In short, in his person there appears the same unconditional authority which Jesus had.[4]

St Paul's jurisdiction in the excommunication of notorious sinners exercised, during absence, *as though I were present*,[5] seems to picture him, when present in the local Church, presiding in the midst of the presbyters; in this respect at all events there is no delegation to them of his authority while he is absent.

Of the actual guidance and control of other local Churches by other original apostles, no documentary record has come down to us. Equally with St Paul they were stewards of the household of God; their apostolic authority was equal to his, and there is no reason to doubt that it was acknowledged and exerted.

What became of this stewardship as the first stewards passed on to their reward, and their pastoral work was carried on by 'apostolic men', evangelists? Our Lord's words indicate that the office of stewardship is to continue to the end in the household, the Church.[6] Our information regarding such apostles of the second generation is incomplete, and is derived mainly from incidental passages in St Paul's letters. Titus, when visiting Corinth as an evangelist or secondary apostle, received strict obedience, and was treated with a

---

[1] B. F. Westcott, *Gospel of St John*, p. 294, note on xx. 21.   [2] II Cor. v. 18–20.
[3] I Cor. vii. 6, 10, 12; II Cor. viii. 8.   [4] *Encycl. Biblica*, III. 3111, s.v. 'Ministry'.
[5] I Cor. v. 3.   [6] Luke xii. 41 ff.

deference amounting to awe.[1] The pastoral epistles more fully indicate the functions and authority committed to evangelists such as
Titus and Timothy. They are to command and teach, reprove, rebuke,
exhort with all authority or command, to set in order the things that
are wanting. They are to maintain the authority of an office that is
independent of personal prestige; *Let no man despise thee. Let no
man despise thy youth.*[2] The power to excommunicate heretics or
schismatics is theirs. They possess disciplinary authority over the local
presbyters, the 'overseers', whom everywhere they are to appoint;[3]
it is possible that the local congregation usually chose its presbyters
and the evangelist ratified the choice. The warning to *lay hands
hastily on no man* is generally understood to refer to the laying on of
hands in ordination.[4]

In the New Testament then, we get a glimpse of the stewardship
beginning already to be handed on from the first generation of
apostles to the second generation of *apostolikoi* or evangelists. The
office is still itinerant. It is not until some thirty or forty years later,
long after the times of the Acts and the Epistles of St Paul, that we
find the place of the itinerant evangelist occupied by a resident
'bishop' with similar functions and authority within his own
parochia*[5] or diocese. The 'mission' in the higher sense endures,
the impulse is continued, although it is not so often geographically
propulsive as it was at the first.

---

[1] II Cor. vii. 15.   [2] Tit. ii. 15; I Tim. iv. 12.   [3] Tit. i. 5.
[4] It has also been understood to refer to Confirmation. Both uses of the laying
on of hands may have been intended.
[5] Note C. Parochia, *diocese, and parish* (p. 105).

NOTES TO CHAPTER XIV

A. 'APOSTLE' IN JEWISH USAGE

Lightfoot, *Apostle*, p. 92. The Syrian equivalent, *shelicha*, 'was the title
of certain legates or commissioners sent from the high priest to visit the
Jews and their synagogues which were dispersed in other countries, with
authority to redress things amiss'. (Lancelot Andrewes, *Minor Works*,
ed. 1846, p. 352.)

B. APOSTOLIC MISSION

'The principle of mission runs through the whole conception of office
in the New Testament. It is so even with Christ himself; it is so with the
Apostles; it is so with all other Christian ministers. "A man takes not

this honour unto himself, but only when called of God, as was Aaron. So also Christ glorified not himself to be made an high priest, but He that said unto him, Thou art My Son" (Heb. v. 4, 5). "As Thou hast sent me into the world, even so have I also sent them into the world" (Jo. xvii. 18). "How shall they preach except they be sent?" (Rom. x. 15). The book of Acts shows us this principle exemplified in the primitive Church by the position of the Apostles; through them alone came the gift of the Holy Ghost, conveyed by the laying on of hands; they, or those commissioned by them, appointed, or ratified the appointment of, even the local officials of each infant community.' (C. H. Turner, *Studies in Early Church History*, p. 12, referring to Acts ii. 42, 43, v. 12–15, vi. 3–6, viii. 14–19, x. 44–8, xi. 15–18, xiv. 23, xix. 5–6.)

C. *PAROCHIA*, DIOCESE, AND PARISH

The word comes from the Greek παροικία, which is short for ἡ ἐκκλησία ἡ παροικοῦσα, the Church 'sojourning' in a place. St Peter calls human life a παροικία, a sojourning (I Pet. i. 17). It meant what was afterwards called a diocese, and the Latin *parochia* is still used for a diocese by Bede in the eighth century. It came to mean a parish, which is the same word in the vernacular. (Wordsworth, p. 145; Bright, pp. 51–53.)

CHAPTER XV. CONTINUING THE MISSION

I

THE book of the Acts begins with a vivid, condensed narrative of the infancy of the new Ekklesia. The Eleven, with the holy women and some brethren, are a band of about one hundred and twenty. Matthias is numbered with the Eleven. The apostles, now Twelve again, are the first stewards of God's Household, the Church; of their commission to that office by Christ Himself no one has ever doubted. On the day of Pentecost there were 'added' about three thousand souls, *and they continued stedfastly in the apostles' teaching and fellowship, in the breaking of the bread, and the prayers.* From that time onward *the Lord added to them day by day those that were being saved.* The return of the Lord is expected at any time. All worldly possessions are possessed in common. Lands and houses are sold and the money realized is laid at the apostles' feet. The only 'ecclesiastical organization' is a rudimentary arrangement for sharing out according to need.

A few years pass by thus, perhaps as many as five or six, before it is found that the original stewardship of the household needs the help of under-stewards. The Seven are chosen by 'the multitude' and ordained by the apostles with prayer and with the laying on of their hands. The *diakonia* or ministry which was their immediate task had no appearance of special sanctity, they were required in fact as mess stewards. It seems unlikely that at the time the Twelve had any thought of founding an order of ministry as that came later to be understood. It is therefore remarkable that they made use of a solemn sacramental form of ordination, but this laying on of hands was an ancient sacrament of the old Ekklesia, an outward and visible sign of accompanying prayer for an inward and spiritual grace. The simplicity of the narrative in Acts suggests that the Twelve used this solemnity without any question or discussion, almost as a matter of course. The account of the Apostolic Council at Jerusalem shows that its members were firmly conscious of direct guidance by the Holy Spirit. Christians who still continue to-day in the apostles' teaching and fellowship are ready to believe that the ordination of the seven *diakonoi*, and its sacramental accompaniment, came about through the same guidance. At all events the order of deacons was at work everywhere before the close of the New Testament, and from very early times the Church has regarded the Seven as the first deacons.*[1]

II

Presbyters were ordinary officers of the old Ekklesia and that is perhaps the reason why their appointment by the apostles in the new Ekklesia seems to be taken so much for granted in the New Testament. The earliest mention of them is when famine relief is sent from Antioch to the presbyters of Judaea about A.D. 47.[2] Then in the first missionary journey of St Paul and St Barnabas in Asia Minor, they appoint elders for the disciples *in every church*.[3] Apostles and presbyters compose the great Council at Jerusalem about A.D. 49.[4] Some seven years later St Paul, while on shore at Miletus, sends for the presbyters of Ephesus, whom he addresses as 'overseers',[5] and when he arrives at Jerusalem and goes in unto James, *all the presbyters were present*.[6] Titus was charged to appoint presbyters in every city in Crete,[7] where his pastoral authority extended over them in the same way as Timothy's did at Ephesus.

There is no express mention anywhere of the laying on of hands in the ordination of presbyters; but there is nothing whatever to suggest that it was omitted, and the probabilities in favour of it are strong. St Luke's method suggests that he intended his account of the ordination of the Seven to be regarded 'as a typical example of ordination in the Apostolic Church'.[8] The rite was in use in the ordination of Jewish presbyters in the apostolic period.[9] It was used by the apostles not only in ordaining to the lower ministry of deacons but also in the bestowal upon all baptized Christians of spiritual gifts in that rite, nowadays called 'confirmation', which is of the nature of ordination to 'the priesthood of the laity'.[10] In the Epistle to the Hebrews, the laying on of hands is even referred to as a foundation, or first principle.[11] The great Congregationalist divine, Dr Dale, has shown that the space given in the New Testament writings to particular doctrines or duties was not determined by their intrinsic and

[1] Note A. *Seven deacons* (p. 112).   [2] Acts xi. 30.
[3] Acts xiv. 23.   [4] Acts xv. 2, 4, 22, 23, xvi. 4.
[5] Acts xx. 17.   [6] Acts xxi. 18.   [7] Tit. i. 5.
[8] E. J. Bicknell in *New Commentary*, s.v. Acts vi. 6, p. 341.
[9] See Note C on p. 70.
[10] This is taught distinctly in the Eastern Orthodox Church; see Dr Sergius Boulgakoff in *The Ministry and the Sacraments* (ed. R. Dunkerley), p. 109.
[11] Heb. vi. 2.

permanent importance, but by the need for the particular teaching at the time.*[1] This applies with particular force to the subject of the ministry and appointment to it, which from its nature was familiar and about which no question seems to have arisen in scriptural times.

There is no indication anywhere in the New Testament that presbyters were ever appointed by anyone other than apostles, or secondary apostles such as Timothy and Titus. At the close of the first century, in the Epistle of Clement to Corinth, there is a striking indication that they had always been appointed by apostles or, later, by 'others' whom the writer classes with apostles without pausing to describe them more exactly. He seems to take it for granted that the Christians he is addressing are familiar with what he refers to.[2]

III

About A.D. 47, perhaps, Herod the king put forth his hands and killed James the brother of John with the sword. Scripture does not record the deaths of others of the Twelve, but it must have come to be understood more and more clearly that their stewardship, if it were not to die out in the Ekklesia, must be handed on to others. They cannot have forgotten the ordination of Joshua by Moses: *Take thee Joshua...and lay thine hand upon him...and thou shalt put of thine honour upon him, that all the children of Israel may obey.*[3] *And Joshua the son of Nun was full of the spirit of wisdom; for Moses had laid his hands upon him.*[4] The New Testament gives clear enough indication that 'colleagues and successors' in the stewardship were actually appointed, both in the description of a number of others as apostles, and also in the more particular record of the position allotted to Timothy and Titus, which so closely resembles that of the later 'bishop', except that their local jurisdiction was not as yet permanent.

As also with regard to the presbyters, the New Testament is silent about the ordination of these secondary apostles. The probabilities are the same.

IV

Commission to ministry, as it is understood in many Protestant denominations, is not a matter of doctrine; it is an affair of prudent organization, comparable to the choice and appointment of a school-

---

[1] Note B. *New Testament silence on the familiar* (p. 112).
[2] See chapter XVI.   [3] Num. xxvii. 18, 20.   [4] Deut. xxxiv. 9.

master. There is no apostolic order of ministry to be perpetuated. In the words of a distinguished leader of Congregational thought, 'The strict successor of the Apostles is the New Testament as containing the precipitate of their standard preaching....The Apostles appointed no canonical successors. They could not....The Apostles could not send as they had been sent by Christ....We hear much question raised whether our ministry is a *valid* ministry. It is absurd. God alone can really know if a ministry is valid....The ministry is valid or regular according as it is effective as a sacrament of the gospel to our experience in a church.'[1] To this attitude of mind, the subject of commission to ministry presents no problem whatever; anyone who is elected as pastor by any group of Christians is as fully a minister as it is possible to be. He has no more continuity with the evangelists or presbyters of the New Testament than his congregation has with the visible Ekklesia of the New Testament; continuity is a matter of no importance whatever.

In a different phase of Protestant belief, the office of ministry is recognized as possessing an authority and sanctity that is different in kind from any mere secular office; yet the commission to it is so entirely a spiritual reality that the warrant and the manner of its outward bestowal are secondary and unessential. No doubt all should be done decently and in order, but how, and by whom, cannot be of great importance. This school of thought fully accepts the need of ministers in a spiritual office for the human mediation of the Word and Sacraments, but rejects the necessity for any particular human mediation in the bestowal of that office. It is not easy to reconcile doctrines such as these with the New Testament, either in its teaching of the nature of the Ekklesia or in its references to the ministers of the apostolic period. They are wholly contrary to the age-long belief of the universal Church, in which its ministry is a continuing stewardship, one with the original stewardship of the household, just as the Ekklesia of the time being is always one with the Ekklesia of Pentecost. This belief has sometimes been given faulty expression; the Church, it is sometimes asserted, depends on the ministry, but that is a half-truth at best. It is as true to say that the ministry depends on the Church. The limbs and members of a physical body depend upon it for their continuity and vitality although it may truly also be said that the limbs and members are vital to the body. In the scriptural doctrine of the Church it may be

[1] Forsyth, pp. 128–31.

seen then that the apostolic ministry, which is its original endowment, is vital to it, and nevertheless is dependent upon the Church for its continuance and vitality.

If then the Christian ministry is a stewardship in the universal Church, if the commission to it is in any sense a continuation of the apostolic mission, by what recognizable human mediation is that commission bestowed? What are the knowable credentials of the steward? From the very beginning that commission has been mediated by the chief pastors of the Church and, as far as can be known, never without them; it has always been recognizably bestowed with the imposition of their hands. A certain type of modern mind sees this rite, or at least any insistence upon its neces-sity, as something material, mechanical, sub-spiritual;[1] to the surer instinct of the early Church and the universal Church thereafter it is prayer made visible, and it is no more 'mechanical' than are the accompanying prayers which are made audible in speech. So far as it is 'material', it may be compared with the appointed elements of the two great sacraments. Could any other way be devised in which the steward of to-day can be correlated in office to the whole Church universal of to-day, scattered as it is (and therefore also to the Church of Pentecost), in which he is numbered with the other stewards of to-day (and therefore with the stewards of the early Church), just as truly as Matthias 'was numbered with the Eleven'? These requirements are fulfilled in the sacramental rite of the Ek-klesia, already hallowed by Old Testament tradition. Unless that solemnity was abandoned and resumed at some time before the end of the second century, which there is not any reason to suppose, it has always been a means and a manifestation of the organic con-tinuity of the Church.

V

It is instructive to compare, with what has here been suggested,[2] what is said by gifted teachers of other views and conceptions of the ministry.

'The primary fact in a true ministry is the personal call of Jesus Christ; and any formal investiture·in name of the community, how-ever suitable and however fortifying it may be, must always be

[1] 'The historical, legal, mechanical, chemical, construction of the Church.' 'A legalistic and Judaic conception.' 'Judaic legalism.' Manning, pp. 75, 133, 135.
[2] See also chapter VI, section VIII.

treated as secondary and subordinate. It is not by churchly forms that ministers of Christ are made.'[1]

'The personal call of God is the indispensable requisite for admittance to the ministry; this call the Church recognizes but does not originate....Gifts, grace, and fruit are the signs by which the Lord has been wont to designate His own called ministers.'[2]

It can be agreed by all that the primary fact in appointment to ministry is the inward and spiritual ordination, not that ordination which is outward and visible. It is equally true that the primary fact in Holy Baptism is the invisible action of the Holy Spirit, not the outward part of the sacrament. But we on earth cannot separate the inward and the outward. We cannot hear the call of the ascended Lord with our mortal ears any more than we can see the action of the Holy Spirit with our mortal eyes.

It can be agreed too that the personal call of God is the inner and indispensable requisite, and that a man may be truly convinced that he has heard that call, but what are the credentials of call recognizable in the universal Ekklesia? Dr Macgregor, whose words have been quoted, pertinently asks: 'Such a view of what is indispensable may be convincing and sufficient to a man himself, but how is the community to be satisfied? And is there not a likelihood that the lighter and vainer a man is, he will the more readily trust to his own inspirations, and thrust himself forward as a God-sent instructor of his fellows? and who is subtle or discerning enough unfailingly to penetrate the self-deceptions to which all men are liable?'[3] But no better answer can be suggested, it seems, than that gifts, graces and fruit are the signs of designation.

Certainly sanctified commonsense would indicate that men should be carefully chosen for the ministry, even if Scripture had not directed it, but human judgement is only too fallible. The teaching quoted above seems to lay upon the community the impossible task of assessing whether each minister has exhibited a sufficient measure of grace to mark him out as truly called. Yet another teacher confesses that 'we cannot begin to classify and grade the manifestations and the means of grace...we do not deal in percentages with the grace of God...our categories fail; our measuring rods are too short; we will not pretend to use them'.[4]

[1] Macgregor, p. 235.
[2] Ibid. p. 200, quoting Methodist Manual of Doctrine for the Use of Candidates, p. 8.
[3] Macgregor, p. 198.   [4] Manning, p. 116.

For those who hold a modern dogma that the apostles could not send as they had been sent,[1] it seems then that commission to the ministry must always be a matter of opinion, and usually therefore of uncertainty. But for others who hold the contrary belief, which seems from Scripture to have been that of the apostles themselves, and which has certainly been the belief of those who came after them in the ministry, there is a certainty of commission afforded by the 'measuring rod' of apostolic ordination by those ministers who represent the universal Ekklesia in imparting it.

[1] Forsyth, p. 129.

NOTES TO CHAPTER XV

A. Seven deacons

Because of the identification of the Seven as the first deacons, it was recorded in the fifth century that 'There are but seven deacons at Rome, answering precisely to the number ordained by the apostles, of whom Stephen was the first martyr; whereas, in other churches, the number of deacons is unlimited'. (Hermias Sozomen, *Eccl. Hist.* book vii, cap. xix.)

B. New Testament silence on the familiar

'It must be obvious to every reader of the New Testament that a mere catalogue of texts in which any great truth is definitely taught can never give a just impression of the place which that truth held in the thought and faith of the Apostles....The space [in the Epistles] which is given to the illustration of particular doctrines or duties was determined, not by the intrinsic and permanent importance of the doctrines or duties themselves, but by the perils which threatened the Christian faith or the Christian integrity of the Churches to which they were written, and by many other circumstances of a temporary character....The frequency and distinctness with which a doctrine is asserted in the apostolic writings is, therefore, no test of its importance. It might even be contended with considerable plausibility that the importance of a doctrine is likely to be in the inverse ratio of the number of passages in which it is directly taught....From the very nature of the apostolic writings these truths which belong to the essence of the Christian creed are, for the most part, implied rather than explicitly taught.' (R. W. Dale, *The Atonement*, pp. 20–22.)

CHAPTER XVI. CLEMENT, AND 'THE OTHER ELLOGIMOI'

THERE is an incidental record about A.D. 95, that presbyters had always been appointed by *ellogimoi* or 'eminent' men (the word is quite general in meaning), at first by apostles and afterwards by 'other *ellogimoi*'. Who were these leading men who came after the first apostles but were apparently classed with them in function and respect?

During the period that has been called 'the tunnel' one conspicuous change takes place in the customary arrangement of ministry. As the New Testament records end, the two orders of presbyters and deacons, found in every local Church, are shepherded by a superior class or order of apostles and secondary apostles or evangelists, whose sphere of ministry is still general, and is only beginning to be associated with particular territory. At the end of that period, in every local Church there are still the same two orders of presbyters and deacons, but the chief pastors who shepherd them are now settled in individual charge of particular Churches. The early Church, down to the time of St Jerome at least, seems never to have doubted that this chief pastorate was identical with the former itinerant chief pastorate. In recent centuries that belief has been directly challenged, and its soundness must be impartially examined. A transition from itinerancy to residency was natural enough in consequence of the extension of the Church throughout the known world, and it tallies with the belief that this reorganization of chief-pastoral work came about without any *organic* change in the ministry, or in the relations of the three orders. It can be said at least that there is no indication of organic change; the 'bishop' of a Church in the latter part of the second century is settled in a pastorate similar to those local pastorates which Timothy or Titus had exercised a century earlier, although not then as permanent incumbencies.

Apart from the implicit belief of the early Church in its own continuity, the absence of any trace of dispute or debate sets up a certain presumption of continuity.*[1] That presumption receives material support from one or two glimpses of the constitutional life of the Church during the period of obscurity.

The first of these glimpses is given four or five years before the

---

[1] Note A. *Constant identity of ministerial principle* (p. 118).

end of the first century, and discloses two points of interest: (1) There were certain 'others' who succeeded to some at least of the pastoral responsibilities of the first apostles. (2) All presbyters of that time had been appointed either by the first apostles or by these 'others'. This information is given quite incidentally in the letter of the Roman Church to the Corinthian Church known as the Epistle of Clement to Corinth.

The first chief pastor or president of the Church in Rome after the martyrdom of St Peter and St Paul was Linus, the same who sent greetings to Timothy on the eve of St Paul's martyrdom, probably a freedman.[1] The second was Anencletus, whose name suggests a similar status. The third was Clement, who presided from A.D. 92 to 100. These have always been retrospectively described as bishops of Rome because their ministerial position was traditionally that to which the name of 'bishop' became attached in the second century. In their own time, the presbyters over whom they presided were still described as 'bishops'. (It was very much later that the bishops of Rome began to receive the Eastern name of 'pope', although the early bishops are also called 'popes' retrospectively.)

Clement was not the fellow-worker of St Paul mentioned in Philippians.[2] He was probably a Hellenist Jew, and a freedman, or a freedman's son, of the household of Flavius Clemens, a consul who became a Christian and was put to death by his cousin the Emperor Domitian.[3] 'Among these freedmen were frequently found the most intelligent and cultivated men of their day.'[4] Later bishops of Rome, Pius (A.D. 140–55) and Callistus (A.D. 218–22), were also freed slaves.[5] The reference by Clement to Peter and Paul as 'the good apostles' harmonizes with the tradition that he was their disciple. The persistent tradition that he was ordained by one of them has been supposed to present a problem, because he did not succeed to the Roman chair until many years after their deaths. But the difficulty is removed when it is remembered that 'mon-episcopacy and diocesan' jurisdiction had not been developed or generally organized at that early date, and Clement may well, like Timothy, Titus and others, have been ordained to the ministry of the chief pastorate without attaining at that time to the chair of Rome. A hundred years after his time he is referred to as an apostle.[6]

[1] Lightfoot, *Clement*, I. p. 76; II Tim. iv. 21.
[2] Phil. iv. 3; Lightfoot, *Clement*, I. p. 22.   [3] Lightfoot, *op. cit.* pp. 59, 61.
[4] *Ibid.* p. 61.   [5] *Ibid.* p. 62.   [6] See above, chapter XIII, section IV.

His letter is written in the name of the Church in the region of the Romans, and his own name does not occur in it. Usual custom may explain this, for when some seventy-five years later, during the episcopate of Soter, a second letter is written from Rome to Corinth, it also is written in the name of the Church, not of the bishop.[1] Dionysius, bishop of Corinth, in replying refers to the epistle 'which you wrote us by Clement',[2] and the authorship of Clement has always been generally recognized.

Just as when St Paul wrote First Corinthians, it was disorder at Corinth that elicited Clement's letter. It was written because the Corinthians had made sedition against their duly appointed presbyters and replaced them by other men. The letter, which is of some length, is far from supporting any theory of universal jurisdiction of the Church in Rome, still less of its bishop. It is written throughout in a tone of loving remonstrance and persuasion. As Bishop Lightfoot says, gentleness and equability, 'sweet reasonableness', was a passion with the writer. There is no citation of exact legal precedent; there is indeed an allusion to Korah, Dathan and Abiram; no more recent parallel to the proceedings of the 'independents' of Corinth seems to come to his mind. He does appeal throughout to what he regards as a divinely appointed orderliness, persisting from the Old Dispensation and merging into the New.

The Apostles received the Gospel for us from the Lord Jesus Christ: Jesus Christ was sent forth from God. So then Christ is from God, and the Apostles are from Christ. Both therefore came of the will of God in the appointed order. Having therefore received a charge, and having been fully assured through the resurrection of our Lord Jesus Christ and confirmed in the word of God with full assurance of the Holy Ghost, they went forth with the glad tidings that the kingdom of God should come. So preaching everywhere in country and town, they appointed their first-fruits, when they had proved them by the Spirit, to be bishops and deacons unto them that should believe.[3]

(It will be noticed that the chief pastor of Rome, about A.D. 95, still speaks of presbyters as bishops.) He urges those whom the people have appointed in place of their presbyters to retire.

Who therefore is noble among you? Who is compassionate? Who is fulfilled with love? Let him say; If by reason of me there be faction and strife and divisions, I retire, I depart, whither ye will, and I do that which

---

[1] Lightfoot, *op. cit.* pp. 71, 72, 83.   [2] Eusebius, *Hist. Eccl.* IV. 23.
[3] Clement, *ad Cor.* 42.

is ordered by the people: only let the flock of Christ be at peace with its duly appointed presbyters.[1]

Ye therefore that laid the foundation of the sedition, submit yourselves unto the presbyters, and receive chastisement unto repentance, bending the knees of your heart. Learn to submit yourselves, laying aside the arrogant and proud stubbornness of your tongue. For it is better for you to be found little in the flock of Christ and to have your name on God's roll, than to be had in exceeding honour and yet be cast out from the hope of Him.[2]

Unfortunately for us, as it seems, and for all present-day scholars and students of the early Church, Clement not only regards the ways of the Church as orderly and constant, but also assumes that they are perfectly familiar to those to whom he is writing. He only refers incidentally therefore to matters that are nowadays in question; nevertheless, these slight references are pregnant with information.

And our apostles knew through our Lord Jesus Christ that there would be strife about the title of the episcopate. Because of this, therefore, having received complete foreknowledge, they appointed the aforesaid [bishops and deacons], and afterwards gave an additional injunction that if they [i.e. the bishops and deacons] fell asleep, other proved men should succeed to their ministration. Those therefore who were appointed by them [i.e. the apostles] or by other *ellogimoi*, with the consent of the whole Church, and have ministered unblamably to the flock of Christ with humility, quietly and unassumingly, and have long borne a good report with all, those we deem not justly to be thrust out from their ministration.*[3]

As Dr Hamilton has pointed out,[4] 'St Clement's witness to the fact of Apostolic appointment is of far higher value than his witness to the historic character of the interpretation which he puts upon the fact'. The tradition of the foretelling that there would be strife over the 'name' or title of the bishop's office may be true, but it was removed by some sixty-five years from his own day. On the other hand, regarding the bare fact of apostolic appointment, he is in an excellent position to give evidence. His letter is only some twenty-five or thirty years later than the deaths of St Peter and St Paul. Orderly succession in the Church is the underlying principle of his appeal to the Corinthian 'independents'. Christ was sent forth from God, the apostles from Christ. They appointed proved men as bishops and deacons and made provision for a succession of ministers.

---

[1] Clement, *ad Cor.* 54.   [2] *Ibid.* 57.
[3] Note B. *Apostles or other* ellogimoi (p. 118).   [4] Hamilton, II. pp. 139, 140.

The only lawfully appointed presbyters hitherto known to the Church, he implies, have been appointed either (1) by the apostles, or (2) by other *ellogimoi*. It is because those recently put into office at Corinth have not been so appointed that he urges them, in all charity, to retire. The whole argument of his letter rests upon that assumption. It does not occur to him that it needs any proof, and, had it been erroneous, 'had St Clement been at fault in his facts regarding either the customs of the Apostles or those of the Church since their day, there were many who would have known it at once'.[1] Actually, the letter seems to have been received with respect and to have carried conviction. At all events there is no further record of Corinthian disorder, and we learn from Dionysius, bishop of Corinth some seventy or eighty years later, that the letter of Clement continued to be read from time to time in the Corinthian Church on Sundays.[2]

It is evidently important to examine the meaning of the adjective *ellogimos*, which is not a word of exact use. The different attempts of scholars show that it is difficult to find a precise translation. The companion verb *ellogeo* means to reckon in, to impute; St Paul uses it in the Epistle to Philemon in the phrase translated as *put that to mine account*. Where the adjective occurs in another passage of Clement's Epistle, already quoted, Lightfoot translates 'to be *ellogimoi*' as 'to have your name on God's roll'. In another passage he translates 'to be *ellogimos* in the number of the saved' as 'to have a name among' them.[3] He renders the passage now under consideration as meaning, appointed by the apostles 'or other men of repute'. The following are translations by other scholars:[4]

other men of account	Dr Darwell Stone
other eminent men	Dr W. K. Lowther Clarke
other distinguished men	Bishop Gore
other honoured men	Dr B. J. Kidd
other notables	Professor C. H. Turner
other men on the roll	Mr W. Lockton
other elect men	Fr. E. Symonds

The very looseness of the phrase in which Clement refers to the

[1] Hamilton, II. p. 140.   [2] Eusebius, *Hist. Eccl.* II. 25; IV. 23.   [3] Clement, *ad Cor.* 58.
[4] D. Stone, *Episcopacy and Valid Orders in the Primitive Church*, 2nd ed. 1926, p. 36. W. K. Lowther Clarke in *Episcopacy A. & M.* p. 29. Gore and Turner, p. 280. B. J. Kidd, *Documents Illustrative of the History of the Church*, I. p. 30. C. H. Turner in *Essays on Early Hist.* p. 112. Lockton, p. 171. E. Symonds, *The Church Universal and the See of Rome*, p. 14.

connexion between the ejected Corinthian presbyters and the apostles—'those who were appointed by them, or afterward by other accredited men'—shows that he was basing his appeal on facts that the Corinthians must know perfectly well already and only need to be reminded of. Fortunately, the indefiniteness of *ellogimoi* does not leave Clement's meaning indefinite. Whatever he meant by *ellogimos*, he applied to the apostles equally with the 'other *ellogimoi*'. That is the inescapable force of the word 'other'. The phrase imports one class of persons by whom all the presbyters have been appointed, composed of the *ellogimoi* apostles and those who, although not themselves primary apostles, were also *ellogimoi*—'other *ellogimoi*'. His whole appeal, based on the orderliness and settled ways of the whole Church rather than on the letter of any enactment, turns on the fact, plainly implied, that neither he nor the Corinthians had ever heard of any presbyters appointed by any except *ellogimoi*, whether the apostles or other *ellogimoi* after them. If he had been mistaken in this, his whole argument would have collapsed.

Who were the *ellogimoi*? On the evidence of the New Testament it can only be conjectured that they were ministers of high authority such as Timothy or Titus, in a pastorate superior to the presbyters whom they presided over and whom, as Clement indicates, they also appointed.

NOTES TO CHAPTER XVI

A.   CONSTANT IDENTITY OF MINISTERIAL PRINCIPLE

'If the constitution of the Church developed in all local manifestations of it into one and the same form of episcopal ministry, there must have been something in the original nature of the Church to account for this identical development.... The unanimity of Christendom on the principle of the transmission of ministerial authority, and upon the form which the hierarchy should assume, is one of the most deeply impressive facts in the history of the Church.' (W. J. Sparrow Simpson, *New Commentary* (N.T.), p. 392.)

B.   APOSTLES OR OTHER *ELLOGIMOI*   (Clement, *ad Cor.* 44)

Some writers have thought to identify the 'other proved men', who replaced the first generation of 'bishops and deacons', with the 'other *ellogimoi*', who are classed with the *ellogimoi* apostles as having appointed the proved men. This identification does not square with the text or the natural meaning.

§ 42. Οἱ ἀπόστολοι ... κατὰ χώρας οὖν καὶ πόλεις κηρύσσοντες καθίστανον τὰς ἀπαρχὰς αὐτῶν, δοκιμάσαντες τῷ πνεύματι, εἰς ἐπισκόπους
καὶ διακόνους τῶν μελλόντων πιστεύειν. § 44. Καὶ οἱ ἀπόστολοι ἡμῶν ... Διὰ ταύτην οὖν τὴν αἰτίαν πρό-
γνωσιν εἰληφότες τελείαν κατέστησαν τοὺς προειρημένους, καὶ μεταξὺ
ἐπινομὴν δεδώκασιν ὅπως, ἐὰν κοιμηθῶσιν, διαδέξωνται ἕτεροι δεδοκιμασμένοι ἄνδρες τὴν λειτουργίαν αὐτῶν. τοὺς οὖν κατασταθέντας ὑπ' ἐκείνων
ἢ μεταξὺ ὑφ' ἑτέρων ἐλλογίμων ἀνδρῶν, συνευδοκησάσης τῆς ἐκκλησίας
πάσης ... τούτους οὐ δικαίως νομίζομεν ἀποβάλλεσθαι τῆς λειτουργίας.

The plain sense is that, ἕτεροι δεδοκιμασμένοι should succeed those
ἐπισκόπους καὶ διακόνους whom at first οἱ ἀπόστολοι δοκιμάσαντες
καθίστανον.

ἕτεροι δεδοκιμασμένοι succeed the first δεδοκιμασμένοι. All δεδοκιμασμένοι (ἐπίσκοποι καὶ διάκονοι) have been appointed either ὑπ' ἐκείνων
(ἀποστόλων) or else ὑφ' ἑτέρων ἐλλογίμων.

CHAPTER XVII. IGNATIUS, BISHOP AND MARTYR, A.D. 110

I

WITHIN twenty years, at the most, after Clement's letter to the Corinthians, a Syrian bishop, journeying to his martyrdom at Rome, wrote seven vivid letters which have been preserved to us. St Ignatius was condemned to death in the persecutions under Trajan, and was sent to Rome to help to supply the demand for victims for the sports of the arena. The provinces were put under requisition to supply convicts to be 'butchered to make a Roman holiday'. He was the bishop of Antioch in Syria, which had been the headquarters of St Paul; he was not 'Bishop of Syria'; at that time 'episcopacy has not passed beyond its primitive stage. The bishop and presbyters are the ministry of a city, not of a diocese. What provision may have been made for the rural districts we are not told.'[1] He was not a Roman citizen, or he would not have been thrown to the beasts of the arena. He was taken to Rome in the custody of a maniple of ten soldiers. They must have had other duties; probably they had to take over other prisoners on their way through Asia Minor. St Ignatius was cheered by the help and sympathy of the brethren of the Churches on the route, but presents made to the soldiers did little to soften their harshness.

From Laodicea to Smyrna there were two routes. The southern road leads past Tralles, Magnesia and Ephesus, reaching Smyrna in about 152 miles. The northern road reaches Smyrna in a slightly shorter mileage, passing Philadelphia on its way; they followed this route. From Laodicea a messenger seems to have hastened along the southern road to tell the Churches of the passage of the martyr to Smyrna, and a number of delegates went to Smyrna to meet him. Ephesus, the nearest to Smyrna, sent its bishop Onesimus, a deacon Burrhus, and three other brethren. Magnesia sent its bishop Damas, two presbyters and a deacon; from Tralles, more distant, its bishop, Polybius, came along. Of the members of the Church in Smyrna with whom St Ignatius came in contact during the halt there, several are mentioned in his letters, the most important being its bishop,

---

[1] Lightfoot, *Ignatius*, I. p. 397.

Polycarp, who himself received the martyr's crown some forty years later in his old age.

Before leaving Smyrna, Ignatius wrote letters to the Churches of the *Ephesians*, *Magnesians*, and *Trallians*, and another to the Church of the *Romans* among whom he was eagerly looking forward to make his witness in the arena; this letter was carried on in advance of him by some Ephesian brethren; it alone bears a date, 24 August.

Burrhus was sent on with St Ignatius to Troas and acted as his amanuensis before he was embarked for Europe, in three letters, to the *Philadelphians*, the *Smyrnaeans*, and to *Polycarp*. Through the labours of scholars, we possess the authentic text of these seven letters. There our knowledge ends. The traditional date of the martyrdom at Rome was 17 October.

'The pitchy darkness, which envelopes the life and work of Ignatius, is illumined at length by a vivid but transient flash of light. If his martyrdom had not rescued him from obscurity, he would have remained like his predecessor [in the bishopric of Antioch] Euodius, a mere name, and nothing more. As it is, he stands out in the momentary light of this event, a distinct and living personality, a true father of the Church, a teacher and an example to all time.'[1]

II

These letters are not long or carefully revised literary efforts, and they show traces of the conditions in which they were written down to dictation, probably in haste. Addressed to Churches mostly in the same districts, exposed to the same dangers, needing the same warnings, the same thoughts occur with some repetition. The dominant personal note is the writer's intense humility and self-depreciation and his burning desire for martyrdom. Indeed in his letter to the *Romans* he entreats them not to try to obtain his deliverance; there were Christians in Rome at that time with influential connexions who might have contrived this. 'I write to all the churches, and I bid all men know, that of my own free will I die for God, unless ye should hinder me. I exhort you, be ye not an "unseasonable kindness" to me. Let me be given to the wild beasts, for through them I can attain unto God. I am God's wheat, and I am ground by the teeth of wild beasts that I may be found pure bread [of Christ].'[2] It has sometimes been objected that the intense eagerness for martyr-

---

[1] Lightfoot, *Ignatius*, I. p. 31.   [2] *Romans* 4.

dom which these letters betray shows a fanaticism inconceivable in an apostolic father. Bishop Lightfoot's comment on this is: 'It is a cheap wisdom which at the study table or over a pulpit desk declaims against the extravagance of the feelings and language of Ignatius as the vision of martyrdom rose up before him. After all it is only by an enthusiasm which men call extravagance that the greatest moral and spiritual triumphs have been won.'[1]

There are two chief topics in the letter to the Churches of Asia Minor: (1) He gives repeated warnings against the then prevalent Docetic and Gnostic heresies, which denied the reality of the Incarnation and maintained that both the birth and death of Christ, and His whole life on earth, were apparitional, not real. St John had written against this same heresy.[2] (2) He treats the threefold ministry of bishops, presbyters and deacons, as the centre of order, the guarantee of unity, in the Church. Again and again he exhorts the Churches to loyalty and obedience, using language that sounds exaggerated to modern ears.

It is therefore necessary, even as your wont is, that ye should do nothing without the bishop; but be ye obedient also to the presbytery, as to the Apostles of Jesus Christ our hope....In like manner let all men respect the deacons as Jesus Christ, even as they should respect the bishop as being a type of the Father and the presbyters as the council of God and as the college of Apostles. Apart from these there is not even the name of a Church.[3]

So then it becometh you to run in harmony with the mind of the bishop; which thing also ye do. For your honourable presbytery, which is worthy of God, is attuned to the bishop, even as its strings to a lyre.[4]

Be ye zealous to do all things in godly concord, the bishop presiding after the likeness of God and the presbyters after the likeness of the council of the Apostles, with the deacons also who are most dear to me, having been entrusted with the diaconate of Jesus Christ.[5]

Shun divisions, as the beginning of evils. Do ye all follow your bishop, as Jesus Christ followed the Father, and the presbytery as the Apostles; and to the deacons pay respect, as to God's commandment. Let no man do aught of things pertaining to the Church apart from the bishop. Let that be held a valid eucharist which is under the bishop or one to whom he shall have committed it.[6]

This striking insistence upon the claims of the threefold ministry to allegiance was secondary to his theological teaching. 'The unity

[1] Lightfoot, *op. cit.* p. 38.   [2] I John ii. 22, 23, iv. 2, 3; II John 7.   [3] *Trallians* 2, 3.
[4] *Ephesians* 4.   [5] *Magnesians* 6.   [6] *Smyrnaeans* 8.

of the body was a guarantee of the unity of the faith. The threefold ministry was the husk, the shell, which protected the precious kernel of the truth.'[1] It is worthy of notice too that the 'mon-episcopacy' of these Churches of Asia Minor was far from being an autocracy. The presbyters are the council of the bishop; obedience is due to them, and even to the deacons. Primitive episcopacy was thoroughly 'constitutional', not what has been decried as 'prelatic'. It should also be remarked that there is no indication that this threefold ministry is being upheld against any other form of Church government, as for instance the presbyteral, or that the distinct ministry of 'the bishop' had originated or developed at the expense of that of the primitive presbyters.

III

The subsequent history of these seven letters of St Ignatius, their fall into obscurity, and their rescue, is a romance of scholarship. Bishop Polycarp of Smyrna preserved copies of some—probably all—and sent copies to the Philippians with a letter of his own, still extant, which he wrote to them immediately after Ignatius had passed on his way to Rome and before intelligence of the martyr's fate had come back.

With the deplorably misguided literary zeal of the early centuries, a mass of spurious and interpolated letters were 'forged', as we should say, under the great name of the martyr. Lightfoot considers that some of these were composed in the latter part of the fourth century, perhaps in Syria, but a long and wholly fictitious correspondence with St John and the Virgin Mary was written in Latin very much later. All these forgeries contain absurdities and anachronisms that could only have escaped detection in an uncritical age. As a consequence, however, 'in the middle ages the spurious and interpolated letters alone have any wide circulation'.[2] St Jerome (who was 'extremely ignorant of early Christian literature', other than works on Biblical exegesis) 'had no personal acquaintance with the writings of Ignatius'.[3] Calvin, in the ignorance prevailing at his time, can hardly be blamed for dismissing St Ignatius with the sole comment that 'Nothing can be more disgusting than the nursery stories which have been published under the name of Ignatius'.[4] In the course of the next century, controversy grew round the

---

[1] Lightfoot, op. cit. p. 40.   [2] Ibid. p. 233.   [3] Ibid. pp. 156, 157.
[4] Calvin, Inst. i. xiii. 29.

writings of Ignatius because of the striking evidence (in the original and genuine letters) to episcopacy at the date of his martyrdom. Milton himself published in 1641 a tract *Of Prelatical Episcopacy* in which he said:

Had *God* ever intended that we should have sought any part of usefull instruction from *Ignatius*, doubtles he would not have so ill provided for our knowledge as to send him to our hands in this broken and disjoynted plight; and if he intended no such thing, we doe injuriously in thinking to tast better the pure Evangelic Manna by seasoning our mouths with the tainted scraps, and fragments of an unknown table; and searching among the verminous and polluted rags dropt overworn from the toyling shoulders of Time, with these deformedly to quilt and interlace the intire, the spotlesse, and undecaying Robe of Truth.[1]

Milton was very soon answered out of his own mouth. For some years before this, Archbishop Ussher had been at work on the letters of Ignatius, and in 1644 he published its results, which clearly exposed the spurious matter and cogently established the genuineness of six of the letters. (That of the epistle to *Polycarp* was established some years later by Bishop Pearson.) The original Greek of the letters was recovered and published by Voss in Amsterdam and Ruinart in Paris. The process of isolating and establishing the seven genuine letters has something of the character and interest of a detective story. It is narrated in three volumes of the monumental work of Bishop Lightfoot on the *Apostolic Fathers*, which is the chief source of the information in this and the preceding chapter. To Lightfoot himself fell the honour of establishing the whole seven letters anew and disproving Cureton's contention that three letters only were genuine which were contained in a Syriac abbreviation published by him in 1845. Lightfoot's exposition is now generally accepted by all scholars as conclusive.

IV

The letter to the *Romans* is addressed to the Church, not to bishop or presbyters. That is the form followed in all the letters to Churches. But *Romans* differs from the other letters because it contains no reference to bishop, presbyters or deacons, such as occurs so prominently in the others. It is also noticeable that there are no warnings in it against heresy. In fact, much of this letter consists of the martyr's

[1] Milton, *Works* (Pickering, 1851), p. 81.

appeals against any influential intervention which might rob him of the crown of martyrdom. From the silence of this short letter on the subject of episcopacy some writers have drawn an inference that there was as yet no bishop of Rome or, at least, that 'the episcopate, though doubtless it existed in some form or other in Rome, had not as yet (it would seem) assumed the same sharp and well-defined monarchical character with which we are confronted in the Eastern churches'.[1]

As against this, it should be noted that the Church of the Romans is addressed in terms of exceptionally high praise, 'the church that is beloved and enlightened—worthy of praise, worthy in purity—having the presidency of love in the country of the region of the Romans—filled with the grace of God without wavering, and filtered clear from every foreign stain—ye were the instructors of others'. Since Ignatius considered that without bishop, presbyters and deacons 'there is not even the name of a church', it is difficult to suppose that the Church in Rome can have been so defective in his eyes. It is quite possible, however, that Alexander, who then presided in Rome as fourth in succession after Clement, may, like Clement, not yet have been distinguished by the epithet of 'the bishop', which in Rome may still have been applied to presbyters in general.

We do not know at what date the bishop of Rome became known as 'the bishop'. The indications are that the transference of the name from the presbyters must have taken place early in the second century, at all events. What is certain is that neither in East nor West is any clear reference to presbyters as 'bishops' found to occur after the first century. The only explanation of this change in the application of the style of 'bishop' is contained in a writing of much later date. It deserves attention because it is intelligible, consistent with the facts as they are otherwise known, and because no other explanation has been suggested that meets the known facts.

Theodore, an Antiochene born about A.D. 350, was an early friend and companion of St John Chrysostom, was ordained a presbyter at Antioch in 383, and was consecrated in 393 bishop of Mopsuestia in Cilicia, a town on the river Pyramus, 12 miles from the sea and 40 miles east of Tarsus, then an important town, but now an insignificant place by the name of Messis. There Theodore worked zealously for the good of his flock until his death in 428, although his great interests were literary and antiquarian. He wrote profusely

[1] Lightfoot, *op. cit.* p. 399.

on subjects pastoral, liturgical and exegetical. 'Of all that the Church had declared to be of faith, he was the staunch defender; and it is characteristic of his honest belief in the Nicene doctrines that he is said to have converted to the Catholic Church the Arian population of his diocese.'[1] Unfortunately, some of his theological writings were at least open to heretical interpretation; more than a century after his death he was accused of being a parent of Nestorianism, and his writings were condemned. From the sixth century onwards they were almost entirely forgotten in the West. His commentaries on the Epistles of St Paul came into notice in the nineteenth century through the rediscovery of old manuscripts.

Theodore observes, as also do other commentators, both earlier and contemporary, that in the New Testament period presbyters were often called bishops. He cites Philippians i. 1, Titus i. 5, 7, and Acts xx. 17, 28 as illustrations. He goes fully into the matter in a long note, almost an excursus, at I Timothy iii. 8, where, as he says, the uninstructed reader might suppose that presbyters had been left out by St Paul, who speaks of 'bishops' and deacons.

There has been, he says, a change of names that ought to be explained, for now the bishop is not called presbyter nor are the presbyters ever called bishops. In the early days presbyters were also called bishops—overseers—because they had to oversee everything in their Churches. Those ministers who had the power of ordaining were not set over a single Church but over a region and were called apostles. Thus to Timothy, Titus, and others, were allotted regions. He describes their work and remarks that it was similar to that of a contemporary bishop in his city and district, visiting all the Churches, teaching and instructing, ordaining, absolving in cases of serious sin. Later on, when believers were greatly increased everywhere and the blessed apostles were dead, these ministers of what he calls the 'universal presidency' felt unworthy to be called apostles and 'divided out the names'. 'They left the name of bishop to him who has the power of ordination in that he has been entrusted with an universal jurisdiction.' He remarks that, since then, in some parts, unnecessarily small towns became bishoprics. A translation of the chief passages will be found in a note.*[2]

---

[1] H. B. Swete, *Theodore of Mopsuestia on the Minor Epistles of St Paul*, I. lxxxvii.
[2] Note A. *Theodore of Mopsuestia on the transference of the name of 'bishop'* (p. 134).

V

Although Theodore's literary style is dull and clumsy, his account of the transference of the name of 'bishop' is clear enough. The name was originally applied indifferently to the presbyters who were in fact the local 'overseers'. It was not applied then to the ministry of 'universal jurisdiction' or 'universal presidency' to which alone ordination pertained, of which Timothy and Titus were members, and to which the general name of 'apostles' was given. But after all the original apostles were dead, this ministry, out of humility, appropriated the name of 'bishop' and dropped that of 'apostles'.

Theodore himself was not born until some two centuries and a half after the changes he wrote of; no implicit reliance can therefore be placed on the accuracy of his antiquarian notes; they call for serious attention however, more perhaps than they have hitherto received. What he says is consistent, at least, with anything that is known from other sources and, if his account can be accepted, it provides a coherent explanation of the incontrovertible fact that presbyters were called 'overseers' during the first century but not afterwards.

It has to be considered whether such indications as are to be found in earlier writings tend to support Theodore's explanation, or not. This has to be set against the well-known theory that the order of bishops was evolved from the presbyterate through the aggrandizement everywhere of a senior or presiding presbyter into a higher ministry. That theory will be separately discussed later.

The letters of St Ignatius must be an important source in which to seek for anything that may throw light on the matter, for the supposed evolution of presiding presbyters, if it took place at all, must have taken place not many years before they were written. It is noticeable that in more than one letter he uses language reminiscent of St Paul's 'not meet to be called an apostle'; he even applies to himself St Paul's own word *ektroma*, one born out of due time.[1] Thus to the Roman Church he says: 'I do not enjoin you, as Peter and Paul did. They were apostles, I am a convict; they were free but I am a slave to this very hour.'[2] If his true position were no more than that of a presiding presbyter, if he had not been one of

[1] *Romans* 9 (cp. I Cor. xv. 8–9), as to which Lightfoot comments, 'Ignatius, like St Paul, we must suppose, had been suddenly brought to a knowledge of the Gospel'. (*Ignatius*, II. p. 230.)
[2] *Romans* 4. Cp. *Trallians* 3.

the apostolic successors, all this would be false humility, or meaning-less at the best.

In the letter to the *Magnesians*, St Ignatius remarks that 'it becometh you also not to presume upon the youth of your bishop'—Bishop Damas—and notes with approval 'that the holy presbyters have not taken advantage of his outwardly youthful estate'.[1] One is reminded by this of St Paul's counsel to Timothy, 'Let no man despise thy youth'.[2] Damas, at all events, can hardly have reached the episcopal order as a senior presbyter who had gradually absorbed authority, in the manner required by the theory referred to. He may, and Timothy may, have earlier been an ordinary presbyter, but, if so, there must in either case have been a definite promotion or transition to a distinct and higher ministry. St Polycarp too, bishop of Smyrna, was aged eighty-six at his martyrdom in A.D. 155, and not a senior in years in the time of St Ignatius. He was appointed by St John.[3]

There is an incidental reference to bishops who are settled or localized 'in the farthest parts of the earth'[4] by which expression Ignatius would be understood to contemplate regions as distant as Gaul on the one hand and Mesopotamia on the other.[5] This remark implies that the threefold 'episcopal' ministry, established in opera-tion in all the Churches of Asia Minor, was not peculiar to that part of the world but was in established operation generally throughout the known world, or at least that Ignatius believed it to be. This may have been true, although there must certainly have been regions and cities still without bishops of their own. The distribution of bishops and dioceses has never been systematic;[6] gaps and anomalies persist to the present day. It seems likely that, up to the time St Ignatius was writing, Philippi had no bishop of its own, because St Polycarp, bishop of Smyrna, in writing to the Philippians shortly after St Ignatius had gone on to Rome, refers to their presbyters and deacons[7] but makes no mention of a bishop. It is possible, though less likely, that there was a temporary vacancy. Neither alternative much supports the theory referred to.

Such slight indications as are to be found in the letters of Ignatius harmonize with what Theodore of Mopsuestia says, and do not fit in with the other theory. Theodore's account itself is entitled to

---

[1] *Magnesians* 3.   [2] I Tim. iv. 12.   [3] Lightfoot, *Ignatius*, II. p. 441.
[4] *Ephesians* 3.   [5] Lightfoot, *op. cit.* p. 40 n.
[6] *Vide supra*, chapter X, section III.
[7] Epistle of Polycarp to the *Philippians* 3.

some weight. He had no axe to grind; the subject was entirely uncontroversial. In the then united Church there was no doubt or dispute to which his information bore any relation. He seems to have felt that his antiquarian notes might be of less interest to others than to himself, for he concludes with a slightly diffident justification of his pause to explain 'the custom of the old days and the cause of its change', which Dr Swete, in editing the text, describes as 'a sort of apology for the foregoing archaeological excursus'.[1] It is not impossible too that there may have survived in Cilicia, down to Theodore's time, authentic traditions of the early Church which were not remembered, or not recorded, elsewhere.

VI

The literature of the tunnel period, then, has yielded several valuable pieces of information.

1.   The presbyters had always been appointed either by *ellogimoi* apostles, or else by 'other *ellogimoi*'. At the end of the first century this was a commonplace fact that needed only to be referred to.

2.   At that time, presbyters, in the West at all events, were still described as bishops; the '*ellogimoi*' were not.

3.   No apostle, 'evangelist', '*ellogimos*', or minister of 'universal jurisdiction', by whatever name described, was then as yet settled in Corinth, or probably in Philippi.

4.   Very early in the second century, one such minister was settled in office in each of the Churches in Asia Minor and, according to St Ignatius, who was such a one himself, in Churches 'in the farthest parts' of the Old World.

5.   This minister, at all events in the East, was now called 'the bishop'.

6.   After the first century, it does not appear that presbyters were any longer described as bishops anywhere.

VII

Concerning Church order, little more can be gleaned from the other literature of the period, although there is a good deal of it. This is hardly to be wondered at. Even to-day, when 'our unhappy divisions' have brought the subject of Church order into frequent

---

[1] H. B. Swete, *op. cit.* II. p. 125 n.

discussion, nine out of ten of the many religious books published contain no reference to it, so that a historian in some distant future would find it difficult to reconstruct from them the Church order (or disorder) of the twentieth century.

Thus the so-called Epistle of *Barnabas* and the Epistle *to Diognetus* are purely religious treatises, although both are directed against tendencies to Judaizing; their authorship is uncertain; the first may have been written as early as A.D. 70 to 80, the latter *c.* A.D. 140, about the same time as the *Expositions of the Oracles of the Lord* of Papias, which have been mentioned before.[1] Papias tells, on the authority of John the Elder, a disciple of the Lord, that Mark, who had not heard the Lord or followed Him, wrote down everything related from time to time by Peter. The Epistle of Polycarp to the *Philippians,* *c.* A.D. 110, has also been mentioned. Justin Martyr[2] addressed his great *Apology* to the Emperor Antoninus Pius at Rome in A.D. 148. His *Dialogue with Trypho* was written later. The first of these was a noble defence of Christianity, at a time when to be a Christian was to court execution as an 'atheist' and a participant in secret and abominable crimes. It contains an account of Christian worship and sacraments in simple informal words, such as 'the washing of him who has professed and given his assent'. In his account of the weekly Sunday Eucharist, 'there is one prominent figure, a person whom Justin, writing for heathen, and all through avoiding the use of ecclesiastical terms, calls the president'.[3] This 'president' is presumably the bishop, as Harnack considers, who counts this mention among the earliest evidences for the 'monarchical episcopate'.[4]

There are two other early documents which have greatly occupied the attention of scholars and have given rise to speculations that may never be finally settled: these are the *Didache* or 'Teaching of the Twelve Apostles', and the *Shepherd* of Hermas.

The value of the *Didache* as an index to early Church ways is weakened by uncertainty as to its date and source. We have noticed

---

[1] P. 75.   [2] See p. 75.

[3] G. Salmon on 'The Christian Ministry' in *Expositor*, June 1887, VI. p. 18. A translation of the *Apology* may be found in the *Ante-Nicene Christian Library*, vol. II, or the *Library of the Fathers*, ed. by D. Stone, vol. XL. Extracts are given by B. J. Kidd, *Documents Illustrative of the History of the Church*, I. pp. 73 f.

[4] A. Harnack, 'On the Origin of the Christian Ministry' in the *Expositor*, May 1887, vol. V, at p. 336. Cp. R. H. Story, p. 23; who supposes the 'president' to be a 'presiding elder'.

already that the genuine letters of St Ignatius were buried under a quantity of spurious matter, written in later centuries and palmed off as his; it needed the industry of great scholars to disinter the genuine letters. There is also a mass of writings, many of them frankly absurd, that were foisted in the name of St Clement of Rome and are known as the *Clementines*. Fortunately his one authentic letter has always stood shoulder-high above this trash. To religious writers in the early centuries this kind of thing did not seem dishonest as it does to us.

From the second to the fourth centuries there appeared a series of 'Church Orders', which were more or less systematic manuals of liturgies and Church customs. Some of them purport to give verbatim speeches of the Twelve Apostles sitting in conclave. They are found in numerous revisions and editions, in Greek, Syriac, Coptic, Ethiopic, etc., and they reproduce each other in whole or part. In 1883 a manuscript entitled the *Didache* or Teaching or Doctrine of the Twelve Apostles was found at Constantinople. The scribe had dated it 1056, and no other copy exists. It was at once recognized as an early nucleus of what is found in a number of these Church orders, and it has supplied scholars ever since with a baffling problem. Their conjectural dates for it range from A.D. 50 to the end of the fourth century.*[1] 'Every one went to the Didache determined to find his pet theories proved by it. Above all it supported those who were in favour of prophets and "charismatic" control of the Church. Hence its great popularity at the time when it was found.'[2]

It begins with a tract of 'the Two Ways', one of life, the other of death. This was probably Jewish in origin; its moral instruction for catechumens about to be baptized is of an intensely Jewish character. Then follow regulations or precepts concerning Baptism, fasting, the Agape and the Eucharist, some prayers for which are given. The next paragraphs relate to the ministry, which appears to be either itinerant and general, or else local and resident. Ministers of the first kind are referred to as apostles, prophets, or teachers, apparently without distinction. The local ministers are 'bishops and deacons', as in Philippians i. 1; they are mentioned in close sequence to directions for the weekly Lord's Day Eucharist: 'elect *therefore* for yourselves bishops and deacons worthy of the Lord...for they also minister unto you the ministry of the prophets and teachers'.

---

[1] Note B. *Conjectural date of the* Didache (p. 136).
[2] Vokes, *The Riddle of the Didache*, p. 220.

The apostles and prophets or teachers are to be received with honour, and counsel is given against the false prophet who seeks for money.

Prophecy, it is true, continued to have a recognized place in Church life long after apostolic times, indeed until it became discredited by the Montanist schismatics at the end of the second century. Yet its place in the *Didache* is suggestive of a very early date; so also is the coupling of 'bishops and deacons'. Dr J. Armitage Robinson deemed the *Didache* to be 'an imaginative picture of the primitive Church' written at a date not earlier than between 140 and 160 A.D.,[1] and a recent analysis adjudges it to be the work of a Montanist towards the end of the second century 'trying to express his Churchmanship in as apostolic language as possible'.[2] The more general verdict, however, assigns a date *c.* A.D. 100, or little later, but holds that 'the work describes, not the conditions in the Church at large, but only those in a remote and backward district, where an imperfect Christianity was taught'.[3]

An interesting passage says that 'every true prophet, who is minded to settle among you, is worthy of his maintenance. . . . Thou shalt take therefore all first fruits. . .and give them to the prophets; for they are your high priests.'[4] This is suggestive of the transition period in the chief pastorate from itinerancy and general oversight to residence and local 'jurisdiction'. Although this transition must have taken place in Asia Minor by about A.D. 100, it may well have come about considerably later in places, such perhaps as some out-of-the-way part of Syria, which has been thought a likely place of origin of the *Didache*.[5]

It was largely from the *Didache* that Dr Harnack deduced the 'charismatic' theory of the early ministry. This word was coined by German theologians from the Greek *charisma*, a gift. According to the theory, which attracted many adherents, there was a general or universal ministry of apostles, prophets, and teachers which was charismatic. Their office was a direct gift of God, not mediated in any way by men, self-evident, and unchallengeable. The local ministry of presbyters or bishops and deacons, on the other hand, was non-charismatic. As gifts died out, only the local ministry remained. But St Paul uses *charisma* for every manifestation of grace in all members of the Church, such as liberal giving, and the showing

---

[1] Armitage Robinson, *Barnabas, Hermes and the Didache*, pp. 44, 45.
[2] Vokes, *op. cit.* p. 209.   [3] Maclean, p. viii.   [4] *Didache*, XIII. 1, 3.
[5] Maclean, p. xxxvii; Gore and Turner, p. 377; Vokes, *op. cit.* p. 217.

of mercy; his teaching does not support the idea that local presbyters or bishops and deacons did not, equally with the itinerant ministry of universal jurisdiction, need the *charisma* of ministry (*diakonia*) which he includes in his list of spiritual gifts.[1] Harnack's theory has been forcibly countered by Dr Armitage Robinson and others, although 'if what is meant is merely that prophets were not appointed by any human instrumentality, whereas bishops and deacons were, that has always been recognized'.[2]

The *Shepherd* of Hermas presents another puzzle, but one that lies within narrower limits. It is the earliest Christian allegory, and it was written in Rome either at the end of the first century or about fifty years later. It consists of three books of visions, in some of which there appears to Hermas an Aged Lady, who personifies the Church. She is aged 'because she was created first of all things. Therefore she is old, and for her sake the world was framed.'[3] In others, there is a man dressed as a shepherd, from whom the work is named. It is full of moral earnestness and simple fervour. There are also bands of young men, old men, some other shepherds, and troops of virgins who 'are the holy spirits, for no man can enter the kingdom of God except these clothe him with their garment'.[4] The visionary personages instruct Hermas at great length on many subjects of morals and conduct. The *Shepherd* was treasured reverently as the teaching of a seer; it was read in church almost as Scripture, and it was used for the instruction of catechumens.

In recent times it has been minutely searched for any clues to contemporary arrangements in the Church. Thus in the course of long sections describing the building of a tower by six young men, who are angels, with various kinds of stones, the Aged Lady, who is the Church and is also the tower, tells Hermas that 'the square white stones...are the apostles and bishops and teachers and deacons who walked in godly gravity, and ministered purely and gravely as bishops and teachers and deacons to the elect of God; of whom some are fallen asleep and some yet are'.[5] Thirty-five stones personify 'the prophets and ministers (or deacons) of the Lord', another forty 'the apostles and teachers of the preaching of the Son of God',[6] who at another place are distinguished.[7] The 'presbyters who preside over the Church'[8] seem to be the same as 'the occupants of the

[1] Rom. xii. 6–8. [2] *Essays on Early Hist.* p. 79. [3] Vis. II. 4. 1. [4] Sim. IX. 13.
[5] Vis. III. 5. 1. [6] Sim. IX. 15. [7] Sim. IX. 16. 5. [8] Vis. II. 4. 3.

chief seat', who in one reference are distinguished from 'the rulers
of the Church'.[1] One of the marks of a false prophet is that he
desires a chief seat.[2] It is nowhere indicated that Hermas himself
held any office of ministry.

Owing to the intensely visionary and symbolic character of this
'quaint' work, as Dr Lindsay calls it,[3] it contributes very little to
our knowledge of the actual ministerial arrangements of its time.
At one point the Aged Lady instructs Hermas to write her words
in two little books and send one to Clement who 'shall send to the
cities which are without, for that is his commission'.[4] It is generally
agreed that this is a reference to the famous St Clement of Rome,
but it may well be merely symbolic, because a bibliographical note
c. A.D. 200 says that Hermas wrote the *Shepherd* while 'his brother
Pius' was bishop of Rome, i.e. A.D. 140-55. It seems clear, at all
events, that the *Shepherd* in its own day was not felt to possess the
anti-episcopal flavour that some modern scholars have thought they
found in it.

[1] Vis. III. 9. 7.   [2] Mand. XI. 12.   [3] Lindsay, p. 176.   [4] Vis. II. 4. 3.

NOTES TO CHAPTER XVII

A. THEODORE OF MOPSUESTIA ON THE TRANSFERENCE OF THE NAME OF 'BISHOP'

From his Commentary on I Timothy, at iii. 8: 'Anyone who is not
familiar with the Holy Scriptures would think that blessed Paul had left
out presbyters. But that is not so; for what he has earlier said of the bishop
he is saying indeed of those who are now called presbyters, because
presbyters of old were called by both these names....

'How then is this? For it is not fitting to pass over the reason for the
exchange of names, and why the names are now distinctly separated, and
neither would the bishop be spoken of as presbyter nor would the presbyter ever receive the appellation of bishop so long as he is a presbyter.

'In the olden days, when converts were few in number, presbyters were
appointed everywhere, so named in point of dignity, as among the Jews
also those who led the people were spoken of as "presbyters": but were
also called bishops (overseers) because of their overseeing all and being
entrusted with the stewardship of all. For they then had complete
authority in church management, and everything depended upon their
judgement....

'Well then, those having the power of ordaining, who are now called
bishops, were not over one Church but were set over a whole region and
were called by the name of apostles. Thus the blessed Paul set Timothy

over the whole of Asia and Titus over Crete. And manifestly too he set others over other regions respectively, so that each, receiving the care of a whole region, should go round and visit all the churches, making appointments as needed for the ministration of the Church, solving their difficulties for them, correcting them with discourse of instruction, healing [i.e. absolving] the more serious of their sins, and in short doing all things fitting for a leading man to do, all the cities having their own presbyters, as I have said, who governed their own churches; so that those who are now called bishops, but were then called apostles, were over the region in exactly the same way as they are now over the city and district over which they received appointment. And at that time this was the arrangement in the Church.

'But after there was a great increase of religion and not only the cities but the country districts were full of believers, and the blessed apostles were dead, those who were preferred to the universal presidency after this were no longer like those former men nor could they have the same testimony from miracles, and perhaps in most things they seemed inferior to them. Deeming it therefore too much to have the title of apostles they divided out the names. They left the name of presbyter to the presbyters, but allotted the name of bishop to him who has the power of ordination, in that he has been entrusted with an universal jurisdiction.'

Theodore's word for ordaining ('the power of ordaining') is χειροτονεῖν, the primary or ordinary meaning of which is merely to appoint, but it came to be used equally with χειροθετεῖν in the technical sense of ordination, the imposition of hands being explicit. (See A. J. Maclean at p. 48 in *Episcopacy A. & M.*, also W. H. Frere at pp. 265, 266, and C. H. Turner at p. 177 in *Essays on Early Hist.*) That Theodore uses χειροτονεῖν in the specific sense appears from his comment on I Tim. iv. 14 (*given thee by prophecy, with the laying on of the hands of the presbytery*), viz. 'He speaks of the meeting of apostles who took part with him, as is likely, in making χειροτονία on him [Timothy], naming it "presbytery" out of honour. And this too is the custom now in the appointment of bishops, for such χειροτονίαι in the church to be fulfilled not by one but by many.'

Theodore has a shorter note on the transference of the name of bishop at Tit. i. 7. 'For while he said "appoint presbyters in every city", he added, referring to the presbyters, "for the bishop must be blameless as God's steward", because he had said that presbyters should be appointed in every city, to execute the stewardship of the Churches. For just on that account they committed whole provinces to those on whom they conferred the power of ordaining, who, travelling throughout the cities as bishops now travel through their districts, ordained those who were seen to be lacking in the ministry of the Church, and instructed them in what they ought to do; ordaining, and at the same time instituting individuals as they thought expedient. At that time those who were set over ordination were called "apostles" indeed out of respect; but they indeed considering it no light thing to be called by that name, preferred, in accordance with the custom that prevails now, to appropriate to themselves the designation of "bishops", because they deemed it greater than their deserts to be called by the name of apostles.'

B. CONJECTURAL DATE OF THE *DIDACHE*

Dr Sabatier, A.D. 50; Dr C. H. Turner, first century or at latest the earliest years of the second (Gore and Turner, p. 377); Dr A. J. Maclean, 'from internal evidence alone', would place it at the very beginning of the first century (Maclean, p. xxxvi); Dr G. Salmon, 120 or earlier; B. S. Easton, second quarter of first century (*The Apostolic Tradition of Hippolytus*, p. 9); Dr T. M. Lindsay, *c.* 135 (p. 383); Dr J. Armitage Robinson, 140–60 (*Barnabas, Hermas and the Didache*, p. 45); F. E. Vokes, *c.* 200 (*The Riddle of the Didache*, p. 210). The problem of date depends for its solution largely upon a scrutiny of the text for quotations from, or allusions to, Scripture and other early documents, and as to these there has been much disagreement. It seems certain at least that the true date must be earlier than a Church Order (the *Didascalia*) of about the middle of the third century.

CHAPTER XVIII. ST JEROME'S THEORY

I

THE Pastoral Epistles, and the other early evidence mentioned in the preceding chapters, portray an apostolic class or order of ministers, referred to indifferently as apostles, or evangelists, or merely as *ellogimoi*, superior to the presbyters or 'bishops' of the local ministry. If the earliest Fathers, and the understanding of the early Church, were not all wrong, it was members of that class or order who became settled individually as chief pastors of Churches. They were successors of the apostles, not of the presbyters from whom the name of 'bishop' was transferred to them.

The Church in the East has never departed from this belief, but historical views in the West have been much influenced by a theory sponsored by St Jerome. According to this theory, which rested on the fact that the primitive presbyters were often called bishops, the 'bishop' of the second century and after was originally only a presiding presbyter whose status had become inflated. St Jerome (A.D. 346–420) was an outstanding scholar of amazing industry who came to Rome as a presbyter in 382 and became secretary to Bishop Damasus. He was pointed out as a probable successor to the bishopric of Rome, but was passed over when Damasus died and Siricius was elected. He never became a bishop. In 385 he left Rome for ever and went East, settled in the Holy Land and lived a life of asceticism and laborious scholarship. The revision of the Latin Bible, the Vulgate, was the greatest of his many works. He was for ever in controversy, in which he was 'violent and acrimonious in a high degree'. His conception of the priesthood was lofty and sacerdotal, and he hotly contested the pretensions of the deacons in some places, particularly in Rome. By a rule peculiar to Rome[1] the number of deacons there was restricted to seven, although presbyters were numerous. Consequently they gained a false pre-eminence, so much so that a presbyter was ordained only on the recommendation of a deacon. In a famous letter,[2] St Jerome rebuked their presumption. 'Must not a mere server of tables and of widows be insane to set himself up arrogantly over men through whose prayers the body

---

[1] Sozomen, *Eccl. Hist.* book VII, cap. xix.   [2] Letter cxlvi, *Ad Evangelum*.

and blood of Christ are produced? Do you ask for proof of what I say? Listen to this passage.' He then cites four familiar texts[1] which show that presbyters were called 'bishops' in the New Testament, and three texts more by way of argument that St Peter and St John were presbyters.[2] 'Subsequently', he continues, 'one presbyter was chosen to preside over the rest, as a remedy against schism. For what function, excepting ordination, belongs to a bishop that does not also belong to a presbyter?' Dr Lowrie makes the following comment:

> St Jerome's theory has contributed more than any other factor to obscure the original conception of the episcopate. We must recognize that it was Jerome's intention to disparage the bishop. He was a disgruntled presbyter. He had also a grudge against the deacons; his letters reveal his pique at the social prestige which they enjoyed, and he believed that the superior power accorded to them in the ecclesiastical administration (especially at Rome) was a usurpation of the rights of the presbyters. He neatly killed two birds with one stone by an interpretation of a passage in St Paul's Epistle to Titus which pointed the deacons to a place below the presbyters and the bishop to a place but little above.[3]

The identity of bishops and presbyters in the language of the New Testament was not a peculiar discovery of St Jerome but was noticed by other fourth-century commentators, Ambrosiaster, Chrysostom, Pelagius and Theodore of Mopsuestia. It was the theories that St Jerome based upon it which were peculiar to him.

Elsewhere, St Jerome amplifies and varies his theories. Churches, he supposes, were governed by a council of presbyters until the devil stirred up religious faction and people began to say, 'I am of Paul, I of Apollos, but I of Cephas'. Then, 'it was decreed throughout the whole world that one should be elected from among the presbyters and placed over the others, and that all the responsibility for the Church should rest upon him.... Among the ancients, presbyters and bishops were the same, but gradually, that the weeds of dissension might be eradicated, all responsibility was devolved upon one.'[4] He seems to imagine that the change was effected by the decree of some Apostolic Council, following upon the disorders at Corinth of which St Paul wrote. This does not square with the fact that Corinth was still without a bishop of its own a generation later on, but St Jerome

---

[1] Phil. i. 1; Acts xx. 28; Tit. i. 5–7; I Tim. iv. 14.
[2] I Pet. v. 1, 2; II John 1; III John 1.
[3] W. Lowrie, *Problems of Church Unity*, p. 230.   [4] Commentary on Titus i.

was probably ignorant of that. At another time, he says that the apostles made presbyters and bishops for each province,[1] and when he is writing against Montanism, not against the deacons, he says, 'With us, again, the bishops occupy the place of the Apostles'.[2] His two guesses, either of a universal decree following the dissensions at Corinth which St Paul dealt with, or alternatively of a gradual devolution, are not very consistent. There is no historical evidence of either. It is clear that St Jerome founds his theories on the Scripture texts but, as Lightfoot says, 'Though well versed in works on Biblical exegesis, which was his specialty, he was otherwise extremely ignorant of early Christian literature'.[3] He had no personal acquaintance with the writings of Ignatius,[4] and probably had never read Clement's Epistle to the *Corinthians*.[5] Living three centuries after the times he wrote of, he was distinctly less well equipped to interpret them than are scholars of to-day. Yet his authority ruled supreme throughout Western Christendom.[6] His detraction of bishops fitted in well with their depression under the papacy, which was already in progress by his time. It had no effect on the Church in the East, but the Church of Rome, since Jerome's time, has been uncertain and confused as to the number of orders of ministry. Nevertheless it still remembers that 'Three orders are of Divine institution, the episcopate, the priesthood and the diaconate....The remaining orders are of ecclesiastical institution.'[7]

St Jerome certainly did not maintain that bishops and presbyters were identical in order at the time when he wrote, but rather that bishops were instituted by the apostles as their successors, and were not 'of the Lord's institution'.[8] 'Wherever there is a bishop, whether it be at Rome or Eugubium, at Alexandria or Zoan, his dignity is one and his priesthood is one....All alike are successors of the apostles.'[9] To St Jerome, this institution of bishops possessed divine authority as the act of the Church.*[10]

In support of his theories, St Jerome mentioned one supposed historical fact. At Alexandria, he says, down to the episcopate of Dionysius in the middle of the third century, 'the presbyters always

---

[1] Commentary on Matt. xxv. 26.
[2] Letter xli, *To Marcella*, 3.   [3] Lightfoot, *Ignatius*, I. p. 157.
[4] *Ibid.* pp. 156, 244.   [5] Lightfoot, *Clement*, I. pp. 370, 410.
[6] Lightfoot, *Ignatius*, I. p. 541.
[7] *The New Catholic Dictionary* (1909, with imprimatur), p. 707.
[8] Commentary on Titus i.   [9] Letter cxlvi, *Ad Evangelum*.
[10] Note A. *St Jerome and Aerius* (p. 146).

named one chosen from among themselves and placed in the higher grade; just as if an army should make a general or deacons should choose one of themselves whom they knew to be diligent and call him archdeacon'. This assertion was commonly accepted, as were also many of Jerome's statements that are known now to be erroneous. Subsequent research has shown it to be likely that this was a legend developed out of a kind of 'Nag's Head Fable', circulated by the opponents of St Athanasius about his consecration to the archbishopric of Alexandria.[1]

II

In 1868 fresh vigour was given to St Jerome's theory when Dr J. B. Lightfoot, bishop of Durham, advanced a somewhat similar hypothesis in his *Dissertation on the Christian Ministry* contained in his Commentary on *Philippians*.

If bishop was at first used as a synonym for presbyter and afterwards came to designate the highest officer under whom presbyters served, the episcopate, properly so called, would seem to have been developed from the subordinate office. In other words, the episcopate was formed not out of the Apostolic order by localization but out of the presbyterial by elevation: and the title, which originally was common to all, came at length to be appropriated to the chief among them.[2]

Dr Lightfoot certainly did not rest his opinion on the statements of St Jerome, in whom he put small reliance as 'not a writer to whom I should look for strict accuracy and frankness'.[3] Dr Lightfoot himself combined these qualities with immense scholarship and learning; it is possible, therefore, to analyse the grounds of his opinion and to judge of their sufficiency. It should first be noticed, however, that when the *Dissertation* was published, the passage quoted above was thought by many people to have undermined the arguments for episcopacy. Dr Lightfoot entirely denied this supposition; he was content to refute it by printing a selection of passages from the *Dissertation* and his other writings, among them the following:

Unless we have recourse to a sweeping condemnation of received documents, it seems vain to deny that early in the second century the

---

[1] For evidence regarding the Alexandrian ministry see Gore and Turner, pp. 115–30 and note B at pp. 315–20; also *Cambridge Medieval History*, I. pp. 159–61.
[2] Lightfoot, *Christian Ministry*, p. 196.
[3] Lightfoot, *Clement*, I. p. 410. In many instances Dr Lightfoot had to correct errors in St Jerome's statements; see the indexes to the five volumes of the *Apostolic Fathers*.

episcopal office was firmly and widely established. Thus during the last three decades of the first century, and consequently during the lifetime of the latest surviving Apostle, this change must have been brought about.

Its maturer forms are seen first in those regions where the latest surviving Apostles (more especially St John) fixed their abode, and at a time when its prevalence cannot be dissociated from their influence or sanction.

If the preceding investigation be substantially correct, the three-fold ministry can be traced to Apostolic direction; and short of an express statement, we can possess no better assurance of a divine appointment or at least a divine sanction.[1]

III

The concern of this book is not so much to establish any one particular historical theory as to urge the essential importance of the organic continuity of the Church. The particular theory of Dr Lightfoot, which closely resembles that of St Jerome, is far from denying an unbroken continuity; indeed it asserts it in tracing the historic and existing threefold ministry to an origin in apostolic direction, with the assurance of divine sanction. In point of historical truth, however, these theories are open to grave doubt. What has been said in the last two chapters need not be recapitulated but, without any derogation of the respect due to Bishop Lightfoot's lofty character and outstanding learning, several reasons can be assigned for doubting the soundness of his opinion as to 'elevation' rather than localization.

(1)   At the back of his mind seems to have been the thought that the office of a bishop is totally different from that of such a one as Timothy, or as one of the first apostles who 'held no local office', who was 'essentially, as his name denotes, a missionary, moving about from place to place, founding and confirming new brotherhoods'.[2] Occupying and adorning the historic see of a prince-bishop palatine, Bishop Lightfoot does not seem to recollect that, even in his own day, there were 'missionaries moving about from place to place' who were as truly bishops in order as he was himself. He thinks of an itinerant chief-pastorate and a resident chief-pastorate as two different orders of ministry. This preconception may have

---

[1] Lightfoot, *Christian Ministry*, pp. 201, 228, 267.
[2] Lightfoot, *op. cit.* p. 196. But a comparable change in the presbyters' sphere of work did not change their office or Order. *Vide supra*, p. 59.

drawn his attention away from the evidence that the bishops were successors of the apostles, not of the 'presbyter-bishops'.

(2)   The presbyters (or local overseers) of a church are thought of as a 'council or college', which, he assumes, 'necessarily supposes a presidency of some kind'. That is the germ of the supposed development.[1] But it is remarkable that Dr Lightfoot, from all his vast store of learning, could not find any evidence for an actual presidency of a presbyter among presbyters. It will be shown later that there is some evidence that points against it.

(3)   In support of the theory, he cites the supposed peculiar custom of Alexandria asserted by St Jerome. He relies on another piece of evidence which is demonstrably a misunderstanding. An old commentator remarked that 'In Egypt, the presbyters seal if the bishop be not present'. Dr Lightfoot took this to mean that in the fourth century the Egyptian presbyters could ordain. Even Homer nods. As has since been shown beyond doubt,[2] the meaning is that they 'sealed', i.e. 'confirmed', anointing at the same time with chrism blessed beforehand by the bishop.

(4)   There are some indications that throw doubt on the whole theory. (a) St Jerome's supposition that the change was effected by 'a decree throughout the whole world' is unsupported by any evidence and is probably now believed by no one. Had this taken place, a Church such as Philippi should not have been still without a bishop when St Polycarp wrote; according to the theory, they should simply have elected a presbyter to the chair. (b) The youthfulness of some early bishops, such as Damas of Magnesia, makes it unlikely that they were merely chairmen-presbyters. (c) If there had ever been chairmen-presbyters, some incidental reference to them might have been expected on one or two occasions, such as when St Paul summoned the presbyters of Ephesus to Miletus, or when he wrote to the Corinthian Church to reprove disorder. Again when St Clement wrote to the same Church a generation later regarding the presbyters and usurping officials, there is no hint that anyone had ever been 'in the chair'. (d) The development of the supposed chairmen-presbyters into a new order of ministry, with the resulting depression of all other presbyters, and their subjection to this new ministry, if it were general, could not have taken place in the short time that known Church history leaves available for

[1] Lightfoot, *Christian Ministry*, p. 207.
Gore and Turner, p. 119; F. E. Brightman in *Essays on Early Hist.* p. 393.

it.*[1] (e) It would have been a revolutionary change that could not have occurred everywhere without leaving some trace.*[2]

It is notoriously difficult to prove a negative, yet these indications go far towards disproving the theory that diocesan episcopacy or 'mon-episcopacy' grew out of the presbyterate by the exaltation of chairmen.

IV

'The development of the ministry was apparently determined by circumstances as they arose, and certainly exhibited variety. But it tended to a uniform pattern.'[3] There was, at all events, the important change from an itinerant to a resident chief-pastorate, which followed upon the colonization of the Old World by the Church. Notwithstanding the serious reasons for doubting St Jerome's theories, we should therefore look into the question of the continuity of the Church upon the assumption that the episcopate was really developed out of the presbyterate. On that assumption, should the episcopate be regarded as a permanent element, an integral feature, of the Church?

The Church is a living society. In early days, at all events, it was so united and homogeneous that it could decide and act unanimously. One example of this was the abandonment of the Sabbath and the substitution of the first day of the week, the Lord's Day, as the holy day of the Church. The New Testament supplies no record of it. The admission of infants to the sacrament of Baptism can also, perhaps, be supported most clearly as the deliberate course of action of a living and Spirit-filled Church. In the words of a distinguished Baptist divine:[4] 'The New Testament theory of baptism, and so far as the records go the practice also, assume faith in the recipient.' At the most, it could hardly be said that there is such clear warrant in the New Testament for the baptizing of infants as to justify its being adopted now if it had not early become the deliberate practice of the Church.[5] Apart from these particular instances in which authority is generally conceded to the unanimous voice of the Church, there are two important instances of wide and sweeping consequence.

---

[1] Note B. *Insufficient time for evolution of a new order* (p. 147).
[2] On the supposed depression of the presbyters, see Salmon, *supra* p. 79.
[3] Gore and Turner, App. p. 395.   [4] H. Martin, *Christian Reunion*, p. 118.
[5] 'The argument *a praxi ecclesiae* is the only, but a sufficient, ground for affirming the legitimacy and laudability of paedo-baptism'; N. P. Williams, *Ideas of the Fall and Original Sin*, p. 221.

For several generations, the canon of Scripture was unsettled. The four Gospels were 'canonized' before the end of the second century, but it was not until the 3rd Council of Carthage, A.D. 397, that the Canon as a whole was fixed. It was not until the Council of Nicaea in A.D. 325 that the Creed was agreed upon which has ever since been the standard of the Catholic Faith. Long before these settled developments, by A.D. 170 or 180 at the very latest, resident 'mon-episcopacy' was universal. Bishop Gore, not long before his death, wrote that

There was a period in the life of the Church which looks precarious.... As regards Order, the period was the shortest. Standardization had taken place by A.D. 180. As regards the Canon of the Apostolic books, the final determination did not take place till the fourth century. The same is true of the Creed. The very odd theology of Hermas or of Justin Martyr was let pass in the second century. The Church became more critical in the third century. It reached decisiveness in the fourth. In all three regions the process was similar. It might have been avoided, we may say, if our Lord had chosen, before He departed, to give the Church written books, to formulate a Creed, to give direction about the form of the ministry. He did none of these things. He left the Church to find its own way under the guidance of the Holy Spirit. He gave to it, or to its leaders the Apostles (as is described in the Gospels), authority, legislative and disciplinary, with a heavenly sanction attached; and we find them in the Acts and in St Paul's Epistles acting in the full consciousness of this authority, which appears to be unquestioned. This is sufficient evidence that it was really given them; but they reach their decisions incidentally, as occasion arose—at first expecting the immediate return of Christ and making no provision for a long future. We can find in the words and actions of apostles the just grounds for the claim later made (1) on behalf of the Nicene Creed, (2) on behalf of the unique and final authority assigned to the original Apostolic teaching (which is the basis on which the Canon rests), and (3) on behalf of the Episcopate; but the 'standardiza-tion' did not take place till from one hundred to three hundred years after Pentecost. All the three standardizations are deliberate, and are intended to be final. All have equal authority.[1]

This particular line of reasoning cannot be expected to weigh with all alike. The Seventh-day Adventist retains the Sabbath. Baptists find no scriptural warrant for infant Baptism, and hold to Baptism of Believers. Many who profess Christianity reject the Creed as an expression of their belief, and some hold themselves at liberty

[1] Gore and Turner, App. pp. 396, 397.

to set aside Scripture in the light of their private judgement. But, says Bishop Gore, 'you can take your choice. You can accept the finality of Canon, Creed, or Episcopate, or you can reject it in favour of fluidity both of Faith and Order.' Thus Professor E. C. Moore of Harvard, writing for the Protestant world, shows that the alternatives are clear, although for himself he accepts fluidity all round. You cannot accept the Canon of Scripture or the Creed as having authority and reject the Episcopate.[1]

Bishop Gore concludes, on the assumption that St Jerome's theory were accepted, '(1) that there was development, reaching what was intended to be finality, in all three departments of standardization, (2) that the authority of the whole Church in the fullest sense lies behind each of the three, so that (3) to reject one and accept the others is unreasonable, and to reject them all is to leave a Christianity without definite meaning, content, or structure'. At least it would leave no clear basis upon which a reunion of Christendom could be agreed. As Dr Hugh Martin has written concerning reunion, 'Much nonsense has been uttered by trying to set "spirit" and "organization" in opposition. A spirit without organization is like a soul without a body, and just as useful....A true unity of spirit would express itself in outer organization.'[2] Looking back to the early Church it can be seen that this unity of spirit existed and found expression. If the threefold ministry universally accepted was a development of the original endowment of the Church, an allocation of the stewardship among three classes of stewards, that development was, at all events, an actual expression of unity. Moreover the reunion of Christendom is inconceivable without a ministry accepted universally as the ministry of the Church, and, except for a ministry linked in equal authority with that of the early undivided Church, universal acceptance can hardly be imagined as possible.[3]

V

After surveying what can be known of the history of the obscure period, it is convenient to summarize its purport, and its bearing upon the central theme of this book, continuity. There are indica-

[1] E. C. Moore, *The New Testament in the Christian Church* (1904), Lectures VI and VIII.
[2] H. Martin, *op. cit.* pp. 51, 52.
[3] See the Resolution of the Faith and Order Conference, Edinburgh, 1937, quoted *infra*, p. 178.

tions, although they fall short of complete proof, that the chief pastorate of the bishop was continuous with that of the secondary apostles which preceded it. There are also indications strongly adverse to the theory that the bishop was merely an inflated chairman-presbyter. Early nomenclature was fluid, however, and the ministerial orders were probably undefined to begin with, at least in name. Thus it is more than likely that the apostles were not consciously establishing the order of deacons, or any 'order', when they ordained the Seven. Perhaps, too, they were not clearly conscious of doing so as they began to appoint more and more of the colleagues, who are described indifferently as fellow-workers, fellow-soldiers, apostles, apostles of Christ, evangelists, *ellogimoi*. It seems likely that the Church actually possessed its orders of ministry before they were clearly thought of as 'orders', or were so described; the fact existed before the name. In whatever stages the lineaments of the Church may have matured, the theme of this book does not stand or fall with any one historical theory. It is enough that there was no revolution or break in the life and order of the early Church, no dissension, no debate even, concerning that order. If the order of the Church and ministry in the second century was in any sense a development, it was unanimous and universal, it was a natural, unforced development comparable to the natural development of adolescence and maturity. Its main features were present, in outline at least, before the Church had lost the sense of direct control by the Spirit, and while it still had the guidance of primary apostles. It follows that any experimental reversion to fluidity, or to some particular system supposed to be still more primitive, even if it could be proved as correct antiquarianism, must be a reactionary break with continuity.

NOTES TO CHAPTER XVIII

A. St Jerome and Aerius

Aerius, an older contemporary of St Jerome, was regarded as an utter heretic, not only for Arianism and other heresies but also for asserting bishop and presbyter to be one order, arguing, as St Jerome did too, from the community of the names in scriptural use. Unlike St Jerome, however, he did not acknowledge that bishops had become a superior order by apostolic institution or custom as successors of the apostles.

B. Insufficient time for evolution of a new order

'Episcopal government is acknowledged to have been universally received in the church presently after the apostles' times. Between the apostles' times and this presently after there was not time enough for, nor possibility of, so great an alteration. And therefore there was no such alteration as is pretended.' (William Chillingworth (*ob.* 1644), *Works*, II. p. 490.)

Part Three

Continuity an essential of the Church
and its unity

—◦—

CHAPTER XIX.   THE PRINCIPLE OF SUCCESSION
IN THE CHURCH

I

THE NEW TESTAMENT, and the evidence of early documents, show how the organic life of the Church inevitably produced an actual succession in ministerial office, in progress almost from the first. On the other hand, it is long before any indication appears of consciousness of the fact, or of its importance. While the Second Coming and the end of all things were still momently expected, the future endurance of the Church in the world naturally received no thought.

So strong in the early days was the conviction of the nearness of the final cataclysm, that the first Christians would no more have cared than did the Irvingite community of the nineteenth century to proceed upon the assumption that the Church militant would outlast the last of the apostles: even the few cities of Israel would not all be evangelized before the Son of Man should return. Only when in fact the first Christian generation was passing away and the end had not come, could the idea grow up that a sequence of office-bearers was necessary to the Church to provide for the continued needs of the Christian Society. There could be no thought of succession, until it was clear that there would be vacant places to which to succeed.[1]

The distinction between the fact of succession, and the principles that underlie it, has been very clearly brought out by Dr Headlam:

As a matter of fact, all bishops in the Christian Church can trace back a succession to a period very shortly after the close of the Apostolic age, and there has been a succession by ordination from then to the present day; nor can there be any reasonable doubt that in some form the succes-

---

[1] C. H. Turner in *Essays on Early Hist.* pp. 108, 109.

sion goes back to the Apostles. The historical fact seems to me sufficiently well proved.[1]

By the end of the Apostolic period there was probably a fixed and universal custom of ordination performed by the Church through its properly appointed ministers....The Church always acts through its regular and duly constituted ministers....There never is wanting a regular ministry, and the Church never acts but through them.[2]

On the principles of succession, however, Dr Headlam takes the distinctive view that episcopal ordination is not 'necessary for valid Orders'; nevertheless it must be the rule of a re-united Church because 'it is necessary to secure Christian unity'.[3]

Whatever may be the value or doctrinal significance of this un-broken succession in the life of the Church with its chief pastors and other stewards, it is clearly an organic succession, although for the early period of its life, corresponding roughly to the first century, it was carried on with probably little or no thought of its significance to the Church of the future. We breathe regularly, many times a minute, yet we do so without paying attention to it unless something occurs to threaten or hinder the regular act of breathing; then indeed we recognize the want. Not until the end of the first century is there a hint of impediment to the regular course of what we now call succession in the Church. The rather disorderly Christians of Corinth had deposed their presbyters and had purported to appoint other office-bearers themselves. This at once, and as far as we know for the first time, brought the *principle* of succession into prominence; that is the whole underlying basis of St Clement's letter; he firmly grasps the principle—explicitly, of the succession of presbyters, im-plicitly, through the survival after the apostles' time of the apostolic function of ordination, of a succession of 'other *ellogimoi*' to apostles.

The fact of succession was never in doubt, so that references to it are casual and rare. Thus, at the beginning of the third century, Hegesippus, writing of the correction of error by the Holy Ghost, and after referring to the apostles who received Him first, says that 'We their successors, who share in the same grace and office of teaching, and are accounted guardians of the Church, do not keep silence but preach boldly'.[4] A generation later, similar language is used by an African bishop, Clarus: 'We have succeeded

---

[1] Headlam, preface, pp. xii, xiii.
[2] Headlam, pp. 85, 87. See also Carnegie Simpson, pp. 154, 156, 157.
[3] Headlam, p. 269.   [4] *Philosophumena*, I. preface.

to the apostles and govern the Church by the same authority as they',[1] and St Cyprian of Carthage says that Christ's words *He that heareth you heareth me*... were spoken 'to His apostles and through them to all His bishops who succeed His apostles by a vicarious ordination'; 'the catholic Church is one and cannot be divided, but is cemented together by the cement of her bishops closely and intimately adhering to each other'.[2]

None of the heresies or schisms that arose in the early centuries threw doubt on the succession or brought it into controversy. The Montanist schismatics followed the supposed prophet Montanus, and prophetesses after him, and they set up no hierarchy or ministry against that of the Catholic Church. The Novatian schismatics, and a little later the Donatist schismatics in Africa, adhered not only to the Catholic Faith but also to the Catholic ministry. Novatian, for example, had obtained episcopal consecration at the hands of three bishops. These schismatics, and some others, possessed an episcopal succession which, apart from the grave fact of schism, was as 'valid' as that of the main body of the Church. In the same way, much later on, the great Schism of East and West has left both Rome and the Churches of the East with a fully 'valid' episcopal succession.

II

It is only since the Reformation that the subject of succession in the Church has received much thought and has become a matter of debate. It is sometimes obscured by confused thinking, particularly in regard to various aspects to which the name of 'apostolic succession' has been attached. We ought to define our terms. As any dictionary will show, the word 'succession' may be used for a series of persons, or things, or events, that follow one another in time, whether or not they are in immediate sequence, or for the principle or quality that links them, as 'the right of succession', or for the process of succeeding, as 'quick succession'. These inflexions of meaning need not detain us, but we ought clearly to distinguish two main types of succession, viz. organic, and notional.

Organic succession implies the existence of some organism, such as a family, within which the members of the succession or series are organically linked. Thus there is succession in the inheritance of name or property by right of blood. This does not depend upon the

---

[1] Cyprian, Epistle lxxv.   [2] Epistle lxvi, *To Florentius*, 3, 6.

individual qualities or merits of the successive heirs, be they great or small. It does depend upon continuity of the organism.

Notional succession or series, on the contrary, depends upon the possession by each individual member in the series of some particular quality or attribute that is chosen as the connective notion. Philosophers may be regarded as a series from Plato and Aristotle onwards; so may all poets be thought of, or all smiths from Tubal Cain until now. Such a notional succession may be set out in chronological order without being continuous; its individual members may be picked out here and there from the history of centuries. It is independent of any organism. Organic and notional succession are perfectly distinct types even when they are brought into combination. A notional succession may be picked out of the members of an organic succession; for example, a notional succession of politicians or of soldiers might be picked out of the organic succession of a particular family.

'Apostolic succession', in any legitimate sense, is of the organic type. The visible Church in the world is an organism, something greater than any organization, a Body of divine establishment, not a man-made association. Its baptized laity, as well as its clergy, are all members of the apostolic succession rightly understood, just as all the particles of a physical body are in the physical succession of its being. Also its chief pastors are, and always have been, organically part of the Body, just as hands and lips are part of a physical body; their mortal wastage is continually renewed by organic replacement from within the Body, just as the specialized members of a physical body are always being organically renewed.

What has been called 'doctrinal succession' is of the notional type, and will be referred to in the next chapter.

III

In the second century there came into prominence a particular aspect of succession which only indirectly involved ministerial succession in the broader sense that has since been called 'apostolic succession'. This was a consequence of the Gnostic heresy. (This heresy, a development of the Docetism against which St John and St Ignatius both wrote so strongly, taught that the taint of evil in the material world is not accidental but essential and that, if the Supreme God is good, He cannot also be the Creator. The human body, being formed of matter, must therefore be evil; the Son of God, manifested as man, could not be so in reality but only in appearance. There could be no true Incarnation, and no true redemption or resurrection of the body.) Gnosticism was widespread, and had affected many Christians who shared in the general 'apostolic succession'; the heresiarch Marcion was the son of a bishop and was probably in episcopal orders himself. Gnosticism claimed to have been handed down as a secret esoteric tradition from the apostles, but it did not capture the chief sees of the Church, those that could claim the earliest foundation by apostles; they were citadels of the Catholic Faith, which could be shown to have been taught by bishop after bishop, reaching back to the founding of each Church. As Dr Headlam says:

> The importance of this succession of bishops was made apparent in the controversy with the Gnostic heretics which was one of the most striking features of the second century. The Gnostics claimed to teach a more profound Christian doctrine, and asserted that they had received it by a secret tradition from the Apostles. To meet this claim Irenaeus and other theologians appealed to the open tradition of the great churches. It was no secret, unknown succession of obscure teachers that had handed on the true Apostolic tradition, but the open succession of well-known bishops. In Rome, in Asia, at Antioch, at Jerusalem, as in other cities, there were churches founded by apostles, and in these there had been since their days a continuous succession of bishops, publicly appointed to their office. These had handed on the true tradition of Christianity, its Scriptures, its faith, its rules of life, and its Church order. Bishop had succeeded bishop. Each had followed the doctrine of his predecessor. This open tradition was a strong testimony to the truth of their teaching.[1]

Shortly after the middle of the second century, Hegesippus from Palestine and St Irenaeus in Gaul were writing against the Gnostics, and both took their stand on the open tradition of faith that had been kept inviolate by the successive bishops of the great sees. Hegesippus had visited Rome while Anicetus was bishop c. A.D. 160, and he 'made a succession', i.e. made a list of its bishops down to Anicetus. *Against Heresies*, the great work of St Irenaeus, is preserved only in a Latin translation. To Irenaeus, Christianity is not a doctrine only but a living institution, a catholic and universal Church in which the essential principle is the 'apostolic succession'.

[1] Headlam, p. 125.

The true Gnosis is the teaching of the apostles, and the ancient system of the Church throughout the world, and the character of the Body of Christ according to the successions of bishops to whom they [the apostles] transmitted the Church in each place.[1]

，In the Church God set first apostles, secondly prophets, thirdly teachers. Therefore where the gifts of God are placed, there should one learn the truth, with those among whom is the succession of the Church from the apostles.[2]

St Irenaeus speaks of the 'succession of the episcopate',[3] but his whole argument is directed towards distinguishing the heresies of the Gnostics from the true Faith maintained in the apostolic sees.

We can enumerate those who were instituted by the apostles as bishops in the Churches, and their successors to our own day, who neither recognized nor taught anything like the ravings of these [Gnostics].

If the apostles had known any esoteric mysteries—

they would assuredly have handed them on to those men to whom they committed the very Churches themselves, for they desired them to be perfect and irreproachable in all things whom they left as successors, handing on their own place of authority.[4]

A well-known passage follows where he says it would be too lengthy to enumerate the successions of all the Churches, so he gives 'the succession of bishops in the Church of Rome, greatest, oldest, and known to all, founded by two most glorious apostles Peter and Paul...they entrusted the office of bishop to Linus...Anencletus followed him. After him, in the third place after the apostles, Clement was appointed bishop'; and so on to nine others ending with 'Eleutherus, the twelfth from the apostles, now occupies the see'.[5] He refers more briefly to the Church at Smyrna, the Churches throughout Asia, and the Church in Ephesus, as tracing their ministry from the apostles in the same way, and bearing witness to the same true Faith.

Professor Turner, Dr Headlam and others have pointed out that St Irenaeus and the other Catholic theologians of the second century were taking their stand upon succession in the teaching chairs of particular sees, not directly upon the succession of ordainers and ordained. It was too obvious to need mention that there could not

[1] Irenaeus, *Adv. Haereses*, IV. xxxiii. 8.　[2] *Ibid.* IV. xxvi. 5.
[3] *Ibid.* IV. xxvi. 2.　[4] *Ibid.* III. iii. 1.
[5] *Ibid.* III. iii. 1, 2, 3 (i.e., *c.* A.D. 175–90).

be succession of a *bishop* to a see without his 'succession' at the hands of ordaining bishops; although in the course of nature these could not include his predecessor in the same see.

'To belong to the succession, a bishop had first to be lawfully chosen by a particular community to occupy the vacant *cathedra* of its church, and secondly to be lawfully entrusted with the *charisma* of the episcopate by the ministry of those already recognized as possessing it.'[1] The more general aspect of succession is implied, rather than asserted, in the language used. It did not enter directly into the argument against the heretics, many of whom could claim to participate in the ministerial succession.

Dr Headlam presses this distinction so far as to say that the argument 'implies no more than a succession of rulers, each lawfully appointed to his office, or a succession of teachers in a school. It does not imply any succession by ordination.... If the manner of appointment to office had been without any religious ceremony the succession for this purpose would have been equally valid';[2] but it is difficult to reconcile this with what he says elsewhere, as quoted already.[3] St Irenaeus, who speaks of 'the sure *charisma* of truth received with the episcopal succession',[4] would have been astonished to be told he had implied that an unordained man could be an 'equally valid' successor in a see.

It will be perceived that the episcopal succession on which the orthodox theologians of the second century took their stand in the struggle against heresy was fundamentally organic in nature. The general organic succession in the apostolic *charisma* of ministry was implicit in it, although their particular argument rested on succession in the chairs of the greater Churches founded by the apostles.

IV

The Reformation brought about an entirely new situation. The Reformers retained the Trinitarian faith of the Nicene Creed, but in many places they abandoned and even deliberately repudiated all organic continuity with the unreformed Church. As to this Lutherans were merely indifferent, but Calvinists were so much set upon severing connexion that priests were compelled to repudiate their

---

[1] C. H. Turner in *Essays on Early Hist.* p. 107. [2] Headlam, p. 126.
[3] *Vide supra*, pp. 148, 149, 154. [4] *Adv. Haereses*, IV. xxvi. 2.

orders as a condition of admittance to the Reformed ministry. A novel theory of an invisible Church in the world, which Ulrich Zwingli seems to have been the first to expound, provided some logical justification for this; if the Church is invisible, no visible organism, however venerable, can be essential to it. Another theory of an invisible 'doctrinal succession'[1] was developed as a changeling for the old organic succession.

During the four centuries since the Reformation 'apostolic succession' has sometimes been misrepresented. Mistaken metaphors have encouraged a false conception of its nature. Thus the bishops have been compared to 'conduit-pipes', leading the fountain of orders from the apostles to their latest successors,[2] or to 'a golden chain, stretching link by link between our modern bishops and the apostles'.[3] Metaphors of this kind do not accord well with the scriptural teaching of the Church as the Body. 'Succession' in the specialized members of a physical body cannot be compartmented or isolated from the organic life of the body as a whole. The man's hand is not the successor of his infant hand only, but of his whole frame. We ought to think and speak of the apostolic succession of the Church, rather than of its bishops alone, however necessary they may be to the Church in the fullness of its life, however indispensable also as the due organs by which the Church accomplishes the continuity of its organic life.

Although the Novatian and Donatist schisms did not bring the subject of succession in the Church directly into discussion, they did raise, and raise fiercely, a question that throws some light upon the principles involved. Could the sacraments, even if administered by a duly ordained bishop or priest, be regarded as valid when they were administered in schism? The validity of Holy Baptism by schismatics was the most pressing problem, but that of ordination was equally involved. In the Baptismal Controversy, as it is called, St Cyprian, bishop of Carthage, and Stephen, bishop of Rome, took the lead on opposite sides, the former insisting that reconciled schismatics must be baptized anew—admittedly there could be no 'rebaptism'. Underlying the thought of the Cyprianic school there can be seen an instinctive realization that the administration of a sacrament is no individual act of the minister, but an administrative

---

[1] Vide infra, chapter XX, section IV.
[2] Francis Mason, Vindication of the Church of England, 1613 (ed. 1728), p. 165.
[3] L. Pullan, History of the Book of Common Prayer, p. 255.

act of the one Church as the vehicle of the Holy Spirit, in which the minister is only the appointed instrument or organ of the Church.

Ultimately, the Roman view came to be accepted throughout the whole Church, that sacraments duly administered by the duly appointed minister, even in schism, are not to be repeated (although a benedictory imposition of hands was given to reconciled schismatics). The formal doctrine of the Roman Church, that it is the whole Church, and that those out of communion with it are outside the Church, has to be reconciled somehow with its recognition of the sacraments of those whom it reckons as schismatics. It certainly leaves room for a somewhat mechanical conception of the sacraments, as if an inherent power resided in the minister in complete detachment from the Church, but reasons have been given earlier[1] for thinking that the formal doctrine of exclusion from the Church is not held consistently, and that, in spite of it, the Church is tacitly recognized as persisting even in a state of division. This agrees with what has been said already in chapter VIII, that the Body of the Church can persist, and has persisted, in division. Although it be impaired and weakened, a recognizable continuity of 'succession' may persist between the Body as it was undivided, and as it is in division.

[1] *Vide supra*, Note A on p. 49.

CHAPTER XX. SOME DISCONTINUITIES

I

FEW if any Christians would disclaim all continuity with the one Church of the New Testament, or would doubt that there must be an essential continuity of some kind from Pentecost until now. There are very many, however, who would deny the need for the organic continuity that has been under consideration here. They are to be found in many denominations ('Churches' in the non-scriptural and modern sense), which do not retain organic continuity with the Church of Pentecost, and most of which lay no claim to it and set no value on it. Yet we not only admit, but firmly and gladly assert, that the grace of God is freely bestowed, and that the fruits of the Spirit often and manifestly appear, in the midst of these denominations. All this sharply raises the question whether there is any real need for the organic unity and continuity of which so much has already been said. That question must be fairly faced, but we should first of all see distinctly where continuity has failed, where, in fact, there has been a break in living continuity between the one Church of the New Testament and the denomination of to-day. That is essential for clearness, because the slight attention generally given to the matter has in some quarters allowed the fact of discontinuity to be forgotten and to remain unacknowledged.

The principle of the denominations which follow the tradition of Independency (represented in modern times chiefly by the Congregationalists and Baptists) is quite clear. Any number of believers, large or small, who choose to associate and combine for worship, create 'a Church' by doing so. This is what is called a 'gathered Church'. The one Church of the New Testament is regarded as a spiritual conception, invisible except in so far as individual believers and congregations or 'Churches' may be said to be visible. It never could have any visible organic existence; therefore it is idle to talk about organic continuity between the one invisible Church and the many visible aggregations or congregations which believers create for themselves and call Churches. Among Christians of this school of thought, there are many 'who look on the minister simply as one of the members of the Church—the talking or presiding member. They think anything else spoils him as a brother. They believe a

Church could go on without a minister, only not so well, with less decency and order.' Even among those Congregationalists who value and revere ministry as 'a prophetic and sacramental office', 'an ordinance of Christ rather than an institution', it is not looked on as part of the organism of the Church. 'The Apostles appointed no canonical successors. They could not....The Apostles could not send as they had been sent by Christ.' 'We hear much question raised whether our ministry is a *valid* ministry. It is absurd. God alone can really know whether a ministry is valid.'[1]

This conception of the Church, failing as it does to recognize the Church as a living organic society in the world, is not easy to reconcile either with scriptural teaching or with the actual life[*2] of the primitive Church. Moreover, in repudiating the visible organism as essential to the Church in the world it rejects the only medium of its visible unity.

The Lutheran wing of the Reformation had for its chief principle the doctrine of justification by faith. Luther had no distinct theory of the Church and he was indifferent, rather than hostile, to its ancient organism. He took upon himself to consecrate new 'bishops' when vacancies arose, as in Naumburg and Merseburg in 1542 and 1544. The Lutherans could easily have preserved continuity through the Prussian bishops who went over to them, if they had cared,[3] but except in Sweden[*4] the Lutheran Churches heedlessly broke away from the ancient organism of the universal Church.

II

The 'Reformed Churches', that is to say those Churches of Switzerland, France, Scotland, and the Netherlands, which followed the teaching of Calvin, have always affirmed in their confessional standards a doctrine that the Church is 'catholick, that is, universal, because it contains the elect of all ages, all realms, nations, and tongues'.[5] This mystical company of the elect of all time, present and future, in the body and out of the body, is of course invisible. The expression 'visible church' is a descriptive epithet for the temporary phenomena of the (invisible) Church perceptible in the world. 'Inasmuch as the faithful gather round the Word and the sacraments,

---

[1] Forsyth, pp. 123, 124, 129, 131.
[2] Note A.   *Apostolic Age without the Apostles* (p. 166).
[3] Ainslie, p. 207.   [4] Note B.   *The Church in Sweden* (p. 166
[5] The *Scots Confession* of 1560.

which are visible, and make a more or less creditable and visible profession of faith, this Church is also visible.'[1] The scriptural conceptions of the elect race, the holy nation, the household of God with its appointed stewardship, the divine Society in the world with its organic life continuously maintained, are hardly acknowledged. This mode of thought is associated with, and probably due in part to, the strange but general oblivion of the Reformers to the existence of the Church in the world in independence of Rome. They ignored the Churches of the Middle East and East. In their perspective, Rome seemed co-extensive with the organic Church. Rome was wholly corrupt. They must come out from her abominations, and be separate, and touch no unclean thing. Dr Ainslie has shown how deliberately and thoroughly the Calvinist Reformers cut off all organic continuity with the unreformed Church, and how consistently the Reformed Churches did so in each country.[2]

Episcopal ordination, of course, was abandoned; but this was from choice, not from necessity. Just as there were bishops in Prussia who joined the Lutherans, there were others both in France and Scotland who went over to the Reformers.[3] 'It was not, then, because they had no former Papal bishops within their borders to carry through ordinations for them that they had ordination by other agents, but because they rejected, or thought nothing of, the theories of ordination and "succession" held in the Papal Church.'[4] Dr Ainslie further shows clearly, what has hitherto been left obscure, that the Reformed Churches deliberately severed all organic continuity with the unreformed Church and its ministry, and repudiated anything of the nature of 'succession' from or through its former presbyters.*[5] The unreformed Church was no Church, but a synagogue of Satan; its ministers no ministers, its sacraments nullities. If a 'reformed priest' was accepted as a Reformed minister, his former orders counted for nothing; in some Churches he was even required to abjure them. The laying on of hands was at first abandoned as a matter of principle, and for long after its reintroduction was employed so casually as to exclude the idea of any essential principle being involved in its use. Actually there has been in the Reformed or Presbyterian Churches a continuous succession of teaching elders, pastors, or ministers (as they have been variously called) for some

[1] Moffatt, p. 97. [2] Ainslie, pp. 159–216.
[3] *Ibid.* p. 216. [4] *Ibid.* p. 217.
[5] Note C. *No presbyterial succession from unreformed presbyters* (p. 166).

three centuries and a half, but the great respect in which their ministry is justly held does not alter the fact that it dates only from the sixteenth century. 'Presbyterians', says Dr Moffatt, 'have allowed freely that *a ministry may originate* without formal ordination.'[1]

Half-way through the next century, among the English Presbyterians, a theory was developed of continuous succession through presbyters. On their premisses, the bishops through whom the ministry of ordination had been mediated for at least fourteen centuries were only presbyters in order. If so, 'episcopal succession' was no more than presbyterial succession under an alias, and presbyters were perfectly competent to carry it on under their own name. Assuming the truth of their premisses, this was almost irresistible. The astonishing thing was that the seventeenth century should have so far forgotten the actual facts of the sixteenth century, should have imagined the orders of the unreformed priests to have been imparted somehow or other to the Reformed ministers, whereas actually they had been regarded as a taint to be carefully eliminated. Dr Ainslie inclines to attribute the novel claim of succession to infection of ideas from the Church of England.[2] Be that as it may, the notion became firmly settled at that period. 'It was one of their commonplaces, that if a person presumed to minister without a valid Ordination, he was to be asked to work a miracle, and if he failed, he was to be rejected as an impostor.'[3] When Oliver Cromwell, lecturing Parliament in 1653, sneered at 'a ministry deriving itself from the Papacy, and pretending to that which is so much insisted on—succession',[4] he was referring sarcastically to the Presbyterian ministers of the day. They could have refuted the taunt conclusively if they had only referred to their sixteenth-century origins; after the deliberate care their ecclesiastical forefathers had taken to guard against any infection of continuity with the unreformed Church and its orders of ministry, Cromwell's jibe was an ironical injustice. Nevertheless the theory of a continuous presbyterial succession remained, and, in Scotland at all events, has been and still is maintained by a few distinguished Presbyterians. *Perpetua successio presbyterorum*, as the theory is called,[5] must be more difficult of acceptance since

---

[1] Moffatt, p. 118 (italics mine).   [2] Ainslie, p. 217.
[3] G. W. Sprott, *Worship and Offices of the Church of Scotland*, p. 193.
[4] Moffatt, p. 30; T. Carlyle, *Letters of Cromwell*, II. p. 353.
[5] The phrase was given currency by Lord Balfour of Burleigh, *An Historical Account of the Rise and Development of Presbyterianism in Scotland* (1911).

its baselessness has been exposed by Dr Ainslie, who for his part regards it as valueless and whose own strong convictions are wholly independent of it. Apart, however, from the careful exclusion of any *successio presbyterorum* in the Reformation period, there are two other difficulties in the way of the theory.

(1) It seems to depend upon the correctness of the hypothesis that the primitive presbyters were rightful ministers of ordination,[1] which in turn rests chiefly upon the familiar fact that in the first century they were often called overseers, 'bishops'.[2] The theory could hardly survive if that hypothesis, for which there is no positive proof, had to be abandoned.

(2) For some fourteen centuries, at all events, power to ordain was not—intentionally at least—conferred upon ministers ordained only to the office of presbyter. So far as the conscious authorization of the Church went, it is certain that presbyters, like deacons, received neither authority nor power to propagate their orders of ministry. To justify a belief that the presbyters of the unreformed Church of the sixteenth century had received power to ordain presbyters to succeed them, it seems necessary, therefore, to propound as doctrine that (*a*) their office carried with it, *sua natura* and by divine appointment, an intrinsic, inherent power to ordain others to it, so inseparable from the office, that (*b*) it was not in the power of the whole united Church to confer the office without (involuntarily) conferring that particular power; such a doctrine is difficult to establish on any scriptural foundation.

III

In Calvinist doctrine, the Reformation was a re-formation or re-construction, on what was regarded as the strict model of the New Testament; form and order therefore received considerable attention. The commissioning of each minister, considered individually, was, just as with the later Independents, a congregational matter.

[1] See *The Presbyterian Tradition*, C. L. Warr, p. 289: 'The historical continuity of the apostolic ministry was not impaired [by abandonment of the episcopal order]. There remained the priests, or presbyters, in whom, *historically*, reposed the essential ministry of Word and Sacrament and *the power and authority to transmit it*' (italics mine).

[2] The Presbyterian delegates at the Second World Conference on Faith and Order in 1937 presented a declaration 'that the conception of the ministry held by their Churches is founded on the identity of "bishops" and "presbyters" in the New Testament'.

A laying on of hands was unessential; in the infancy of the Reformed Churches there could in fact be no 'ordained' man to administer the rite. The Holy Orders of any former presbyter were a corruption to be sloughed off or, at the best, a nullity to be ignored. Yet it was always desired that other congregations or their ministers should in some way be associated with the election; there was from the first a feeling after an authority wider than that of the electing congregation alone. There could be no 'presbyteries' at the beginning, but in the course of a generation the Presbyterian system became settled in its high and serious orderliness. Since then 'ordination is the act of a presbytery'.[1] The problem of originating this continuity of ordained 'preaching elders', without any ordained elders to originate it, seems never to have been felt or even noticed. One reason of this, perhaps, is that a 'teacher or doctor', who has never been considered to need any ordination, was counted equivalent to a 'minister';[2] it was probably in this character that such leaders as Andrew Melville and Robert Bruce ministered without ordination. In the *First Book of Discipline* of the Scottish National Church, the provision 'concernying Ministeris and thair Lauchfull Electioun' is that 'It apperteneth to the Pepill, and to everie severall Congregatioun, to Elect thair Minister'. Admission 'must consist in consent of the pepill and Kirk quhairto thai salbe appointed, and in approbation of the learned Ministeris appointed for thair examinatioun'. Even in the *Westminster Form of Church Government* of 1644–5, it is declared ('Touching the Power of Ordination') that 'It is very requisite, that no single congregation, *that can conveniently associate*, do assume to itself all and sole power in ordination'. The necessary implication, that a single congregation has power of ordination when associates are not to be had, shows an unexpectedly close approach to Congregationalist principle. 'The calling and ordaining of a minister, like the election of a deacon or any other spiritual act, is within the competence of the local church, but it is the unbroken custom of Congregationalists to associate with the ordaining church the representatives of other churches.'[3]

It has been claimed that 'The people of the particular congregation which were electing one to be their minister...were virtually acting as *representative* of the Church as a whole',[4] but 'representative' is

[1] *Westminster Form of Church Government* ('Touching the Power of Ordination').
[2] *Ibid.* s.v. 'Teacher or Doctor'.   [3] Manning, p. 156; see also p. 183.
[4] Ainslie, p. 234.

another of the ambiguous words that are traps for incautious thinking. In the sense of 'typical', no doubt, individual believers or congregations may be representative, but not, surely, in the sense of holding a special delegation or authority to act on behalf of others. In the latter sense, 'the people of any particular congregation' are not representative of the Ekklesia. As a matter of organization, the careful and orderly Presbyterian constitution can invest any of its congregations with representative authority within the great Presbyterian communion; yet no ordinary individual, and no congregation, however *typically* representative, is an *authoritative* representative of the Church Universal.

Ordination to sacred office in the universal Church requires that appointment to the ministry must, in some way, carry with it the authority of the universal Church. In the infancy of the Church this offered no difficulty. At the very beginning, the Church and the ministry were identical, *and there were added unto them day by day those that were being saved.* The first ordination of under-stewards was administered by the chief stewards, the Twelve, at the declared will of *the whole multitude.* During the lifetime of the Twelve, no question of the universality of the ministry could arise, and for centuries it was never in question, although the Church had multiplied over all the old world so that never again could any ordaining possibly receive the assent of the whole multitude. There is no trace of any early controversy as to the principle of universality. So silent, indeed, is the early Church that principle must be looked for in its actual and consistent practice. Just as the first stewards, who appointed others to come after them, were organically part of the whole Church, so their successors are an organic part of the Church as a whole. Ordination by the authorized stewards and ministers of ordination is thus an act of the whole Body of the Church, just as speech is a function of the whole man, not only of the vocal organs. Those ministers of ordination are representative of the whole Church in an organic quality that would be impossible for them to receive by any mere organization, however world wide.

IV

As has recently been made very clear, the Reformed Churches in the sixteenth century had not the slightest intention to preserve a ministerial succession in continuity with the unreformed Church and its ministry and, indeed, the methods of admission to their ministry were designed to bar the door against the very idea. Early in the controversies of that time, and in rejoinder to the strictures of Roman Catholics, they developed a theory of a 'doctrinal succession' as an attestation and credential for the Reformed ministry, supposedly better than the despised and repudiated 'apostolic succession' of the unreformed. Dr Ainslie traces this idea of doctrinal succession as far back as Balnaves in 1543 and Beza in 1565.[1] It cannot be better explained than in his words:

There has been in the Church a succession of preachers and teachers of 'the most perfect doctrine of all', the Gospel. This is a very real succession for the Christian Ministry. It is a 'Doctrinal Succession',... produced by a series of men in the Ministry down through the ages, who have truly known in some measure the Christian Gospel and have proclaimed it. They are in the 'succession' simply by reason of being such preachers and teachers....Every generation of the Church has had its members of this 'Succession' or 'Series'....This Series might be called the Apostolic Succession of preachers.[2]

In the last chapter, organic succession was distinguished from notional succession. It is at once apparent that this doctrinal succession is of the latter kind. It contrasts sharply with that succession of Church and ministry before the Reformation which is organic and, as Dr Ainslie points out, would cease to be a succession if it ceased to be an organic continuity. 'On the other hand,' as he says, 'this Doctrinal Apostolic Succession described above, made up of a continuous [sic] series of receivers and preachers...can never be broken in such ways.'[3] That is plainly true. A notional continuity is not broken for want of an organic continuity that it never possessed; but it is misleading to call such a series 'continuous' unless in a purely notional sense. Dr Ainslie sees, of course, that 'there may have been gaps in this series caused by the difficulty of obtaining the true Word, when in some centuries it was not readily available in any purity'.[4] Gaps, whether of years or centuries, matter nothing to a series that is only notional, mental, artificial. Any preachers of the past whose doctrine fails to satisfy the compiler of the series 'automatically fall out of the Series or Succession without impairing it'.[5] This doctrinal succession of preachers is, by its own nature,

[1] Ainslie, pp. 219, 220. It may also be found in the *Orthodoxa Responsio* of the 'reformed Jesuit', Thomas Seton (1536–83), at pp. 29, 107.   [2] Ainslie, pp. 221, 222.
[3] *Ibid.* pp. 222, 223.   [4] *Ibid.* p. 222.   [5] *Ibid.* p. 223.

eclectic and arbitrary; its membership is as much beyond human ken as the invisible membership of the Church is in the Calvinist conception. Dr Ainslie's own comment, although made in another connexion, brings out the valuelessness of such a compilation, even if it could be made, to anyone but the compiler: 'By a "petitio principii" it will be affirmed that these "successions" must be the true apostolic successions because they hand down the true apostolic doctrine.'[1] No one will doubt the importance of adhering stead-fastly to 'the faith that was once for all delivered to the saints', but 'If it were attempted to insist on succession in doctrine as the sole condition of the essence of a Church,...that which would be thus perpetuated would not be a society at all, but a creed or body of tenets'.[2]

In the valuable recent study of the Reformed ministry here referred to, the central fact is emphasized that *preacherhood* 'is the constituting essential of the Reformed Ministerial Order',[3] as contrasted with *priesthood*. It 'was essentially an Order of Preachers'.[4] This is not a place to discuss any distorted conceptions of priesthood that may have prevailed; it need only be said that the Church at large recog-nizes a priestly element in its ministerial office. The whole Church is priestly, and just as the hand and the mouth particularly express the body of which they form part, so the ministers of the Church in some ways particularly express the priestly Body of which they are members.*[5] In the mind of the Calvinist Reformers, however, priest and priesthood had the exact significance that they had acquired in contemporary Rome, and no other meaning or value whatever. For them, priesthood connoted all the accretions of the Roman Pontifical, suggested the outwardness of Old Testament priest and sacrifice, or even crude paganism, to the exclusion of all the inner and spiritual meaning of sacrifice under the New Covenant.

So far as this vocation of 'preacherhood' can be regarded as an 'order', it is in the prophetic line, not the priestly, an order of prophets. 'There must always be something of the prophetic gift direct from God about the true preacherhood.'[6] Calvin's teaching embodies this principle,[7] and when the ministers or 'preaching elders' began to shake off the authority of the 'ruling elders' over

---

[1] Ainslie, p. 206.
[2] W. E. Gladstone, *Church Principles considered in their results*, p. 193.
[3] Ainslie, p. 241. [4] *Ibid.* p. 243.
[5] Note D. *Ministerial priesthood* (p. 168).
[6] Ainslie, p. 251. [7] *Inst.* IV. i. 5; Ainslie, p. 49.

them in the kirk sessions, we find them quite naturally claiming the status of prophets and citing Scripture in their support—'the spirit of the propheits is subject to the propheits'.[1] The actual style of 'prophet' was sometimes employed.[2]

Now it does not appear in Holy Scripture that any one becomes a prophet by any ecclesiastical appointment. A prophet needs no ordination. Indeed there can be no credentials for a prophet other than the measure of prophetic utterance divinely bestowed on him. Prophecy is its own credential. Dr Ainslie perceives and points out, with a novel clarity, that an order of preachers has no need whatever for any recognizable 'apostolic succession'. 'The validity of the Reformed Ministry has no need of such supports. They would be superfluous or irrelevant.'[3] Therefore he has no regret or misgiving in ruthlessly demolishing the theory of *perpetua successio presbyterorum*.

[1] Ainslie, p. 135, I Cor. xiv. 32.
[2] D. Calderwood, *History of the Kirk of Scotland*, IV. p. 513.
[3] Ainslie, p. 249.

NOTES TO CHAPTER XX

A. APOSTOLIC AGE WITHOUT THE APOSTLES

'Presbyterianism and Independency are both sixteenth-century anti-quarian reconstructions of the Apostolic Age without the Apostles. So far as we can see, no individual presbyter ever ruled a Church, nor did a college of presbyters function without oversight (episkopé) of either the larger Church, or later, a local bishop.' (W. K. Lowther Clarke in *Episcopacy A. & M.* p. 43.)

B. THE CHURCH IN SWEDEN

The reformation of the Church in Sweden was the most gradual of all the reformations, and it has retained its organic continuity with the universal Church. It ultimately adopted the Augsburg Confession and its doctrine is Lutheran, but the word 'Lutheran' has never formed part of its name, *Svenska Kyrkan*, the Swedish Church.

C. NO PRESBYTERIAL SUCCESSION FROM UNREFORMED PRESBYTERS

'A notable fact about the Reformed Churches of the Reformation time and the period following, was the wonderful agreement and uniformity amongst them.' (Ainslie, p. 255.) Calvin had written that the Popish priesthood is an impious profanation of the true ministry; the character of the priestly office must be eradicated and obliterated. (Ainslie, p. 210;

Calvin, *Letters*, III. p. 107.) The Reformed Church of the Netherlands required that any priest who desired to embrace the Reformed ministry must not only renounce Popery but also his own Orders. (Ainslie, p. 211.)

The standards of the Reformers in Scotland are set out in the *Confession* of 1560, which calls the Catholic Church in the West 'the pestilent synagoge of Sathan', and declares that 'thair ministeris ar no ministeris of Christ Jesus'. (Cap. XXII, *Of the Rycht Administratioun of the Sacramentis*.) The Assembly of December 1565 enacted that baptism 'administrat be ane papist preist sal be reiterat', treating it apparently as a nullity. (Ainslie, p. 245.) The *Confession* denies that 'Linealle discente' is one of 'the Notis by which the True Kirk is descearned from the fals...that horrible harlote the Kirke malignant'. (Cap. XVIII.) In a Latin translation of the *Confession*, lineal descent was rendered by *successio episcoporum*, whence it has been suggested that the Reformers did not mean to reject *successio presbyterorum* (a phrase then unheard of), but neither Dr Ainslie nor Dr Moffatt finds any substance in that suggestion. (Ainslie, p. 213; Moffatt, p. 31.) Thus in Scotland also, the orders of the unreformed presbyters were deemed worthless and null by the considered judgement and the system of the new National Church and by the 'reformed priests' themselves. (Ainslie, pp. 163, 214; Lord Balfour of Burleigh, *An Historical Account of the Rise and Development of Presbyterianism in Scotland*, p. 44.) Few of the reformed priests were ever admitted as Reformed ministers, and those who were so received had to undergo the same process of admission as any other men. (Ainslie, p. 214.) As a rule they were only allowed to be Readers, not ministers. (Ainslie, p. 174; Story, pp. 243, 251.)

In order to lock the door securely against any idea of continuity between the Reformed Churches and the unreformed 'Kirke malignant', or of any community of office that might be thought of as imparted to the Reformed ministers through the former priests ('no ministeris of Christ'), the laying on of hands was expressly excised from the form of their admission. It was discarded in the Genevan *Ordonnances* of 1541 (although Calvin gave it a guarded approval 'provided it be not superstitiously abused', *Inst.* IV. iii. 16, xix. 28, 29), and by the Reformed Churches of France and the Netherlands. (Ainslie, p. 166.) In Scotland, the *First Book of Discipline* of 1560 forbade it, 'for albeit the Apostollis used the impositioun of handis, yet seing the mirakle is ceassed, the using of the ceremonie we juge is nott necessarie'. This First Book was accepted by the General Assembly, although neither it nor the *Second Book of Discipline* was sanctioned by Parliament. (Story, p. 273.) 'It was issued as if with the "imprimatur" of the Church' (Ainslie, p. 171) and, significantly, it had been drawn up chiefly by 'reformed priests' and reflected the abjuring of their former orders as presbyters. It declared that 'The Papisticall Preastis have neather power nor authoritie to minister the Sacramentis of Christ Jesus'. Thus Knox repudiated his priest's orders

(Ainslie, p. 214) and protested that he ordained no one (*ibid*. p. 233). He believed that he had no title to preach the Gospel until he was admitted to the Reformed ministry by a 'vocatioun' or call (J. Cunningham, *Church History of Scotland*, vol. i, p. 293; Knox, *Works*, ed. D. Laing, vol. i, pp. 186–188). The modern theory of a *successio presbyterorum* through the unreformed priests to the Reformed ministers has no foundation of fact. The *Second Book of Discipline*, accepted in 1581, provided for the laying on of hands in ordination, which seems to have been used occasionally as early as 1572, and generally (though not at all invariably) after 1581. Andrew Melville was apparently never thus ordained. (Ainslie, p. 176.) As late as 1598, Robert Bruce, 'an honourable, very conscientious, and devoted man', only accepted imposition of hands under protest after eleven years of ministry. (T. McCrie, *Life of Melville*, 2nd ed. 1884, II. p. 451; D. Calderwood, *History of the Kirk of Scotland*, v. pp. 714, 715, 723.)

From the latter years of the sixteenth century, at all events, a regular succession of Presbyterian ministers has been maintained, although they have not always looked upon themselves as an *order* of ministry; thus James Melville said 'that distinctioun of yours betwixt the clergie and laicks, smelles of the pride of Papistrie' (Calderwood, *op. cit.* IV. p. 513), and George Gillespie the theologian called it 'popish and anti-Christian' to draw the distinction (*An Assertion of the Government of the Church of Scotland*, 1641; see G. D. Henderson, *The Scottish Ruling Elder*, p. 188). My pamphlet on *Presbytery and Apostolic Succession* at pp. 42–7 deals further with the subject of this note, and at pp. 31–9 considers whether constitutional Presbyterian doctrine includes any principle of succession, in the light of confessional standards, the writings of theologians, and practical observance (Drummond Tract Depot, Stirling, 1s. by post, or through any bookseller).

D.   MINISTERIAL PRIESTHOOD

'The idea of priesthood in Christianity needs to be constantly purified by reference to the sense in which Christ was a priest...the safeguarding of the idea of priesthood lies partly in the maintenance of the corporate conception of the priest's office—viz. that he is the divinely constituted organ of a body which is throughout priestly: partly also in the true conception of sacrifice.' (Bishop C. Gore, *Orders and Unity*, p. 164.)

Dr R. C. Moberley's study of *Ministerial Priesthood* brings out the deeper Christian meaning of the terms. 'The sacrificial priesthood of the Church is really her identification with the priesthood and sacrifice of Christ...by outward enactment ceremonially, and by inwardness of spirit vitally....The whole body of Christ is priestly' (p. 254). 'If Christ is King the Church is royal. If Christ is Priest, the Church is priestly.... Priesthood is not abolished but consummated in Christ's Church' (p. 251).

The passages in the New Testament teaching the holy priesthood of the Church and its members (particularly I Pet. ii. 5, 9; Rev. v. 9, 10, xx. 6) 'are not used of apostles or of presbyters distinctively, but of the body as a whole, and of it just because it is the body of Christ' (p. 253). 'The priesthood of the ministry is nothing distinct in kind from the priesthood of the Church. The ordained priests...have no greater right in the sacraments than the laity: only they, and not the laity, have been authorized to stand before the congregation in the ministerial enactment of the Sacraments which are the Sacrament—and the life—of both alike' (p. 258).

'Priesthood' in its catholic meaning stands not only for outward functions but for the spirit of sacrifice, which is 'the spirit of love in a world of sin and pain, whose expression in the inner soul is priestly intercession, and whose utterance in the outward life is devotion of ministry "for others": for others, from the Christ-like point of view, as for those for whom Christ died' (p. 260). 'Now the priestly spirit is *not* the exclusive possession of the ordained ministry; it is the spirit of the priestly Church. But those who are ordained "priests" are bound to be eminently leaders and representatives of this priestliness of spirit, and they have assigned to them an external sphere and professional duties which constitute a special opportunity, and a charisma of grace which constitutes a special call and a special capacity, for its exercise' (p. 261).

Throughout Christendom, the sacrament of Baptism, admitting to the Church, has always been completed by the laying on of hands (generally accompanied by unction), with prayer for the gifts of the Holy Spirit to endow the already baptized with grace for their work as laymen and laywomen. This New Testament sacrament is, in essence, ordination for their life-work, as members of the Church, of 'the holy priesthood' of all the baptized (I Pet. ii. 5, 9). In the Eastern Orthodox Church it is expressly taught that Confirmation (as it is called in the West) is ordination to that priesthood of all the baptized, cleric and lay, which is often called 'the priesthood of the laity' (Rev. Fr Sergius Boulgakoff, D.D., in *The Ministry and the Sacraments*, ed. R. Dunkerley, p. 109); but those who receive further ordination to the ministry obtain an external sphere and a special lifelong opportunity for its exercise (Moberley, *op. cit.* p. 261). The priesthood of the ministry, and the priesthood common to all the baptized, are not really inconsistent; they are complementary and mutually indispensable ideas. Such expressions as 'the priesthood of all believers', when used to discredit the idea of ministerial priesthood, are found to be divested of any meaning that is denied to the ministry, and become little more than empty phrases.

CHAPTER XXI. 'THAT THEY ALL MAY BE ONE'

I

THE need for Christian unity has long been clamant in the mission-field, and it has come increasingly to be felt in the half-pagan 'Christian lands' of to-day. No one who is not already convinced of the need is likely to have read through the previous chapters of this book; if any required convincing I could not match the force and eloquence of many workers for unity who have done much in recent years to awaken us to a sense of the need. Moreover no eloquence can have the appeal of our Lord's expressed will for His disciples, that they all may be one that the world may believe. If that does not move us to prayer and thought and action, nothing will. It is only too plain that the world does not believe; we must bear the implication and the reproach that our disunity is a cause of unbelief in the world.

Our Lord's saying concerning the *two or three gathered together* has always been relied upon as an argument against any duty of adherence to the ancient Church, or even any need of 'organized religion'. It was invoked by Tertullian after he joined the Montanists about A.D. 200,[1] and it has even been interpreted to mean that the gathered two or three are given 'full authority to judge on moral questions'.[2] St Cyprian long ago showed that the text was misunderstood, and that in reality it teaches the need for agreement and unity in prayer.*[3]

Yet it is recognized on all sides that divine blessing has been given to Christians who have formed new associations for themselves, whether these are called 'Churches' or not, and to the new ministries instituted by them. Those who themselves stick to the old ways gladly acknowledge the 'fruits and graces' that have often followed the new.

If then the denominations, the 'Churches' in the modern sense, have been unmistakably used by God, can there be such sanctity or virtue in the ancient and organic stewardship of the Ekklesia as to justify insistence upon it? Can it be a *sine qua non* of Christian union? It is natural enough for many Christians to hold a contrary

---

[1] See *Essays on Early Hist.* p. 21 n.   [2] Macgregor, p. 26.
[3] Note A. '*Two or three gathered together*' (p. 180).

opinion. 'They cannot understand why any person who professes
the Christian name should boggle at the surrender of what they take
to be a matter of mere administrative convenience.' Thus it is urged
persuasively by Dr Carnegie Simpson that there is no appreciable
difference in history in the recognition and use by the Holy Spirit
of different 'types of ecclesiastical order,...a fact', he says, 'of really
far-reaching significance'.[1] Certainly it is impossible for us to measure
or assess the divine blessings that have signalized this or that association of Christians; an attempt to do so would be unseemly and
foolish; but one thing is plain, that the blessing of unity is lacking,
and the fruits of unity.

II

We cannot tell that God's will for His Church has been carried out
because He has followed with blessing both us and others who are
separated from us. Indeed, a difficulty of discerning His will is due
in part to the very abundance of His grace. In *The Church and the
Bible* Dr Goudge draws a lesson for the Christian Ekklesia from
God's way with the Ekklesia of Israel. He did not forsake Israel
when they wandered from the right path. According to several
passages of Scripture,[2] 'the demand for a king was an act of apostasy,
since it was inconsistent with the crown rights of God Himself'.

A theologian would here distinguish between God's 'antecedent' and
His 'consequent' will. He would say that antecedently God desired His
people to have no visible head; but that, being what they had come to
be, it was best for them to have one. He would take a similar view
of the Great Schism under Jeroboam. The loss of visible unity was contrary to the divine ideal; it turned the hands of God's people against one
another; and, until the evil was abolished through common disaster, God's
purpose for them could not be fulfilled. But 'the thing' was none the less
'of the Lord', since it was the best which human sin allowed; it deprived
neither section of Israel of their relation to God as His people. He continued to send His prophets to both, and both had their contributions to
make to law, prophecy, and psalmody alike....

God follows His people on the path which they have chosen for themselves, and makes even their unfaithfulness to 'turn to His praise', just
as He will do when similar events take place in the story of the Christian
Church.[3]

[1] Carnegie Simpson, p. 139; but see note B (p. 180).
[2] I Sam. xii. 12; Judg. viii. 23; Hos. viii. 4.
[3] H. L. Goudge, *The Church and the Bible*, pp. 89, 90.

There is only one divine grace, which is not confined to appointed channels and paths, to sacraments or to the sacramental Church. The outpouring of this grace cannot therefore be taken as proof that the paths which have been followed were the appointed paths. We cannot tell what more abundant grace would have been given, what world-blessing would have come about, if we and those who have gone before us had been able to remain in unity. We must be one because it is God's will, not because His mercy does not follow us while we are scattered in disunion, for it does; we must be one, not so much for our own individual salvation as because it is His will, that thereby the world may believe.

III

The abundance of the free grace of God, which no boundaries can confine, suggests to many that all outward demarcation of the Church is unnecessary or even wrong. But if this were true of the Church, must it not be equally true of the sacraments of the Church? The need of the visible Church for man's salvation is like the need of the sacraments as separate channels of grace; they are necessary for mankind in this world of matter as they are 'unnecessary' to God; we know that God's grace is not restricted to them, yet we are not presumptuously to abandon them.

We may conjecture what St Paul would have said on this question if it had arisen in his day. He pre-eminently teaches of the free grace of God, freely poured down on us; yet, although *where sin abounded grace did abound more exceedingly*, he said emphatically that we must not *continue in sin that grace may abound*. It seems reasonable to think that St Paul, who saw to the careful administration of Baptism and who wrote for our admonition some of the greatest teaching both on the sacrament of Holy Communion and also on the sacramental nature of the Church, would have rebuked and put down any decrying of 'institutional religion', any holding aloof from the visible community of the Church in reliance on the free outpouring of grace outside its life and fellowship.

The supposed disproof of the need for the organic and visible Church goes too far for most of those who rely upon it.*[1] It equally implies that the visible sacraments are also unnecessary, which indeed is the belief of the Friends, who do not observe them. If we were

---

[1] Note B. *Fulfilment of God's will not proved by His blessing* (p. 180).

pure spirits, we should be altogether independent of forms and sacraments, our needs would be met in a Church invisible; but the Church of the New Testament must be visible, its religion is the religion of the Incarnation, the Word made flesh, a religion of the spirit expressing itself in matter. Just as an outward part is a necessity of a sacrament, so the outward organism is necessary to the sacramental Church. It is *a body fitly framed and knit together...according to the working in due measure of each several part,*[1] and the apostolic stewardship is indispensable to this fit framing and knitting in unity. Indeed no ministry with more limited credentials could be 'universally recognized by all to act on behalf of the universal Church'. At last, there is a general acknowledgement by Christians of every school of thought that such a ministry is necessary 'to act on behalf of the universal Church in the administration of the sacraments'.[2] The 'fit framing' of the Body is the outward part of the sacramental Church in the world. A necessary component of this outward part has now been plainly acknowledged.

The Church as a continuing society is and must be one, not only in space but also in time. Those who are in the Church must be in unity not only with all brethren now living in earth's remotest parts, but also with the membership of the Church in the past. In a human family, it is ancestral continuity with the past that is the family bond of unity in the present. In a somewhat analogous way the Church must be united in continuity in order that it may be united in the present. We can be in communion with one another to-day only if we are likewise in communion with the early Church. Lateral unity, we may say, comes from vertical unity, and it is the continuous organic life of the society, the Body, that joins and unites the Ekklesia of the present time with the Ekklesia of Pentecost.

IV

When we have dropped the word 'validity' from our vocabularies because of the misunderstandings it creates, when reverent and thankful acknowledgement has been made of the 'gifts, graces, and fruit' the bestowal of which is not confined to sacraments or to the outward fellowship of the sacramental Church, the inescapable fact remains, on the last analysis, that unity of the Church *in the world* requires organic unity.

[1] Eph. iv. 16. [2] Resolution of Edinburgh Conference on Faith and Order, 1937.

How that is to be regained is not at present clear. It is not by 'submission' to Rome, or, for that matter, to Athens or Canterbury or Constantinople or any part of the divided Body. Certainly full and ultimate unity must include the millions of the Roman Church, but such a consummation is far out of sight at present. The ex-crescences that Rome has added to the Faith once delivered to the saints (to say no more) cannot be essential to unity because they were not part of the common faith of the undivided Church. They block the way to union as a mountain in the path, a veritable Hima-laya. Because all things are possible with God, we can trust only that this mountain will some day be removed. For other Christians who hold the Catholic Faith of which the Nicene Creed is the expression, the approach to unity is rather less obstructed. All are maimed and crippled by division. Any 'submission' can be only to the Head of the Body, and it can only follow from a persuasion of what is His will. For that will, there must most surely be a way, one that will be found if only it is sought for by all with earnest prayer and thought.

The *Appeal to All Christian People*, which has already been referred to, was sent out by more than two hundred and fifty bishops of the Anglican Communion from all over the world, in conference at Lambeth in 1920. In it they said:

VI. We believe that the visible unity of the Church will be found to involve the whole-hearted acceptance of:

The Holy Scriptures, as the record of God's revelation of Himself to man, and as being the rule and ultimate standard of faith; and the Creed commonly called Nicene, as the sufficient statement of the Christian faith, and either it or the Apostles' Creed as the Baptismal confession of belief:

The divinely instituted sacraments of Baptism and the Holy Com-munion, as expressing for all the corporate life of the whole fellowship in and with Christ:

A ministry acknowledged by every part of the Church as possessing not only the inward call of the Spirit, but also the commission of Christ and the authority of the whole body.

In view of proposals recently advanced in the United States of America, it is of interest to notice that these four elements, of Scrip-ture, Creed, Sacraments, and Ministry, are taken, with a little altera-tion of wording, from a reply given as long ago as 1886 by the bishops of the Episcopal Church in the U.S.A. to a memorial on

Christian union. They affirmed their belief that Christian unity

can be restored only by the return of all Christian communions to the principles of unity exemplified by the undivided Catholic Church during the first ages of its existence; which principles we believe to be the substantial deposit of Christian Faith and Order committed by Christ and His Apostles to the Church unto the end of the world, and therefore incapable of compromise or surrender by those who have been ordained to be its stewards and trustees for the common and equal benefit of all men.

As 'inherent parts of this sacred deposit' they accounted these four elements, which were later approved of by the Lambeth Conference of 1888. Since 1920, they have gone by the name of the 'Lambeth Quadrilateral'.

The vision of a Church 'within whose visible unity all the treasures of faith and order, bequeathed as a heritage by the past to the present,... possessed in common, and made serviceable to the whole Body of Christ'[1] is still only a vision. 'Within this unity Christian Communions now separated from one another would retain much that has long been distinctive in their methods of worship and service.' The scattered and separated members of the Ekklesia might come together again with rejoicing, bringing their sheaves with them; but no smooth or easy road to this regaining of unity has yet been found.

V

Any full and real sharing of the life of the household and its stewardship seems to call for the imparting of the world-wide commission of apostolic ordination to ministers who have not already received it. This should not be regarded as a repudiation or denial of commissions already received and fruitfully exercised. Moreover, seeing that within the unity of the Faith there is room for difference of outlook and belief in many respects, a unanimous and loyal acceptance of the ancient outward organism of the Church is possible without requiring it to be an article of doctrinal belief. Actually that very reconciliation—of unanimous observance with diversity of belief as to the necessity for it—is found in the Anglican Communion.

St Paul himself, *an apostle not from men, neither through man: not a whit behind the very chiefest apostles*,[2] who would not for a moment

---

[1] *Appeal to All Christian People* from the Lambeth Conference of 1920.
[2] Gal. i. 1; II Cor. xi. 5.

have disowned or cast a slight upon the commission he had received, did not scruple at Antioch to accept ordination in some sort for the great work then beginning of spreading the Church through the world. There have been many saintly men, such as Robert Leighton, who have not felt that the receiving of an ordination as a wider commission throughout the whole fellowship implies the repudiating or the slighting even of orders already received. 'No one of us could possibly be taken to repudiate his past ministry. God forbid that any man should repudiate a past experience rich in spiritual blessings for himself and others.'[1]

'Re-ordination' is the expression generally used; it is perhaps open to objection because it may be understood as a begging of a question which, it is thought, may be left open. A better expression would be 'ulterior ordination', one that is added to what has gone before, and in some sense goes beyond it. There need be no doubt or scruple in any quarter in accepting a new ordination in this sense. Dr Broomfield recently has written: 'If ordination were solely a mark of an inward call by God, there would be no reason for its repetition. A second form of ordination or commission might truly imply doubt about the previous ministry. But when the receiving of ordination or commission is regarded also as admission to a particular status within a Christian fellowship, there need be no such misgivings. To receive "recognition" in this way from a body other than one's own is to extend the sphere within which one holds that status.'[2]

Nevertheless it seems at present to the majority of those who have considered the idea of 'conditional re-ordination', no matter how carefully guarded against any implied denial of ordinations or commissions already bestowed—'ulterior ordination', in fact, not 're-ordination'—that it would be 'a disowning of past ministries', and that therefore 'there can be no question of re-ordination'. So long as that is the voice of conscience, it blocks this pathway to unity.*[3]

VI

Concrete proposals of great interest and importance have been framed on the basis of two main ideas: (1) That all *future* ordinations to ministry in such communions as may agree to combine in a 'united Church' should be conferred in a manner 'universally

[1] *Appeal to All Christian People*, supra.
[2] G. W. Broomfield, *Revelation and Reunion*, p. 122.
[3] Note C. '*Re-ordination*' (p. 181).

recognized by all' as on behalf of the universal Church. This admittedly calls for 'episcopal ordination'. (2) That all existing ministries of the communions uniting should be acknowledged as 'presbyters in the united Church', without any re- or ulterior ordination. On the basis of these two main ideas, a project of union between the dioceses of the Anglican Church in South India, and two great Protestant Churches there, has been in preparation for many years and has now been revised.[1] The same two main ideas are embodied in a more tentative scheme, drafted by a joint conference of ministers of the Church of England and the Federal Council of the Evangelical Free Churches,[2] to encourage thought and discussion. This pamphlet, and also the South India scheme, deserve to be widely read and considered; they show how in many ways union presents less difficulty than might be supposed, and that it holds out a promise of enrichment from 'the spiritual treasures at present treasured in separation'. The acceptance of episcopal ordination for the future 'neither affirms nor excludes the view that Apostolic Succession determines the validity of the Ministry and Sacraments'. This careful reservation only gives expression to what is the tacit position in the Anglican Communion.

Yet the combination of these two main ideas involves serious defects or drawbacks. It implies that about half a century must elapse before all the ministry can be at one in the possession of the wider ordination, until which time discriminations will be inevitable and may be dangerously divisive. It has been said that the scheme 'seeks to create a united Church with a merely federated ministry'. It seems to many also that acceptance as presbyters of those who have not received, and are unwilling to receive, the traditional and ancient ordination, far from leaving any doctrinal view of episcopacy an open question, in effect affirms dogmatically that it is unnecessary, and thus denies a view that is said not to be excluded. Although there are many with whom these difficulties weigh heavily, the longing for union in South India is so intense that most of them feel able to acquiesce in a period of 'irregularity' preceding a final consummation of complete union. Unfortunately the revised scheme for South India contains a provision postponing complete organic union to a future that is both distant and uncertain.*[3]

[1] *Proposed Scheme of Church Union in South India*, seventh edition (revised), 1942.
[2] *Outline of a Reunion Scheme for the Church of England and the Evangelical Free Churches of England*, 1938, Student Christian Movement Press, 6d.
[3] Note D. *The scheme of Church union in South India* (p. 182).

Proposals of a less specific kind have been suggested for the future 'co-ordination' of ministers of still separate communions in such a manner—which implies the episcopal co-operation—as will qualify them as possessors of a universal commission to ministry, although the communions in which they will continue to serve, with the rest of their individual ministers, remain in separation. This plan, which seems to relegate any hope of a real Christian union to a remote future, is open to more objections than its authors may have perceived; yet it too calls for earnest consideration as a possible means towards even a distant end.

There has for a long time been wide agreement upon the first three points of the so-called Lambeth Quadrilateral, i.e. the common acceptance of Scripture, Creed, and Sacraments. It is the fourth point that has been found so difficult, viz.

A ministry acknowledged by every part of the Church as possessing not only the inward call of the Spirit, but also the commission of Christ and the authority of the whole body.

Hitherto, both adherents and opponents of 'episcopacy' have inclined to regard it too much as a method of 'government'. The South India scheme and the Outline scheme have made it clear at least that, in that aspect, the episcopal system of Church administration, restored in its primitive character, has none of that imagined despotism which has for long made it a bugbear in some quarters, that in fact it can happily accommodate valuable Presbyterian and Congregational elements.

The resolution of the 1937 Faith and Order Conference may be quoted again here, because of its great importance; it is a finger-post to the essential principle of episcopacy, which goes deeper than the mere method of government associated with it:

We believe that every Sacrament should be so ordered that all may recognize in it an act performed on behalf of the universal Church. To this end there is need of an ordained ministry recognized by all to act on behalf of the universal Church in the administration of the Sacraments.

That is essential to organic unity. According as the South India scheme furthers that principle, or falls short of it, so must be our hopes and expectations of that scheme.

Since this concluding chapter was written, a document of very great importance and interest, entitled *Basic Principles for the Union* *of the Presbyterian Church in the United States of America*[1] *and the Protestant Episcopal Church in the United States of America,* has been made public. Its proposals go further than those for South India, because they make a new and striking provision for the transition period of coalescence, in the form of 'supplemental ordination', to be administered to all the existing ministers of the uniting communions, with the laying on of hands by 'the bishop of the diocese concerned, with attendant presbyters' in the case of a Presbyterian minister, and by the Presbytery in the case of an Episcopalian. It has at length been perceived that organic unity requires that *all* of a ministry must be so ordered that *all* can recognize it to act on behalf of the universal Church. The principles which have been agreed upon by conferring delegations are now to be submitted to the dioceses and to the presbyteries for study and report. They contain much that will demand anxious thought,*[2] yet they are a welcome and heartening sign that the minds of Christians are awaking more and more to a sense of the need for the organic unity of the apostolic Ekklesia, and to a clearer perception of what that implies.

The road to unity is not yet clearly visible. In searching for it, it is of utmost importance that we all should recognize at least the direction of the goal to which it must lead. 'It cannot be disputed', an eminent Congregationalist has said, 'that the Church of England is a comprehensive Church, though what it is that holds it together I have never been able to discover. I sometimes think that, if the Free Churches could discover what holds them apart, and the Anglican Church could discover what holds it together, we might find the secret of reunion.'[3] I believe that the secret is its possession—blindly often, undogmatically, but loyally maintained—of continuity with the one undivided Church of Pentecost. That is an objective reality; even when it is unvalued it remains a potent fact. I have been impelled to write this book by the conviction that the sought-for medium of unity, the great essential of that unity in diversity for which we yearn and pray, is the ancient and enduring outward organism of the Ekklesia.

[1] This is considerably the largest of thirteen separate Presbyterian Churches in the U.S.A.

[2] Note E. *Supplemental ordination,* p. 183.

[3] Rev. K. L. Parry, Chairman of the Congregational Union, at its meeting on 12 May 1942. Cp. C. F. Rogers, *A Church genuinely Catholic,* p. 180: 'There are wide divergences of opinion, of temperament, of practice, in the English Church, but her unity in spite of it all is a very real thing.'

NOTES TO CHAPTER XXI

A. 'TWO OR THREE GATHERED TOGETHER'

'Neither let certain persons beguile themselves by a vain interpretation in that the Lord hath said, *Where two or three are gathered together in my Name, there am I in the midst of them.* Those who corrupt and falsely interpret the Gospel lay down what follows, but omit what goes before; giving heed to part, while part they deceitfully suppress; as themselves are sundered from the Church, so they divide the purport of what is in one passage. For when the Lord was impressing agreement and peace upon His disciples, He said, *I say unto you, that if two of you shall agree on earth as touching anything that they shall ask, it shall be done for them of my Father which is in heaven. For where two or three are gathered together in my Name, there am I in the midst of them,* showing that most is given, not to the many in number when they pray, but to oneness of heart. *If,* He saith, *two of you shall agree on earth*; He places agreement first; hearts at peace are the first condition; He teaches that we must agree together faithfully and firmly. Yet how can he be said to be at agreement with others who is at disagreement with the body of the Church itself, and with the universal brotherhood?' (St Cyprian on Matt. xviii. 19, 20 in Treatise V, *On the Unity of the Church,* § 11.)

In *The Nature of Catholicity,* by the Rev. Daniel T. Jenkins, the author, a Congregational minister, says at pp. 105, 106: 'Modern Independency... has misunderstood the text...and has overlooked the fact that it is only the presence of the Word, Sacraments, and Apostolic Ministry with Dogmatics which can insure that the gathering together is in fact in Christ's name.' He considers that all these are present in 'a modern properly organized Congregational Church'.

B. FULFILMENT OF GOD'S WILL NOT PROVED BY HIS BLESSING

'The appeal to spiritual results as giving sanction to an initial "irregularity" cannot stop with the case of the first Reformed churches or their lineal successors. This appeal applies to no body more conclusively than to the Society of Friends, who reject the most indisputable ordinances of Christ, baptism and the eucharist. It applies in our own time to the Salvation Army, who do the like. It applies perhaps to some movements which own no exclusive allegiance to the name of Christ. Thus the argument from good fruits can indeed be used to prove that God is not tied to His own ordinances; but it cannot be used to destroy the authority of these ordinances, if there is to remain any standard of institutions of Christ which we are constrained to maintain, or to which we are bound to recur.' (Bishop C. Gore, *Orders and Unity,* pp. 185, 186.)

'A distinction must be drawn between Divinely blessed and Divinely intended. The Divine blessing has not only rested on those who have no ministry of bishops and of priests but also upon those who have no ministry at all; upon those who maintain the Sacramental principle, and also upon those who reject it; upon those who maintain the doctrine of our Lord's Divine Person and also upon those who regard His person as human and created; indeed, upon adherents of other religions besides the Christian. But while we acknowledge that they have all been Divinely blessed, most of us would by no means be prepared to conclude that they are all alike Divinely authorized.' (W. J. Sparrow Simpson, *The Ministry and the Eucharist*, pp. 118, 119.)

'The great Christian communions which possess neither bishop nor priest possess the Christian Gospel; and the blessing which has rested upon their labours may well be attributed to the truth that they retain rather than to the departures they have made from the ministerial principles of the centuries.' (*Ibid.* p. 120.)

C. 'RE-ORDINATION'

'There can be no question of reordination' is the *non possumus* of a distinguished champion of Christian reunion, Dr Hugh Martin (*Christian Reunion*, p. 156), but a different view has lately been expressed by Mr Archibald W. Harrison: 'Quoting one of the Puritans, Nonconformists are inclined to say that the whole idea of reordination "hurts the mind". If ever we achieve unity, some one's mind will have to be a little wounded. It might, however, be an honourable wound in so great a cause. If it were clearly understood that the Free Church minister was receiving no new grace in a second ordination, which he had not already received in the first, but that he was thinking of the tender conscience of the "weaker brethren" of the Anglican Church, there ought to be no impassable barrier there. The times demand courageous and sacrificial action.' (*The Evangelical Revival and Christian Reunion*, pp. 199, 200.) It is appropriate here to recall that part of the Lambeth *Appeal* where the assembled bishops said:

'we who send forth this appeal would say that if the authorities of other Communions should so desire, we are persuaded that...Bishops and clergy of our Communion would willingly accept from these authorities a form of commission or recognition which would commend our ministry to their congregations, as having its place in the one family life. It is not in our power to know how far this suggestion may be acceptable to those to whom we offer it. We can only say that we offer it in all sincerity as a token of our longing that all ministries of grace, theirs and ours, shall be available for the service of our Lord in a united Church. It is our hope that the same motive would lead ministers who have not received it to accept a commission through episcopal ordination, as obtaining for them a ministry throughout the whole fellowship.'

Notwithstanding the different conceptions of ordination that prevail in the Christian communities which are seeking a road to unity, there could surely be prayerful sincerity in some such reciprocal ordination and commission. Each separated community believes that its particular witness to some aspect of Christian doctrine has hitherto justified its separation, and there is to-day an increasing mutual recognition of the sheaves that others can bring into a common store. The grace received in a sacrament cannot be weighed or measured; the Giver has always more to give. Is it too great a thing to ask of anyone, however ordained, to bow the head in willingness to receive just what further grace the Lord of infinite grace may see fit to bestow upon brethren who are coming into a unity in accordance with His will?

D. The scheme of Church union in South India

For thirty years after the inauguration of union ministers may be received from 'any Church whose missions have founded the originally separate parts of the united Church', and even after these thirty years it is to be an open question whether exceptions shall continue to 'the rule that its ministry is an episcopally ordained ministry'. The scheme declares at one point that 'continuity with the historic episcopate shall both initially and thereafter be effectually maintained', but this fundamental principle of agreement is so much undermined that the whole scheme is sadly endangered. It has been truly said 'that it is really useless to press for reunion in outward order by methods which, when examined, seem to imply that matters of outward order are spiritually unimportant'. (O. C. Quick, *The Christian Sacraments*, p. 153.)

The original basis of the scheme was a hopeful one, viz., frank acceptance of primitive catholic episcopacy, without assertion of it as a doctrinal necessity. The scheme, as developed and revised, rightly excludes any undue episcopal domination (for that is not primitive or catholic), but it goes on to empower its synod, in certain events, to overrule the bishops on matter of faith and doctrine. This would have been unthinkable in the early life of the Church. Then, and ever since, an important part of the unitive function of the chief pastorate has been its steadying guardianship of doctrine. These provisions might lead to a new schism. The scheme, in the process of revision, has shifted from its basis.

E. Supplemental ordination

In a pamphlet entitled *Anglican and Free Church Ministries* (S.P.C.K. 1944) Canon G. W. Broomfield develops the idea of 'supplemental ordination' on constructive lines. There should be no reluctant acceptance of reciprocal ordination but rather a *positive desire* for it. Thus

'Anglican bishops and priests would, for their part, receive ordination at the hands of the Free Churches....' 'For my part...I should love to become a Free Church minister...should count it a privilege to be linked, outwardly as well as inwardly, with the corporate lives of the Communions which have manifestly been spheres of divine activity'. But he urges strongly that supplementary ordination 'should be accomplished by the use of the *same* rites and ceremonies as are normally employed by the ordaining Church in its ordinations: and that its special character should be indicated by a formula such as the following, which would come immediately before the actual words of ordination: "Seeing that thou hast been ordained to the ministry in the......Church, and dost desire to exercise thy ministry in union with the......Church, we do now, on behalf of this latter Church, confer ordination upon thee according to its customary rites and ceremonies"'.

INDEX OF REFERENCES TO HOLY SCRIPTURE

GENERAL INDEX

Prime Minister, no official title until
1905, 88
nominates bishops in England, 54, 98
Prophecy, not an office, 97, 166
in second century, 132
bishops chosen by, 98
Prime Minister substituted for, 98
Prophets, 72, 97, 98, 131, 132
Presbyterian ministers as, 165, 166
Pullan, L., 155
Puller, F. W., 99
Pusey, E. B., 6

qahal, 16, 28
Quick, O. C., 48, 183
Quod semper, ubique, ab omnibus, 10

Ramsey, A. M., 20
Readers, minor order of, 63
lay, 63
in Reformed Churches, 167
Reformed ministry, no continuity with
unreformed, 154, 159, 163, 164, 167
congregational in origin, 160-3
confused nomenclature, 89
traditional dress, 43
Re-ordination, conditional, 176
ulterior, 176
supplemental, 179, 182
grace not measurable, 182
H. Martin on, 181
A. W. Harrison on, 181
Representative, an ambiguous word, 162,
163
Robinson, J. Armitage, 132, 133
Roman bishop, aggrandizement of, 64
Roman Church doctrine: the whole
Church Roman, 10, 44, 49, 156
ex hypothesi indivisible, 44
schismatics outside Church, 44
inconsistent practice, 49
schismatic sacraments valid, 156
priesthood, 68, 165, 166
confusion regarding orders, 64, 70,
139
Roman denials of Anglican orders, 63,
68
Ruinart of Paris, 124
Ruling-elders of Reformed Churches, no
laying of hands on, 89
authority over preaching-elders, 165
whether presbyters in theory, 89, 168
valuable ministry, 89, 90
resemblance to apostolic diaconate, 60

Sabbath replaced by Lord's Day, 143,
144

Sacrament, nature, 2
the Holy Incarnation the greatest, 2
the Church sacramental, 31 f.
barriers to grace of, 35
administered in schism, 155, 156
catholic, held invalid by Reformers,
159, 167
irregular forms, 36, 37
modern abandonment, 37, 47
and see Grace not confined
sacramentum and mysterium, 5
Salmon, G., 72, 79, 96, 99, 100
Salvation Army, 9, 19, 46, 180
Schism, in Old Testament, 171
effect on sacraments, 155, 156
Roman attitude to, 44, 49, 156
Novatian, 54, 150, 155
Donatist, 150, 155
East and West, 42, 46, 150
Great Schism of the West, 49
Schmiedel, P. W., 103
Scots Confession (1560), 158, 167
Second Book of Discipline, 167
Second Coming, the, 27, 80, 144, 148
Secular grandeur of bishops, 11, 55, 58,
141
Septuagint, 16
Seton, Thomas, 164
Seven, ordination of the, 26, 101, 106,
107, 146, 163
Seventh-day Adventists, 144
Seventy Apostles, the, 92, 93, 96, 101
Severus, Emperor, 77
shelicha, 104
Shepherd of Hermas, 100, 130, 133, 134,
144
Silence on the uncontroversial, see Un-
questioned things
Silvanus, an apostle, 11, 61, 93, 98
Simpson, P. Carnegie, 65, 171
Simpson, W. J. Sparrow, 6, 118, 181
Smyrna, 75, 120, 121, 128, 153
Society for Propagation of Gospel, 9
Sosthenes, an apostle, 94
South India, Scheme of Church Union,
177, 178, 183
Sozomen, Ecclesiastical History, 55, 112
Spiritists, 18
Spiritual Communion, 4-6
Sprott, G. W., 160
Stewardship of the Household, the
Church: Gospel teaching, 23, 40, 43
strongly impressed on apostles, 26
continuing endurance of, 5, 43, 63, 64,
103
must be handed on, 23, 24, 43
credentials of stewards, 36, 51, 110-12

For EU product safety concerns, contact us at Calle de José Abascal, 56–1°,
28003 Madrid, Spain or eugpsr@cambridge.org.

www.ingramcontent.com/pod-product-compliance
Ingram Content Group UK Ltd.
Pitfield, Milton Keynes, MK11 3LW, UK
UKHW010046140625
459647UK00012BB/1634